FIVE
VIEWS
ON

THE EXTENT OF THE ATONEMENT

Books in the Counterpoints Series

Church Life

Evaluating the Church Growth Movement
Exploring the Worship Spectrum
Remarriage after Divorce in Today's Church
Understanding Four Views on Baptism
Understanding Four Views on the Lord's Supper
Who Runs the Church?

Bible and Theology

Are Miraculous Gifts for Today?
Five Views on Apologetics
Five Views on Biblical Inerrancy
Five Views on Law and Gospel
Five Views on Sanctification
Five Views on the Church and Politics
Four Views on the Church's Mission
Four Views on Christian Spirituality
Four Views on Christianity and Philosophy
Four Views on Creation, Evolution, and Intelligent Design
Four Views on Divine Providence
Four Views on Eternal Security
Four Views on Hell
Four Views on Moving Beyond the Bible to Theology
Four Views on Salvation in a Pluralistic World
Four Views on the Apostle Paul
Four Views on the Book of Revelation
Four Views on the Historical Adam
Four Views on the Role of Works at the Final Judgment
Four Views on the Spectrum of Evangelicalism
Genesis: History, Fiction, or Neither?
How Jewish Is Christianity?
Show Them No Mercy
Three Views on Creation and Evolution
Three Views on Eastern Orthodoxy and Evangelicalism
Three Views on the Millennium and Beyond
Three Views on the New Testament Use of the Old Testament
Three Views on the Rapture
Two Views on Homosexuality, the Bible, and the Church
Two Views on the Doctrine of the Trinity
Two Views on Women in Ministry

FIVE VIEWS ON THE EXTENT OF THE ATONEMENT

Andrew Louth

Matthew Levering

Michael Horton

Fred Sanders

Tom Greggs

Adam J. Johnson, general editor
Stanley N. Gundry, series editor

COUNTERPOINTS
► BIBLE & THEOLOGY ◄

ZONDERVAN
ACADEMIC

ZONDERVAN ACADEMIC

Five Views on the Extent of the Atonement
Copyright © 2019 by Andrew Louth, Matthew Levering, Michael Horton, Fred Sanders, Tom Greggs, Adam J. Johnson

ISBN 978-0-310-52771-8 (softcover)

ISBN 978-0-310-52773-2 (ebook)

Requests for information should be addressed to:
Zondervan, *3900 Sparks Dr. SE, Grand Rapids, Michigan 49546*

Cover design: Tammy Johnson
Cover photo: Masterfile.com

Printed in the United States of America

19 20 21 22 23 24 25 26 27 28 /LSC/ 15 14 13 12 11 10 9 8 7 6 5 4 3 2 1

CONTENTS

CONTRIBUTORS ▆▆▆▆▆▆▆▆▆▆▆▆

Andrew Louth—is emeritus professor of patristic and Byzantine studies in the Department of Theology and Religion, Durham University. His research interests lie mostly in the history of theology in the Greek tradition and Russian and Romanian (Orthodox) theology. His books include *Origins of the Christian Mystical Tradition* and *Discerning the Mystery*, as well as books on Dionysius the Areopagite, Maximus the Confessor, and John Damascene.

Matthew Levering—is James N. and Mary D. Perry Jr. Chair of Theology at Mundelein Seminary, codirector of the Chicago Theological Initiative, and a longtime participant in Evangelicals and Catholics Together. Among his more than thirty-five published books are *Engaging the Doctrine of the Holy Spirit*, *Dying and the Virtues*, and *The Theology of Augustine*.

Michael Horton—is J. Gresham Machen Professor of Systematic Theology and Apologetics at Westminster Seminary, California. In addition to his work at the seminary, he is the founder and host of the White Horse Inn, a nationally syndicated, weekly radio talk show exploring issues of Reformation theology in American Christianity. Some of his most recent books include *Rediscovering the Holy Spirit, Core Christianity*, and *The Christian Faith*.

Fred Sanders—is professor of theology in the Torrey Honors Institute at Biola University. He is a systematic theologian who studies and teaches across the entire range of classic Christian doctrine but with a special focus on the doctrine of the Trinity. He has edited and published a number of books, including *The Deep Things of God, The Triune God*, and *Wesley on the Christian Life*.

Tom Greggs—is Marischal Chair of Divinity at the University of Aberdeen. He is currently working on a three-volume series on Protestant ecclesiology. His principal publications include *Theology against Religion, Barth, Origen, and Universal Salvation*, and *New Perspectives for Evangelical Theology*.

Adam J. Johnson—is associate professor of theology in the Torrey Honors Institute at Biola University. He focuses on the doctrine of the atonement, exploring the many ways in which the death and resurrection of Jesus Christ effect the reconciliation of all things to God. He is the author and editor of several books on the atonement, including *Atonement: A Guide for the Perplexed* and the *T&T Clark Companion to Atonement*.

INTRODUCTION

ADAM J. JOHNSON

Doctrine: A Basilica unto the Lord

Saint Peter's Basilica is one of the most awe-inspiring churches in which I have worshiped. While the design of the building itself is a marvel, it was the profound feeling of holy space, dedicated to the Lord, that so moved me. Along with that came the painful awareness that this parti-cular building was in many ways at the heart of the events surrounding the Protestant reformation of the sixteenth century, making for a pain-ful, yet perhaps appropriate, dual motion of worship and contrition, which I will never forget.

Outside of the basilica stands an ancient Egyptian obelisk. At the time of Pope Sixtus V, however, this obelisk stood disharmoniously to the south side of the basilica. "More than three hundred architects, engineers, scientists, and savants from all over Europe submitted plans" to move it to the center of Saint Peter's Square—no small feat, for the obelisk weighs some 320 tons and stands eighty-three feet tall. The problem was to lift, reposition, and reestablish the monolith without damaging it. Eventually, Domenico Fontana came up with a plan using seventy winches and a sort of land-raft on wheels that could roll the obelisk into place. Things appeared to go smoothly at first, but as the obelisk was slowly lifted from its ancient foundation, the ropes began to give way. The voice of a sailor "cried out, 'Acqua alle funi!'—'Water the ropes!'" Fontana followed the advice, the ropes did not break, and the obelisk was successfully moved.[1]

The engineering challenges faced in this task were immense but in some ways quite simple, for the challenge lay in the proportions involved in a single, monolithic object, which needed to be lifted, moved, and repositioned. In other words, it was a relatively simple and one-dimensional task made difficult by the massive scope of the object

---

1. R. A. Scotti, *Basilica: The Splendor and the Scandal; Building St. Peter's* (New York: Penguin, 2007), 203ff.

involved. An altogether different set of challenges lay in constructing the basilica itself—and above all its 448-foot dome. Bramante irrevocably set the proportions of the basilica by means of the four immense pillars supporting the dome. But in some ways, this was the easy part, for the challenge lay in building a dome to fit these pillars, a task begun by Michelangelo and finished by Giacomo della Porta. Here, the trials were altogether more complex than with the obelisk, for the forces at play were far more diverse. The weight of the dome was massive, calling for reinforcement of the pillars and foundations. Beyond that, depending on the shape and structure of the dome, its weight could either rest on the pillars supporting it or become outward-pushing forces that would tear apart the church. The materials used, the shape of the dome, the role of the pillars—these and a host of other factors, not to mention the aesthetic of the whole, coalesced into a monumental challenge in which there could be no trial runs.

The difference between these two challenges, moving the Egyptian obelisk and building the dome of Saint Peter's, is a helpful one to keep in mind when it comes to thinking about the extent of the atonement, which resides at the intersection of predestination and the cross. We are asking who Christ died for, whether for all or for the elect alone.[2] Answering this question may seem to resemble the challenge of moving the obelisk: a monumental task, laden with implications for faith and practice, but nonetheless a fairly simple one of finding the pertinent passages in Scripture and formulating a biblical view. But as we will see over the course of this book, the challenge is much more akin to the building of the dome of Saint Peter's.

---

2. It would be typical to heavily footnote an introduction such as this, guiding the reader to a range of scholarly sources on the topic. In this case I have chosen not to do so for two reasons. First, I am focusing my efforts and available space to equip the reader to benefit maximally from the essays that follow rather than offer my own guidance into the doctrine. Second, many of the sources directly addressing this topic presuppose one of a small handful of entrenched positions that range from variations within the Reformed position to the Wesleyan responses, but the purpose of this book is to push the debate beyond these circles by inviting traditions that do not address the topic directly, for their own very good reasons, to offer their contribution. I will, however, make one concession. Though clearly favoring a limited or definite view of the extent of the atonement, David Gibson and Jonathan Gibson's book stands as a monumental contribution to the subject. Its arguments and bibliographies will offer ample guidance for further research on the topic, though, to be sure, the book is not meant to give equal representation to the range of views within the ecumenical church. David Gibson and Jonathan Gibson, eds., *From Heaven He Came and Sought Her: Definite Atonement in Historical, Biblical, Theological, and Pastoral Perspective* (Wheaton, IL: Crossway, 2013).

A noteworthy point of comparison is the fact that this question, much like Saint Peter's itself, has been the occasion for worship and joy for some and pain, repentance, and suffering for others. Many find themselves caught up in wonder and appreciation as they gaze upon the architectural wonder that is classical Reformed teaching, with its vaulting chambers and beautiful mosaics of doctrine, known to many by the acronym TULIP (total depravity, unconditional election, limited atonement, irresistible grace, and perseverance of the saints). Others, touring the same theological structure, find themselves grieved at the harm it has done to the teaching and preaching of the church, casting the faithful into fears and doubts about their salvation ("how do I know if I am one of the elect?") and raising significant theological questions of no small existential force, such as evangelism ("am I right to tell someone God loves them?") and prayer ("why should I pray for the salvation of a friend if this has been determined from the dawn of time?"). But the similarities go on from there, granting us a deeper and more helpful insight into these matters.

When some consider the question, "For whom did the Father send Jesus to die and rise again?" they think in terms of the monolithic Egyptian obelisk. As they envision it, the answer forms a massive, singular whole. Granted, it may take an immense amount of work and theological courage to move it into place, but it stands in Scripture nonetheless, whether or not one has the wisdom (and daring) of Fontana to allow it to rest in its proper place within one's theological system. The difficulty is not so much the doctrine itself, but the challenge of getting it into its proper position. The cry, "Acqua alle funi!" is a matter of treating with proper care the different exegetical and theological tools one uses to get the doctrine into place, but the doctrine itself is relatively straightforward (albeit colossal).

As you read the different views expressed in this book, I invite you to a different way of thinking about this question—one that attends to the range of complex theological forces at play within potential answers to this question, forces that can come together to form holy doctrinal space in which to worship the Creator and Re-Creator of heaven and earth, or forces that can work against each other, collapsing the whole into a catastrophic pile of wreckage and rubble. Inasmuch as we think of "the extent of the atonement" as a singular whole, we fail to acknowledge the many vital factors comprising this doctrine—to our very great detriment (and perhaps to the detriment of those worshiping under the roof of our doctrinal systems).

The Forces at Play

Scripture does not offer a monolithic position regarding the extent of the atonement. On the one hand, Scripture seems to say that God loves the whole world and sent his Son to save any who respond to him in faith (John 3:16). On the other hand, the Bible seems to say that God ordains specific individuals to eternal life (Acts 13:48). This simple contrast already makes for a challenge, but as we will see, this is only a brief introduction to the forces that constitute a proper doctrinal account of the extent of the atonement.

The doctrine of the extent of the atonement, I would like to suggest, is not one we pluck, ready-formed and ripe, from the branches of Scripture. Rather, it is a synthetic doctrine, built from a range of passages throughout Scripture, along with a host of doctrines, which together shape our view. To come to grips with this doctrine is no mere matter of wrestling with one or two passages of Scripture to reach one's conclusion. Far from it! This is a matter of forming a whole system of Christian doctrine, the kind of system whose careful interworkings can support such a dome both safely and with the unique aesthetic proper to the Maker of heaven and earth. In this introduction, I hope to pave the way for the chapters that follow so as to heighten your awareness of the theological forces at play in what follows. In the conclusion, I will look back on what we have seen, inviting you to answer a series of theological questions, each grounded in specific exegetical projects—for one of the great purposes of theology is to facilitate and nourish the interpretation of Scripture, upon which the Christian faith stands.

Doctrine of God

What then are some of these forces that shape our understanding of the extent of the atonement? Chief among these is the doctrine of God. Speaking of God, of the triune God, might seem like a straightforward task, but although God is one, it does not mean that he is easy to know, to speak of, or to think rightly of.

One way to see this difficulty is by answering the following question: Does God change? Of course God does not shift from being good to bad, from being a Trinity to being a quaternity, or some other change like that. But did God change when he created or has he always been Creator in some sense? Was there any change in God when he made his covenants with the people of Israel or when, at the end of the book of Jonah, God seems to relent?

While some positions certainly do fall at the extremes—from a nearly Platonist view in which God is utterly unchanging (more of a benevolent force of goodness than a personal, unchanging God) to a Hegelian, process, or open-theist position—most Christians, working somewhere within these extremes, must grapple with whether and in what sense change is becoming of the God of Abraham, Isaac, and Jacob, the God who raised Jesus from the dead, the living and active God of the gospel. And of course it is not hard to see how this shapes our understanding of the extent of the atonement. Those emphasizing the way God related to the people of Nineveh will tend to think more broadly or universally of the extent of the atonement, while those dwelling more on the constancy and unchangingness of God will be more likely to limit the scope of Christ's atoning work. But note: neither of these is unbiblical. The challenge is far greater than simply choosing a favorite text and claiming to know God thereby.

Doctrine of the Divine Attributes

This brings us to a related though distinct doctrine: the divine attributes, particularly love, freedom, constancy (unchangingness), and sovereignty. For the purposes of this introduction, I will focus on the latter.

As Abram notes in Genesis 15:2, God is sovereign. That much is a given. But what does it mean for God to be sovereign? Is there more than one possible or plausible answer in the Bible? Does it mean that God wills everything that happens, sin and evil included? What does it mean for the wills of the creatures God made? Does sovereignty rule out all or just some forms of change? What do 1 and 2 Samuel reveal about the kingship and sovereignty of God? And when God tells Moses that he will destroy the nation of Israel and fulfill his covenantal promises through Moses in Exodus 32 after the Golden Calf incident, what does this reveal about the nature of his sovereignty?

Understanding the question of the extent of the atonement presupposes a whole set of commitments regarding the character or attributes of God. Part of the burden of discussions on this topic is to do the theological and biblical work that makes these commitments clear, and then submit that work to scrutiny. For how God is sovereign—the unique nature of the triune God's sovereignty as revealed in the person and work of Jesus Christ—is a question that can bring life to and deeply shape how we understand the extent of Christ's saving work (the same being true of other divine attributes such as love and freedom).[3]

Christology

The same is true for Christology. How we think of Jesus deeply shapes our other theological commitments. If Jesus is a solution to a problem, then naturally our attention is drawn to the problem. For a solution is only as interesting and important as the problem it solves. But what if we turn things upside down? What if Jesus is not merely the problem-solver? What if he is the source of all creation? Colossians 1:15–20 is invaluable here (though John 1 and Ephesians 1 belong in a fuller treatment):

> The Son is the image of the invisible God, the firstborn over all creation. For in him all things were created: things in heaven and on earth, visible and invisible, whether thrones or powers or rulers or authorities; all things have been created through him and for him. He is before all things, and in him all things hold together. And he is the head of the body, the church; he is the beginning and the firstborn from among the dead, so that in everything he might have the supremacy. For God was pleased to have all his fullness dwell in him, and through him to reconcile to himself all things, whether things on earth or things in heaven, by making peace through his blood, shed on the cross.

What if Jesus is the firstborn over all creation? What if creation was made "in him," and all things were created "through him" and "for him," and "all things hold together" in him? Such a view still allows for Jesus to be the solution, for through him God "reconcile[s] to himself all things,"

---

3. One attribute that probably should receive more attention than it does in these discussions is that of divine simplicity, which demands, among other things, that we not separate the divine attributes, as though God could be just and not wise, or loving and not holy, towards the same person. The God who is one is likewise one in his character, and divine simplicity plays a vital role in guiding our thinking about other attributes and how we relate them to each other.

but it emphasizes the way that the one who is the origin of all things is simultaneously the one who is the solution and goal of all things.

Why does this matter for the extent of the atonement? For two reasons: First, perhaps you have noticed the way in which discussions on this topic focus mainly on the doctrine of God (whether he changes, the nature of his will, the content of his election and determination, the nature of his sovereignty) and only later turn to Christology and soteriology to wrap things up. But this is surely a misstep. Any theological conversation that seeks to formulate its key commitments without reference to the person and work of Jesus, building them on the doctrine of God alone, is surely making a grave mistake, for Jesus is how we know the Father, how we know God. In response to Philip, Jesus said, "Anyone who has seen me has seen the Father. How can you say, 'Show us the Father'? Don't you believe that I am in the Father, and that the Father is in me?" (John 14:9–10). Any theology that operates from the vantage point of the doctrine of God, without reference to the way that Jesus reveals this God, runs the grave risk of distorting the doctrine of God.

Second, Christology is the key to anthropology. One of the goals of the doctrine of the extent of the atonement is to consider the anthropological implications of God's electing and saving work—but how we do this is of great consequence. If Jesus is a solution, then that leaves much of the anthropology to be developed on its own terms. What it means to be human, the purposes of humans—these and other questions can perhaps be answered apart from the solution to the problem of sin that they face. But what if the answer to the question, "What does it mean to be made in the image of God?" lies in Colossians: "The Son . . . in whom we have redemption, the forgiveness of sins . . . is the image of the invisible God" (Col. 1:13–15)? What are the implications of the claim that to be human is to be connected to and related to Christ as Colossians seems to argue? Jesus moves, then, from being a solution, from being *the* solution, to being much more. Jesus is the origin, the pattern, the one in whom and through whom, we are human. While this does not necessarily settle questions about the extent of the atonement, you can begin to see how it shapes them; it begins to pull together and synthesize parts of a picture that could, on other views, remain fairly separate. Remember that the challenge here is not simply to formulate an answer to the extent of the atonement but to learn to think systematically, to weave together the different theological commitments that together, as a whole, answer this question. And surely the center of such an approach must be our faithfulness to and understanding of our Lord Jesus Christ.

Atonement

The atonement is the fourth force we consider, for it is by no means a simple and straightforward doctrine. Is our salvation from sin, death, or the devil? Are we saved by imputation, representation, vicarious satisfaction, or deification? Is the atonement about the human condition, the plight of all creation (including our own), or is it cosmic in scope? Different ecclesial traditions have different emphases and doctrines when it comes to explaining the death and resurrection of Jesus (as is particularly evident in Louth's chapter), which influence their understanding of the extent of this work. It is a distinctive feature of debates on the extent of the atonement that they tend to focus on the question of "extent" and only then consider the implications which follow for the "atonement" rather than working the other way around, but this runs the risk of minimizing the role of Christ, allowing other factors to control and shape our understanding of his passion—a dangerous move indeed.[4]

Predestination

A fifth force at play (and the last one we will consider here) is that of predestination. The temptation, of course, is to think that we know what the word means, and read that meaning into the biblical text. But what *does* it mean? Does it mean an inviolable plan set before the foundation of time for the salvation of some and the damnation of others, or does it mean something roughly parallel to the role of fate in the ancient Greek stories? Perhaps it means something altogether different?

The challenges here are numerous. First, which texts do we use to help us interpret others? Paul seems to use the potter and clay imagery in Romans 9 in a deterministic way. Yet in 2 Timothy 2:20–21 he uses the same imagery in a very difference sense, akin to the parable of the sower

---

4. On the topic of the atonement in general, I commend my works on the subject: Adam J. Johnson, *Atonement: A Guide for the Perplexed* (New York: T&T Clark, 2015); and Johnson, ed., *T&T Clark Companion to Atonement* (New York: T&T Clark, 2017).

(Matt. 13:1–23), in which the objects in question (dishes or soil) seem to have some role in shaping or changing themselves to become better or more honorable. This is no mere matter of submitting to Scripture; it is a matter of holistic and synthetic scriptural interpretation where we seek to embrace the overall vision, which can be difficult to discern in individual passages.

Second, who is the audience of the texts in question? While this is important to understanding any text in Scripture, it is particularly vital here. Are the most extended passages on predestination, such as Romans 9–11 and Ephesians 1–3, writing to the Christian in general? Or are they writing to congregations of Jews and Gentiles? And if the latter, how does that change our understanding of what is being said? It is vitally important to consider the relationship of Jew and gentile within the gospel in general (esp. Rom. 9–11 and Eph. 1–3) and the extent of the atonement in particular. As we will see in the following chapters, Catholics and Calvinists are slightly more inclined to affirm a general audience in these passages, while the Orthodox and Wesleyans are slightly more inclined to emphasize the Jew/gentile relations at the heart of Paul's concerns.

Finally, what end do these passages have in mind? It is easy to assume when we see the word *predestination* that the end in mind is heaven or hell. But is that the case? The challenge is to have a sober approach to the text in which we allow the text to shape our understanding of the meaning it gives to predestination. Part of doing this is listening carefully to what is and is not said in key passages pertaining to predestination of the elect. What did God elect them for according to those passages? Eternal salvation, damnation, or some other, more specific purpose, perhaps one within this earthly life?

The Task at Hand

The purpose of this introduction is to equip you to read the chapters that follow by providing certain categories, questions, and strategies that enable you to benefit maximally from each chapter. I have tried to pull back the curtain and point out some of the key places in the doctrine of the extent of the atonement where important decisions and distinctions are being made so that what seems like a monolith can become, in your eyes, much more of a structure. For this, more than anything, is what I hope you will gain from this introduction: a clear sense that the extent of the atonement is a synthetic doctrine, one developed by sets of commitments in a range of different doctrines, many of which have a range of possible meanings and come together to form the doctrine.

And this brings us to what I take to be the greatest contribution of this volume: its ecumenical approach. As a college student, I understood there to be two positions on the extent of the atonement: the Reformed (stretching back to Augustine), which emphasized, among other things, the Pauline view of predestination, and the Wesleyan, which emphasized the scriptural passages that seem to affirm the free will with which God endowed his creatures. Now of course the reality is far more complex than this (not only because most Calvinists affirm some understanding of free will and Wesleyans eagerly affirm their understanding of predestination), and one way it is more complex is in its history.

Once we introduce both the Orthodox and the Catholic positions into this mix, we find ourselves presented with a far more nuanced, balanced, and stimulating picture, characterized less by polarization and more by breadth. And this is key, for where there is breadth of well-meaning and charitable interpretation of Scripture, there is an invitation to learn and consider. However, polarization tends to promote defensive stands and overzealous offenses, which is dangerous, for a war on this turf is a civil war of brother against sister, each wielding passages of Scripture against the other. And this will not do. Our challenge is not to win but to submit to the whole testimony of Scripture and therefore to face and embrace those passages we find most awkward and offensive. I know of no way more nurturing for such an approach to Scripture than to read widely across the history of church, to read ecumenically, to be confronted by the unity and diversity of positions across the church in each of the doctrines that together influence the one we have in question.

It is for this reason that we have asked representatives of the Orthodox, Catholic, Reformed, and Wesleyan traditions to offer their representative voice for your consideration, as well as a representative from a position that has not had official ecclesial support in the way these other views have but has always found a voice among members of the church: universalism. My hope is that these representatives and their arguments will equip and invigorate your further work in that great synthetic task which is the doctrine of the extent of the atonement.

EASTERN ORTHODOX VIEW

ANDREW LOUTH

One problem faced by Orthodox seeking to participate in almost any discussion of theological topics with fellow Christians of Western traditions is that what one might call the linguistic and conceptual geography appears strange. Terms are used that are difficult to translate into Greek, the originary language of Eastern Orthodoxy, something made even more difficult when one is considering the way these theological terms or concepts relate to one another: the theological terrain, mapped out by the concepts expressed in (ultimately, for the West, generally Latin), often seems quite unfamiliar. To ask what Orthodox theology makes of original sin, or the atonement, is to ask first for an effort of translation of an unfamiliar concept into something recognizable on the terrain of Orthodox theology. Of course, it was the other way around in the formative years of the church; then the terminology of theology was primarily Greek—one might indeed argue that the aboriginal language of Christianity, once it realized its mission to the nations, is Greek; indeed, Latin was late to emerge. So it was that Latin thinkers struggled to represent Greek terms and distinctions in Latin, something that was often very difficult. Latin theologians were aware of this: Augustine is quite conscious that the terminology of Greek Trinitarian theology, involving the distinction between *hypostasis*, the word that came to be used for the members of the Trinity, and *ousia* ("being" or "essence") or *physis* ("nature"), used for the divine unity, was poorly expressed by the traditional language of Latin Trinitarian theology, which distinguished between *persona* and *substantia*. Indeed the confusion was in danger of being further confounded by the fact that *substantia* in Latin, representing the unity of the Godhead, corresponded most closely to—what linguists call a "calque" of—the Greek *hypostasis*, used in Greek theology to represent the three members of the Trinity, Father, Son, and Holy Spirit.

The case of the atonement represents a further problem, for *atonement* is one of the few theological terms that is aboriginally English. The earliest use of the word, in a theological context, seems to occur in Tyndale's translation of the New Testament, where it was used to translate 2 Corinthians 5:18 (τὴν διακονίαν τῆς καταλλαγῆς: "ministry of atonement"). This use of atonement did not survive in the later English translations of the Bible. In the King James Version, *atonement* is only used once in the New Testament, in Romans 5:11; generally, the word *reconciliation* is used to render καταλλαγή (*katallagē*). In the KJV *atonement* is used much more widely in translating the Old Testament, especially in connexion with the sacrificial ceremonies laid out in the Pentateuch.

The regular use of the word in English theology seems much later (according to the online *Oxford English Dictionary*), in the mid-nineteenth century, to which belongs the spelling out of its meaning as at-one-ment. The word "atonement" looks as if it is derived from the verb "to atone," but the evidence of use does not support this (our expectations are often undermined by the lexicographers' craft). The early uses of "atonement" and "atone" were not religious and often very general: bringing together estranged parties into unity, reconciliation, and so forth. However, the *Oxford English Dictionary* reveals that the older, more general meanings become obsolete; it is the fourth meaning, listed, as usual, chronologically in terms of attestation, that became normal: making amends, satisfaction, expiation. In other words, the meaning of *atonement*, once close to what the etymology of the word suggests, that is, "bringing into one, to unify," fairly quickly gravitated towards a forensic meaning.

Atone is not, however, the only verb related to atonement. In Middle English there is another etymologically close word: the verb *to one*—that is, the noun *one* used as a verb. Its provenance is interesting. The first example given in the *Oxford English Dictionary* comes from a treatise called *Aʒenbite of Inwit* dated to about 1340.[1] More familiar examples

---

1. *Aʒenbite of Inwit*, or *Ayenbite of Inwyt*, can be translated "remorse of conscience," or more literally "biting again of conscience." Notably, the title attracted James Joyce's ludic imagination.

can be found. For example, in the long version of Julian of Norwich's *Revelations of Divine Love* (c. 1395), she says that "than shall our blissid saviour perfectly helyn us and one us to him."[2] *The Cloud of Unknowing* (late fourteenth century) also speaks of the soul as "onyd Þus to God in spirit."[3] To think of *atonement* as related to this use of the verb *to one* suggests a very different linguistic career for the word *atonement*—being drawn less into the forensic orbit, as actually happened, and instead coming to belong to the language of the spiritual ("mystical") experience of union with God, of "oning" to God, envisaged by the Middle English mystics. "Atonement," at-one-ment, would in this case suggest deification (θέωσις). This—in what must seem like a—flight of linguistic fancy is not irrelevant to this essay, but I shall leave its relevance to emerge in what follows.

Atonement, then, set out on its linguistic path with a forensic meaning of making amends, satisfaction, something that could be demanded and supervised by legal process and the courts. In its eventual theological use, it picked up the tendency of Western theology, present arguably since Tertullian, to frame our relationship with God, and especially its restoration, in legal terms. This is hardly a surprising development: the prophetic tradition of the Old Testament makes much of the Day of Judgment of the Lord, when all will appear before God's judgment seat. Forensic language of being found guilty or acquitted becomes commonplace and enters deeply into devotional language; it is frequently found in the Psalms—"blessed is the one whose unrighteousness is forgiven, and whose sin is covered" (Ps. 31/32:1).[4] The forensic language merges with ritual language, as in the verse just quoted: "covering" of sin belongs to the Hebrew language of sacrifice.[5] That the language of atonement attracted such forensic connotations is scarcely surprising if

---

2. "Then shall our blessed saviour perfectly heal us and one us to him." Julian of Norwich, *Revelations of Divine Love*, ed. Barry Windeatt (Oxford: Oxford University Press, 2016), 78.2.17–18.

3. "Oned thus to God in spirit." *The Cloud of Unknowing* and *The Book of Privy Counselling*, ed. Phyllis Hodgson, Early English Text Society (London: Oxford University Press, 1944), ch. 25, p. 60.

4. Ps. 31:1 in the translations used by the Orthodox Church, which follow the Septuagint numbering of the Psalms; Ps. 32:1 in most English translations, which follow the Masoretic Text. Unless otherwise indicated, Scripture quotations in this essay are the author's own translation.

5. See Louis Jacobs, *The Jewish Religion: A Companion* (Oxford: Oxford University Press, 1995), *s.v.* Yom Kippur, 613–14.

one thinks that the development of this term belongs to the later Middle Ages, which, under the influence of the covenant theology of that period and fostered jointly by the popularity of nominalism in philosophy and the "two-powers" doctrine in theology, discouraged ontological and metaphysical ways of understanding the relationship of the creature to God and laid all the emphasis on the covenant, established by God's will, as determining the creature's relationship to God. The focus of theology in this late phase of scholasticism shifted from metaphysics, as with Aquinas (*analogia entis*), to canon law, understood as exploring how God's will for his creatures is set forth. In this context, forensic concepts, such as justification, came to the fore and were finally confirmed in the centrality of the doctrine of justification by faith for the Reformers, especially Luther. The language of atonement is part of this way of understanding the relationship between the human and God.

It is a theological development that has little resonance with the theological development of the Orthodox East. This is manifest from Alister McGrath's early work *Iustitia Dei*.[6] In the first volume, which leads up to the Reformation, McGrath skips from Latin theologian to Latin theologian and only begins to settle down to the development of justification in the later Middle Ages. The Greek Fathers are passed over in a few pages. The second volume, which starts with the Reformation, finds itself pursuing a proper subject, led by the Reformers and their successors, with Catholic theology responding to what Catholics perceived to be errors in this essentially juridical notion. Luther's point of view—nurtured in this to a degree by his reception of late medieval theology, but inspired by the analogy he perceived between his protest against the medieval Catholic Church and the apostle Paul's polemic against the place of the law in the thought of the Pharisees, from whose ranks he had come—made justification by faith central and read Saint Paul's letters in the light of this doctrine. This led to making Romans and Galatians the core of the Pauline corpus, the other epistles being treated as satellites in this theological constellation. Once put like that, it is evident that other ways of conceiving of the Pauline corpus are possible: focusing on the epistles to the Corinthians, for example, would hardly lead to justification being regarded as central—the Eucharist

6. Alister E. McGrath, *Iustitia Dei: A History of the Christian Doctrine of Justification*, 2 vols. (Cambridge: Cambridge University Press, 1986).

would assume a more central place, along with Paul's reflection on his own transforming experience of God's grace, leading from glory to glory, and working out a dialectic of death and resurrection, of human dying to the "flesh" enabling human resurrection and transformation by grace and by the Holy Spirit (see 2 Cor. 3–4; 12; and esp. 3:18; 4:7–12; 12:1–10).

Another more systematic and less historical way of locating the place of atonement in the theological landscape would be to observe that the Scriptures and, following and interpreting them, theology use a wide range of metaphors in interpreting God's action in Christ. One of these metaphors is judgment and acquittal, which is inhabited by the language of atonement and justification. But there are others: Christ as victor, on the cross engaging in a mortal struggle with death, manifest as victorious in the resurrection (*mors et vita duello / conflixere mirando / dux vitae mortuus / regnat vivus*); Christ as a sacrificial victim, making expiation for the sins of humanity but also as priest offering sacrifice (*Victimae paschali laudes / immolent Christiani. / Agnus redemit oves. / Christus innocens Patri / reconciliavit / peccatores*);[7] Christ as healer (cf. Julian, quoted above: "than shall our blissid saviour perfectly helyn us and one us to him");[8] Christ as teacher; Christ as perfect example of what it is to be human (these last two examples rarely appear alone, at least in the Fathers).

There is a further point to be made about these images for interpreting God's action in Christ. They are all, in different ways, paradoxical. The cross was an instrument of painful and prolonged execution; no one would naturally think of it as an altar, nor an emblem of victory. The death of a man on a cross does not suggest, in itself, victory over death; it looks all too like subjection to death, the fate of all mortals. To see Christ on the cross as "riding the Axile Tree"[9] is a heroic bringing

---

7. The quotations are from Wipo's Easter Sequence (eleventh century): "Death and life have grappled / in a wondrous duel. / The leader of life, dead, / does reign, alive; / To the paschal victim, praises / let the Christians sacrifice. / The Lamb has redeemed the sheep. / The sinless Christ / has reconciled sinners / to the Father." Peter G. Walsh with Christopher Husch, trans., in *One Hundred Latin Hymns: Ambrose to Aquinas*, Dumbarton Oaks Medieval Library 18 (Cambridge, MA: Harvard University Press, 2012), 267.

8. For an extensive (Orthodox) account of Christ's healing work, extending into ascetic and mystical theology, see Jean-Claude Larchet, *Thérapeutique des maladies spirituelles* (Paris: Éditions du Cerf, 1997).

9. The last line of *The Anathemata* of David Jones.

together of metaphors, fusing Yggdrasil—the cosmic tree of Nordic myth—with a cruel instrument of Roman execution. Even what might seem such a straightforward metaphor of Christ as the healer insists on paradox. When Eusebius of Caesarea, in his festal oration at Tyre, compares Christ to "a devoted physician [who], to save the lives of the sick, sees the horrible danger yet touches the infected place, and in treating another's troubles brings suffering on himself"[10]—anticipating T. S. Eliot's "wounded surgeon," whose "steel . . . questions the distempered part."[11] The indirectness of the metaphor, the way in which it invites other metaphors that conflict or set it off, is important to note. There is danger in limiting the range of imagery in interpreting Christ's saving work, as one of the great Orthodox theologian of the last century, Vladimir Lossky, warned:

> Nevertheless, when the dogma of the redemption is treated in isolation from the general body of Christian teaching, there is always the risk of limiting the tradition by interpreting it exclusively in terms of the work of the Redeemer. Then theological thought develops along three lines: original sin, its reparation on the cross, and the appropriation of the saving results of the work of Christ to Christians. In these constricting perspectives of a theology dominated by the idea of redemption, the patristic sentence, "God made Himself man that man might become God," seems to be strange and abnormal. The thought of union with God is forgotten because of our preoccupation solely with our own salvation; or rather, union with God is seen only negatively, in contrast with our present wretchedness.[12]

That Lossky has in mind Western theology (and maybe the impact of such Western theology in the kind of textbooks traditionally used in Orthodox theological faculties and seminaries) becomes apparent in the following section, which traces this narrowing of theology to Anselm of Canterbury and his *Cur Deus homo.*

---

10. Eusebius, *Ecclesiastical History* 10.4.11.
11. Eliot, "East Coker," part IV.
12. Vladimir Lossky, "Redemption and Deification," in *In the Image and Likeness of God* (Crestwood, NY: St. Vladimir's Seminary Press, 1974), 97–110, at 98–99.

Anselm does seem to mark a watershed in Western theology of the atonement (and in other areas, notably the question of the *filioque*). In the case of the atonement, Anselm's contribution has two dimensions. The first is manifest in Anselm's unhappiness with interpreting the work of Christ in terms that are less than cogently rational, thus rejecting all analogies, imagery, and symbolism, not least the typological exegesis of the Scriptures. Right at the beginning of *Cur Deus homo*, Anselm exposes what he regards as the inadequacy of argument based on what is fitting, appropriate—*convenienter*.

> For it is right that, just as death entered the human race by human disobedience, so life should be restored through the obedience of a man. And to the extent that sin, which was the cause of our damnation, had its beginning from a woman, so the author of our justice and salvation should be born of a woman. And as the devil, who conquered through the taste of a tree that persuaded man, should himself be conquered by the passion of a tree which was borne by a man. Likewise there are many other things that might be carefully considered, which show the untold beauty of our redemption procured in this way.[13]

But for Anselm all these analogies are inadequate, which leads to the second dimension of his thought on the atonement (and other aspects of theology, too). What needs to be demonstrated, as Boso brightly says in response to Anselm, is "solid rational truth" (*veritatis soliditas rationabilis*), that is, the "necessity" (*necessitas*) that underlies God's action, to which Anselm responds: "Is it not enough for the necessary reason (*necessaria ratio*) to be seen, why God must do those things that we say?"[14]

Where "necessary reason" leads Anselm is to an understanding of the atonement in which human sin constitutes an infinite offence against God's honour, amendment for which cannot be made by humankind because of its finitude. Amendment, however, can only be made by a human being. Therefore God must assume humanity so that, as human, he can make amendment for the offence made by humans and so that,

---

13. Anselm, *Cur Deus homo* 1.3, *S. Anselmi cantuariensis archiepiscopi opera omnia*, vol. 2, ed. F. S. Schmitt (London: Thomas Nelson, 1946), 51; my translation.

14. Anselm, *Cur Deus homo* 1.4.

as God, he is able to make amends, since he is himself infinite and can make such infinite recompense.

Anselm's argument has attracted much criticism. The terms in which he finds the "necessary reason" for the atonement are not as independent of cultural conditions as his argument suggests. The notion of God's offended honour seems to belong to the feudal society of Anselm's time. Even if the presuppositions of the argument are found more immediately in the penitential system, introduced throughout the West by Irish monks with their complex notion of amendment for sin through penitential works, this is just as likely to reflect ideas of honour attached to office and person, ideas characteristic of an essentially feudal society. For the purposes of this essay, however, what is important to observe is the way Anselm's search for "necessary reason" drives him towards a way of understanding the atonement that is measurable; it is the vagueness and mere suggestiveness of metaphorical ways of understanding reconciliation between God and the human, as well as the indirectness of imagery, from which Anselm seeks to free theology. One might well think that reason, *ratio*—necessarily human, limited reason—overreaches in seeking an exhaustively rational account of God's relation to humankind and therefore is likely to find itself trapped in human conceptual schemes that are in no way adequate to the manifold ways God is in the incarnate Christ reconciling the human to himself.

The subject of this essay is not, however, simply the atonement, but the *extent* of the atonement, which, I would argue, is a notion that arises from the cast of mind that is confident of success in exploring the ways of God with humans. There seem to me to be three considerations behind thinking of the extent of the atonement. The first arises from the way in which the notion of the atonement, with the idea of making amends, seems to conceive of the matter in quantitative terms; we are thinking about *amounts*: amounts of amendment, of satisfaction (which literally means doing *enough*). If atonement is thought of in quantitative terms, it is natural to think not just how much is needed (in terms of amendment, satisfaction) but how far it will go, its extent. In this sense, the notion of the extent of the atonement is part and parcel of a notion of atonement that thinks in terms of amends. This first consideration is strengthened by the fact that salvation and redemption have come to be considered, in some Christian traditions, in terms of God's predestination or election.

The idea of salvation as election is a fundamental notion: "you have not chosen me, but I have chosen you," as the Lord says to his disciples (John 15:16). The notion of election, of being chosen, was radicalized in the Pelagian controversy. Against Pelagius's conviction that grace is, at best, an assistance to our following God's commands and thus achieving salvation, Augustine insists that only by God's grace are we saved. This grace is undeserved; we can do nothing to elicit or attract it—grace is given freely (*gratia gratis data*). All that the human can do is believe in Christ and thus receive grace by faith. If there is nothing we can do to attain salvation, and it is all a matter of God's grace, which we accept through faith, then the only agent in human salvation is God: salvation is a matter of God's choosing, his election. And this election, belonging to God, belongs also to eternity. To be saved is to be eternally predestined for salvation by God. It follows that not to be saved is to be eternally not predestined for salvation, that is, rejected by God, so that to be damned is to be eternally consigned to damnation by God. Augustine accepts this conclusion with some reluctance. He does not dwell on eternal damnation of the eternally reprobate, but it can be said to haunt his later thought.

Second, if those to be saved are those who have been eternally predestined to salvation by God, then, as the number of human beings created by God is finite, so we are to think in terms of a defined number of the elect. The "hundred and forty-four thousand" of the Apocalypse, "the servants of God" who have been "sealed . . . upon their foreheads" (Rev. 7:3), the "hundred and forty-four thousand who had [the Lamb's] name and his Father's name written on their foreheads" (Rev. 14:1), and who alone can "learn the song" that "they sing . . . before the four living creatures and before the elders" (Rev. 14:3)—these "hundred and forty-four thousand" show a limited, though ample, number of the redeemed.

Third, there is the notion that the redeemed will make up the number of the celestial community, diminished by those angels who fell. Augustine mentions this idea in his *Enchiridion*, a brief summary of the main points of the Christian faith that he composed near the beginning of his final decade. There he states that restored humanity will "fill up the gap left in the society of the angels by the fall of the demons" so that "Jerusalem on high, our mother, the city of God, will not be deprived of the number of its citizens, or even perhaps reign with a more copious number."[15] That last comment suggests that the number of the elect is not exactly determined by the number of the fallen angels, for it may perhaps exceed it. And it should be noted that Augustine goes on to remark that "we know neither the number of the saints nor the number of the impure demons, whose place will be taken by the children of the holy mother, who appeared barren on the earth, those children who will remain in that peace, from which [the demons] have fallen, without any temporal end,"[16] which, while discouraging any computation of the number of the elect, at once affirms the status of the redeemed as substitutes for the fallen angels. Augustine repeats this later in the *Enchiridion*, "by this redemption of humans the losses of that angelic fall is made up,"[17] and again in the *City of God*, which says, God "by his grace gathered together a people so numerous as to replace and renew the gap left by the fallen angels, and thus that beloved city on high will not be deprived of the full number of its citizens, indeed may perhaps rejoice in a more abundant number."[18] Augustine's idea that the elect fill up the diminished celestial community, which does not restrict the number of the redeemed to the number of the fallen angels, is found in Gregory the Great[19] and became a *theologoumenon* discussed by later Latin theologians, not necessarily with agreement. For example, Anselm, in *Cur Deus homo*, rejects the notion on the grounds that it would make the redemption of humankind dependent on the fall of the angels.[20]

If this analysis of the notion of the extent of the atonement in Western Latin theology is correct (I have only sketched what seem to me the main points, as the other essays in this volume develop this theme at greater length and from various perspectives), then it is not surprising that concern about the extent of the atonement is rarely found in the

---

15. Augustine, *Enchiridion* 9.29: *ex eius parte reparata, quod angelicae societati ruina illa diabolica minuerat, suppleretur.... Ita superna Jerusalem mater nostra, civitas Dei, nulla civium suorum numerositate fraudabitur, aut uberiore etiam copia fortasse regnabit.*

16. Augustine, *Enchiridion* 9.29: *Neque enim numerum aut sanctorum hominum aut immundorum daemonum novimus, in quorum locum succedentes filii sanctae matris, quae sterilis apparebant in terris, in ea pace de qua illi ceciderunt, sine ullo temporis termino permanebunt.*

17. Augustine, *Enchiridion* 16.61: *et ex ipsa hominum redemptione ruinae illius angelicae detrimenta reparantur.*

18. Augustine, *De civitate Dei* 22.1.2: *tantum populum gratia sua colligit ut inde suppleat et instauret partem quae lapsa est angelorum, ac sic illa dilecta et superna civitas non fraudetur suorum numero civium, quin etiam fortassis et uberiore laetetur.*

19. Gregory the Great, *In Evangeliis* 24.11.

20. See Anselm, *Cur Deus homo* 1.16–18.

theologies of the Orthodox East, for none of these considerations—predestination springing from the Pelagian controversy, the hundred and forty-four elders of the Apocalypse, the notion that redeemed humans will make up the loss in the angelic society caused by the fall of the angels—has much, if any, resonance in the Orthodox East. The Pelagian controversy passed the Greek East by.

The Apocalypse, though regarded, with some hesitation, as Holy Scripture, has no part in the lectionaries of the Orthodox East, and the notion of redeemed humanity filling up the gap left by the fallen angels is never, to my knowledge, even considered (there is no mention of such an idea in the two relatively long chapters devoted to angels and demons in John Damascene's *On the Orthodox Faith*).[21] Nor is predestination made much of in the theology of the Greek East; allied notions of providence (πρόνοια) and predetermination (προορισμός) were the subject of much discussion throughout the patristic and Byzantine period, but this discussion was largely philosophical, lacking the theological concern with human redemption that lay behind the Latin reflection on predestination. The notion of providence was not purely abstract, however, as can be seen from Saint Maximos the Confessor's response to the opening greeting of his interrogator, Bishop Theodosios of Caesarea in Bithynia, at the dispute in Bizya. Theodosios had opened the proceeding by asking Maximos how he was (Πῶς ἔχεις, κῦρι ἀββᾶ), only to get the reply, "As before all the ages God predetermined for me a way of life in his providence [τὴν περὶ ἐμὲ προνοητικὴν διεξαγωγήν]—so I am."[22] The (brief) discussion that follows is conducted in philosophical terms; Maximos's evident confidence in God's providence can only be construed from his demeanour.

It is perhaps worth dwelling on this.[23] The Western notion of predestination finds support in several passages from the New Testament, most notably Romans 9–11 but also Ephesians 1, which seems to speak directly of predestination (the Latin translation has *praedestinavit* in verse 5 and *praedestinati* in verse 11). The Greek terminology is different: πρόνοια, πρόγνωσις, and προορισμός, meaning providence (or more

---

21. John Damascene, *Expositio fidei* 17–18.

22. *Dispute at Bizya* 3, in *Maximus the Confessor and His Companions: Documents from Exile*, trans. and ed. Pauline Allen and Bronwen Neil (Oxford: Oxford University Press, 2002), 78.

23. This excursus was suggested by Adam Johnson, to whom I am indebted for directing me to the passages from the Damascene.

generally "care"), foreknowledge, and predetermination, respectively. Each term has a rich philosophical heritage in which there was a well-developed understanding that the πρόνοια (providence) of the gods (or of God) does not overrule human freedom. A variety of Greek terms likewise correspond to *freedom*—αὐτεξουσία (sometimes simply ἐξουσία), προαίρεσις, and γνώμη, meaning self-determination, (free) choice, and intention, respectively. For Christians this understanding of πρόνοια (providence) was rooted in their understanding of the human as created in the image and likeness of God (cf. Gen. 1:26). The dominant Greek patristic view understood this to mean that the human was created according to the Word of God (κατ᾽ εἰκόνα Θεοῦ = κατὰ τὸν Λόγον) and manifest in the fact that the human is λογικός ("rational," but with the richer connotations of "participating in the Logos, or Word of God"). Freedom is fundamental to being human. Losing one's freedom was not a consequence of the fall; only the further step of surrendering to the passions could lead to such slavery, which would deprive one of humanity.

It is with this in mind that the Greek Fathers interpret Scripture. Saint John Chrysostom, who preached homilies covering the whole Pauline corpus (Romans to Hebrews), approaches these passages with these firm convictions (and a clear sense of what these passages are really about, that is, Chrysostom is under no doubt that Romans 9–11 is about Israel and the church, not about the predestination of the individual). Nevertheless, he devotes time to dealing patiently with the imagery used by the apostle, especially in Romans 9. For example, homily 17, a long sermon on Romans 9, is primarily concerned with clarifying Paul's argument rather than, as was Chrysostom's normal practice, with drawing practical conclusions, as he himself comments at the close of the homily. On the example of the potter making pots, "one vessel for beauty and another for menial use" (RSV), Chrysostom's overall point is that such examples have a specific purpose, which we must discern and not ascribe to them some kind of universal application. Virtually his first comment on the example is that "God [the real author of the sacred text] seeks not only a demonstration of works, but also the nobility of choice and right intention." On Romans 9:16, which states, "It is not up to him who wills or who runs, but to God who shows mercy," Chrysostom comments, "When it says, 'not to him who will or who runs,' this does not take away self-determination, but shows that it is not all down to him, but needs grace from on high. For it is indeed necessary to will and to run; but not to be confident in one's own labours, but in God's love for humanity (φιλανθρωπία). As he said elsewhere, 'not I, but the grace of God within me' (1 Cor. 15:10)." Similarly, Ephesians 1:5, which says, "in love he predetermined us to the adoption of sons through Jesus Christ in him," must be understood with respect to those who are thus predetermined:

> For it is not from labours or virtuous achievements, but from love; neither from love alone, nor from our own virtue. For if it were from love alone, it would be necessary for all to be saved; if again from our virtue alone, then his presence would be superfluous, and all his dispensation. But neither from love alone, nor from our virtue, but from both. "For he chose us," it says; the one who chooses knows what he is choosing. "In love, it says, he chose us." But virtue saves no one, love being absent.

For Chrysostom, the mystery is the engagement between God's love and the free human response, not one without the other. Others among the Fathers draw on the arsenal of Greek philosophy. Saint Maximos, in his aforementioned interrogation, is asked by Bishop Theodosios to justify his trust in providence. In his reply, Maximos draws on the philosophical distinction between what is up to us (ἐφ' ἡμῖν) and what is not up to us: what is up to us is within our will, and what is not up to us is the realm of God's providence. There is a mysterious interaction between what is up to us and what is up to providence, but human freewill remains sovereign in all this. Saint John of Damascus draws on this in two chapters of his *On the Orthodox Faith* (chs. 43–44; or in the Latin enumeration, 2.29–30), which close his discussion of human nature and concern providence (ch. 43) and foreknowledge and predetermination (ch. 44). There the Damascene repeats Maximos's distinction: "What is up to us does not belong to providence, but to our own self-determination." Much later on, in a chapter concerning whether "God Is Not the Author of Evil," he discusses the Romans passage about the potter. There he reads the potter's making of vessels both beautiful and menial (Rom. 9:19–22) in the light of 2 Timothy 2:20–21, where purification on the part of the individual enables one to become an honourable vessel, purification that of its essence is voluntary.[24] Again, as with Chrysostom, the mystery of free human engagement with God concerns John, not God's will overriding human self-determination: "It must be understood not as of God's own activity, but as of God's allowing through self-determination, furthermore the good is not to be forced."[25]

So far I have argued that a forensic notion of atonement is not prevalent in Eastern Orthodox theology, as it became in the West, and furthermore that consideration of the extent of the atonement hardly gets off the ground, for the concerns and sources relevant to this topic in Western Latin theology have little or no resonance in the Greek East, nor, I would add, in the Syriac East. Having said that, I acknowledge that there has been a tendency among Orthodox theologians to play down the crucifixion and lay all the emphasis on the resurrection, and this is a tendency to be resisted. In some of its manifestations, it is part of a more general anti-Western bias that tends to regard anything that belongs to the Western tradition as, in principle, suspect. Perhaps, in relation to the atonement, the most famous example is to be found in the great Russian churchman and theologian at the turn of the nineteenth century, Metropolitan Antony Khrapovitsky, the founder of the "Russian Orthodox Church Outside Russia," who sought in his understanding of redemption in Christ to shift the focus from the cross to Christ's agony in the Garden of Gethsemane.[26] Fr. Georges Florovsky set himself stoutly against any such sidelining of the cross and has found disciples in the generation of theologians that came after him.[27] Nevertheless, without ignoring the cross or diminishing the centrality

---

24. John's "chapter title" echoes a famous homily by Saint Basil the Great on which John draws, especially on the voluntary nature of the purification.

25. This latter phrase a close echo of Plato's conviction that "virtue knows no master."

26. On Khrapovitsky, see Vladimir Tsurikov, ed., *Metropolitan Antonii Khrapovitskii: Archpastor of the Russian Diaspora*, Readings in Russian Religious Culture 5 (Jordanville, NY: Foundation of Russian History, 2014), which includes a contribution on his soteriology by Archpriest Nikolai Artemov (in Russian), 19–68.

27. See Matthew Baker, Seraphim Danckaert, and Nicholas Marinides, eds., *On the Tree of the Cross: Georges Florovsky and the Patristic Doctrine of Atonement* (Jordanville, NY: Holy Trinity Seminary Press, 2016), the proceedings of a symposium, which includes some hitherto unpublished pieces by Florovsky, including *"In Ligno Crucis,"* a lecture originally published in Swedish. For all Florovsky's emphasis on the centrality of the cross, it does not seem to me that he ignores the other aspects of the Christian doctrine of redemption.

of the cross in the mystery of redemption, it seems to me that what I have argued stands. It is not that the cross is not central, it is rather that an understanding of the cross in the context of a narrow doctrine of sacrifice, or of a way of understanding the work of Christ as primarily making amends for human sin—as the very term "atonement" tends to do—narrows down the variety of ways in which the work and person of Christ have been understood in the Christian tradition. It is the richness of the Christian tradition of expressing the cross and resurrection of Christ that needs to be celebrated and that the patristic and liturgical tradition acknowledges. Any attempt, such as Anselm's, to narrow down the atonement to some necessary rationale expressed, almost inevitably in quantitative terms, seems to me to be taking a dangerous step. And I believe that in making such an assertion that I am representing what the patristic-liturgical-Orthodox tradition unmistakably affirms.

What is there to add? I think it might be worth exploring how the notion of any delimited extent of atonement is sidelined by more central concerns in Orthodox theology. A good place to begin in exploring Orthodox notions of the atonement is with the prayers we find in the divine liturgy. The "prayer of the first antiphon" that accompanies the first litany, said quietly by the priest, reads thus:

> Lord, our God, whose might is beyond compare and whose glory is beyond understanding, whose mercy is without measure and whose love for mankind is beyond all telling, look upon us and upon this holy house, Master, according to your loving kindness, and bestow on us and on those who pray with us your acts of rich mercy and compassion.

It is the first part of the prayer that is most relevant to our concerns: the God from whom we seek redemption is one "whose might is beyond compare and whose glory is beyond understanding, whose mercy is without measure and whose love for mankind is beyond all telling." Redemption then is the expression of God's "love for mankind" (φιλανθρωπία), which is "beyond all telling" (ἄφατος), and is the love of One whose "might is beyond compare," whose "glory is beyond all understanding," and whose "mercy is without measure." This is not simply the conventional "apophatic" ascription to God of his qualities or attributes: apophatic in the sense that they deny that these ascriptions—might, glory, mercy, love—are beyond human understanding and need to be denied in any human sense if they are to be appropriate to God. Rather, it expresses the conviction that God's love is the love of One of boundless might, glory, and mercy. From such a perspective, what is perceived in God is his overwhelming love, and redemption is an expression of this love, which is not qualified by any impotence on God's part in manifesting this love. So, too, from such a perspective the "extent of the atonement" (an unnatural term in this context) is not so much about the limits of the atonement as it is about what is entailed by the *unlimitedness* of God's redeeming love. The suggestion is less that few are chosen and more what limit could there be to God's love—who could possibly fall outside such overwhelming love?

The problem from this perspective is what to make of the repeated assertions of the gospel, on the lips of the Lord, of the "furnace of fire" or the "outer darkness" where "there will be weeping and gnashing of teeth." And consider the quotation from Isaiah 66:24 in Mark's Gospel about being cast "into Gehenna, into the inextinguishable fire, where the worm will not die, nor the fire be quenched," and on one occasion the conclusion says, "for many are called, but few are chosen."[28] It would seem that it is passages such as these that have prevented any unqualified endorsement of universalism in the Orthodox tradition, although pressure to affirm universal salvation (the restoration of all: ἀποκατάστασις παντῶν) is not uncommonly manifest. These passages could be interpreted as an uncompromising way of asserting the radical choice presented by the gospel, as a kind of homiletic warning (it is noticeable that several times the reference to the place of "weeping and gnashing of teeth" occurs in parables, where it could be argued conventional ideas about the afterlife are being adopted).

To understand this approach to the extent of atonement, it is necessary to step back and look at the ways the relationship between God and humankind has been understood in the Christian tradition. Patristic and Orthodox theology begins its understanding of this relationship with the creation of the cosmos and humankind by God. Athanasios,

---

28. See Matt. 8:12; 13:42, 50; 22:13–14; 24:51; 25:30; Mark 9:44, 46, 48 (note that the apparatus suggests that the full formula occurs in later MSS and the Latin versions); Luke 13:28.

for example, says that if we are to proceed with an exposition of the incarnation and the cross, then "it is necessary to speak first about the creation of the universe and its creator, God, so that in this way it may be seen to be fitting that its renewal should take place by the Word who created it in the beginning."[29]

God created the whole universe or cosmos, including human creation "in the image of God," in order to bring the whole created order to the perfection of union with him. Central to this purpose is the creation of humankind, for the human, on the one hand, constitutes a "small cosmos" (μικρὸς κόσμος, or "microcosm" in the coinage of the Renaissance) whose function is to represent the cosmos to God and God to the cosmos, and to act as "bond of the cosmos" (σύνδεσμος τοῦ κόσμου). As Maximos the Confessor put it,

> [The human] was introduced last among beings—like a kind of natural bond mediating between the universal extremes through his parts, and unifying through himself things that by nature are separated from each other by a great distance—so that, by making of his own division a beginning of the unity which gathers up all things to God their Author, . . . he might reach the limit of the sublime ascent that comes about through the union of all things in God.[30]

The role of the human within the cosmos was to bring the whole of creation to union with God, to deification (θέωσις). God's purpose for creation remains—his will and purpose are not frustrated—so that what one might think of as the "greater arc" of theology runs from creation to deification. Humankind, in Adam and Eve according to the biblical account, failed in this role of mediation. Through their sin, death and corruption were introduced into the created order; the created order lost the coinherence secured by human steadfastness to God and became opaque to God's purpose for it (though Maximos stresses that, even in its fallen state, nature remains as God intended it: "nothing natural is

---

29. Athanasios, *De Incarnatione* 1.
30. Maximos the Confessor, *Ambigua* 41:1305BC, in *On Difficulties in the Church Fathers: The Ambigua*, vol. 2, trans. and ed. Nicholas Constas, Dumbarton Oaks Medieval Library 29 (Cambridge, MA: Harvard University Press, 2014), 105.

opposed to God"). The created order became opaque, that is, to the disordered apprehension of fallen humanity. God's solution was—initially through the Law and the Prophets and finally by the incarnation—to draw fallen human nature back to union with him. In the words of the prayer of Anaphora in the liturgy of Saint John Chrysostom: "You brought us out of non-existence into being, and when we had fallen you raised us up again, and left nothing undone until you had brought us up to heaven and had granted us your Kingdom that is to come." Finally, in the incarnation, God assumed human nature in the person of his Son and once again fulfilled the mediating role of the human in the cosmos, and this he did through love. Again in the words of the Anaphora of St. John Chrysostom, "This is how you loved the world: you gave your only-begotten Son, so that whoever believes in him might not perish, but have eternal life," adopting the words of the Fourth Evangelist.

So there is, as it were, a "lesser arc," running from the fall to redemption, the purpose of which is to restore the greater arc, running from creation to deification. Redemption from sin and death is necessary, if the greater arc of God's intention for his creation is to be fulfilled, but redemption is not an end in itself: its purpose is to facilitate God's original and eternal purpose for his created order, to draw it into union with himself, to deify it. This is made clear in the lapidary assertion of Saint Athanasios in *On the Incarnation*, "The Word of God became human, so that the human might become God,"[31] or more fully in *On the Decrees of Nicaea*, "For *the Word became flesh* that he might offer it for all and that we, partaking of his Spirit, might be able to become God."[32] This is an assertion found in the whole Greek patristic tradition, from St. Irenaeus in the second century to St. Gregory Palamas in the fourteenth and beyond. The purpose of the incarnation is not simply redemption from sin and death, but deification (θέωσις). The lesser arc from fall to redemption must be accomplished in order to establish the greater arc from creation to deification. Redemption is essentially an act of God's love for humankind, love which is essentially unitive, and the

---

31. Athanasios, *De Incarnatione* 54.
32. Athanasios, *De Decretis Nicaenae Synodi* 14.4: «ὁ γὰρ λόγος σὰρξ ἐγένετο», ἵνα καὶ προσενέγκῃ τοῦτο ὑπὲρ πάντων καὶ ἡμεῖς ἐκ τοῦ πνεύματος αὐτοῦ μεταλαβόντες θεοποιηθῆναι δυνηθῶμεν.

purpose of this love is not just to make amends for human sin, or even simply to heal the wounds inflicted by sin and death, but to draw the human—and through the human the whole created cosmos—into union with God, which entails deification.

This sense that the goal of God's love is not just the redemption of the human but the deification of the whole cosmos is found in all the major Orthodox theologians of the last century. It was the subject of an article specifically on this theme by Vladimir Lossky, "Redemption and Deification," in a posthumous collection of articles, *In the Image and Likeness of God*, but is found in a more discursive mode in other Orthodox theologians such as Sergii Bulgakov and Dumitru Stăniloae.[33] Although in *The Lamb of God* Bulgakov devotes many pages to redemption,[34] the doctrine is presented as a step on the way to the transfiguration of the human. Indeed, his discussion of redemption significantly includes a treatment of the transfiguration of Christ. As he puts it in the summary he provided of the volume, included at the end of the English translation: "The Divine Incarnation is not only a means to redemption from sin but also the elevation of man to divine-humanity, to which he was summoned when he was created."[35] Stăniloae, too, insists that we see redemption in a broader context: "This transformed Jesus has a decisive role in the saving work after the Resurrection. This means that the world benefits not only from an external forgiveness on the basis of a juridical satisfaction offered by Christ on the cross, but it, too, is subjected to a transformation through the present work of Christ, who is full of the divine life at the right hand of the Father."[36] It is important to note that both Bulgakov and Stăniloae discuss the redemptive work of Christ in the context of his dual roles as high priest and sacrifice. Vladimir Lossky's more focused consideration of the relationship between redemption and deification closes with this reflection:

---

33. And in Georges Florovsky. See n27 above.

34. Sergius Bulgakov, *The Lamb of God*, trans. Boris Jakim (Grand Rapids: Eerdmans, 2008), 342–72, in the section on "The High-Priestly Ministry of Christ," preceded by a subsection on "Christ as High Priest," and followed by subsections on "The Death of Christ and His Descent into Hell" and "The Glorification of Christ."

35. Bulgakov, *Lamb of God*, 446.

36. Dumitru Stăniloae, *The Experience of God: Orthodox Dogmatic Theology*, vol. 3, *The Person of Jesus Christ as God and Saviour*, trans. Ioan Ionita (Brookline, MA: Holy Cross Orthodox Press, 1989), 122. It is really impossible to separate out Stăniloae's treatment of the atonement from his whole discussion of the saving work of Christ.

Considered from the point of view of our fallen state, the aim of the divine dispensation can be termed salvation or redemption. This is the negative aspect of our ultimate goal, which is considered from the perspective of our sin. Considered from the point of view of the ultimate vocation of created beings, the aim of the divine dispensation can be termed deification. This is the positive definition of the same mystery, which must be accomplished in each human person in the Church and which will be fully revealed in the age to come, when, after having finally reunited all things in Christ, God will become all in all.[37]

What I have argued so far is that, from the point of view of the patristic-Orthodox theological tradition, the notion of the extent of the atonement, foreign though it is to the idiom of Orthodox theology, if considered is found to turn upside-down the way this notion is understood in Western theology, where the extent of the atonement is equivalent to the (limited) number of those predestined to salvation or to glory. From the perspective of Orthodox theology, the notion of the "extent" of the atonement is rather understood as unlimited—as unlimited as the "mercy [of God] is without measure and whose love for mankind is beyond all telling," in the words of the prayer already quoted above.

If God's love for humankind is unlimited, then it would seem appropriate that humankind's response to this love will be a love similarly without limit. Often quoted in this context is a passage from Saint Isaac the Syrian (Saint Isaac of Nineveh):

And what is a merciful heart?—It is the heart's burning for the sake of the entire creation, for men, for birds, for animals, for demons, and for every created thing; and by the recollection and the sight of them the eyes of a merciful man pour forth abundant tears. From the strong and vehement mercy which grips his heart and from his great compassion, his heart is humbled and he cannot bear to hear or to see any injury or slight sorrow in creation. For this reason he offers up tearful prayer continually even for

---

37. Lossky, "Redemption and Deification," 110.

irrational beasts, for the enemies of the truth, and for those who harm him, that they be protected and receive mercy. And in like manner he even prays for the family of reptiles because of the great compassion that burns without measure in his heart in the likeness of God.[38]

If a human being can aspire to such limitless compassion, because he is "in the likeness of God," how much more abundant must be God's love for his creation? Such human love and compassion is not easily attained. The whole spiritual wisdom of the Byzantine East, of which the *Philokalia* of 1782, compiled by Saint Nikodimos of the Holy Mountain and Saint Makarios of Corinth, is but a selection, has the ultimate purpose of "purifying, illuminating, and perfecting" the soul so that nothing distracts it from such limitless love and compassion.[39] Jean-Claude Larchet's *Thérapeutique des maladies spirituelles*, already mentioned,[40] provides a thorough introduction to this spiritual wisdom.

I want to conclude by considering two passages from what we should regard as monastic literature: the first from Dionysios the Areopagite's *Epistle 8*; the second from the writings of the twentieth-century Russian monk and starets of the Holy Mountain, Saint Silouan. Dionysios, in his eighth letter, writes to an abbot who sought to prevent a priest absolving someone whom he, the abbot, felt was unworthy of such forgiveness. The abbot, clearly (as would not be uncommon in Dionysios's day) a monk but not a priest, was violating hierarchy in trying to prevent a priest from performing his priestly duty, but the point of the letter goes deeper than that, for the purpose of hierarchy, as Dionysios makes clear, is the drawing of all creation into union with God in love. The abbot, Demophilos, is acting unhierarchically, but more profoundly, he is setting himself against the unitive purpose of hierarchy, which springs from love. Towards the end of the letter, Dionysios illustrates his message by recounting the story of a vision granted to a monk called Karpos, whom he claims as a friend. This monk had been grieved by an

38. Isaac the Syrian, Homily 71 [from "Part One"], in *The Ascetical Homilies of Saint Isaac the Syrian* (Boston, MA: Holy Transfiguration Monastery, 1984), 344–45.

39. *Philokalia*, compiled by Saint Nikodimos of the Holy Mountain and Saint Makarios of Corinth, 4 vols. (London: Faber and Faber, 1979–95), see the title page.

40. See n8.

unbeliever who led a member of the church into apostasy, and he went to bed full of bitterness. At midnight he got up to pray, according to his custom, but he was still plagued by anger and resentment at what had happened. So, in his prayer,

He besought God, by some stroke of lightning, suddenly, without mercy, to cut short the lives of them both. But, while saying this, he declared that he seemed suddenly to see the house in which he stood, first torn asunder, and from the roof divided into two in the midst, and there appeared many-coloured flames of fire before his eyes (for the place now seemed under the open sky) borne down from the heavenly region until it reached him. Then, heaven itself gave way, and he saw, on the vault of heaven, Jesus with countless angels in human form standing around him. This was what he saw above and he marvelled. But below, as Karpos bent down, he said that he saw the very foundation ripped in two, revealing a sort of yawning and dark chasm, and those very men, whom he had cursed, standing before him, on the mouth of the chasm, trembling, pitiful, barely not yet carried down by the slipping of their feet. From below the chasm, there were serpents, creeping up and gliding from beneath, around their feet, now contriving to drag them away, and weighing them down, and luring them; and then again arousing their desire or titillating them with their teeth or their tails, and all the time contriving to pull them down into the yawning gulf. There were certain men also in the midst, colluding with the serpents against these men, at once tearing and pushing and beating them down. And they seemed to be on the point of falling, partly against their will, partly by their will; little by little overcome by the calamity, and at once resigned. And Karpos said that he himself was glad, as he looked below, and careless of what was above. Furthermore, he was vexed and made light of it, because they had not already fallen, and many times attempted to get them to fall, and when he did not succeed, was irritated and swore. Then, when he barely lifted up his eyes, he saw the heaven again, just as he had seen it before, and there Jesus, moved with pity at what was taking place, was getting up from his throne above the heavens and bending down towards them, stretched out a helping hand; while the angels, assisting him, took hold of the two men, from one place or another. And, with his hand still stretched out, Jesus said to Karpos, "Strike me then, for I am ready, even again, to suffer for the salvation of human kind; for it pleases me to prevent others from committing sin. But see, if it is good for you to exchange your place in the chasm and with the serpents for a dwelling place with God and the good angels who love humankind."[41]

The notion that Jesus would be prepared to come again to save humankind is not without parallel in the theology of the East; it is the stuff of much Orthodox folklore. But the story of Karpos raises another point: If there are those consigned to perdition in hell, what should be the reaction of those who have found their way to heaven? Are they aware of the damned? What is their reaction to be? Regret, satisfaction, even joy at the fulfilment of God's purposes? This question seems to be posed very acutely by any doctrine of the atonement that limits its extent, especially by the doctrine of predestination, but it can arise anyway. A certain ungodly glee at the fate of the damned is not unknown in Orthodox circles, as William Dalrymple discovered on his visit to the monastery of Mar Saba in the Judaean Desert, when he met a monk who spoke to him of a "River of Blood . . . full of Freemasons, whores, and heretics: Protestants, Schismatics, Jews, Catholics . . . ," and said that "Fire—fire that will never end, terrible, terrible fire—will come from the throne of Christ, just like on the icons."[42] Nevertheless, it seems to me that such an attitude is at odds with the fundamental temper of the Orthodox tradition.

Fr. Sophrony remarks that Saint Silouan, by living out the word of Christ that was revealed to him, "Keep your mind in hell, and despair not," was led to a kind of limitless prayer: "His prayer reached out beyond the bounds of time, and all thought of the transitory phenomena of human life, of enemies, vanished." Fr. Sophrony continued,

41. Dionysios the Areopagite, *Ep.* 8: 1100A–D. My translation, based on (at some distance) John Parker's translation in *The Works of Dionysius the Areopagite* (London: James Parker, 1897–99), 1.164–66.
42. William Dalrymple, *From the Holy Mountain: A Journey in the Shadow of Byzantium* (London: HarperCollins, 1997), 280–81.

I remember a conversation between him and a certain hermit, who declared with evident satisfaction, "God will punish all atheists. They will burn in everlasting fire." Obviously upset, the Staretz [now Saint] said; "Tell me, supposing you went to paradise and there looked down and saw somebody burning in hell-fire—would you feel happy?" "It can't be helped. It would be their own fault," said the hermit. The Staretz answered him with a sorrowful countenance: "Love could not bear that," he said. "We must pray for all."[43]

I have argued that the notion of the extent of the atonement sits ill within the perspective of Orthodox theology. This is mainly because the notion of the atonement, with the suggestion that salvation is to be understood in terms of making amends, satisfaction, and expiation as the dictionary suggests, narrows down the myriad ways in which the saving work of Christ is understood in the biblical and patristic tradition. Focus on the atonement understood in such terms seems to entail an approach to salvation that is forensic and quantitative. In the mind of Anselm and his successors such an approach offers a way of understanding the *ratio* (the inner logic) of God's *oikonomia*, which might well be thought to be beyond human grasp. Furthermore, focus on the atonement too easily restricts theological reflection to an arc running from the fall to redemption, either obscuring the full story of God's dealing with the world that begins with creation and runs through to deification, which is the consequence of union with God that he intended for creation through the human, or simply regarding the created order as a kind of backdrop to the real story of the redemption of fallen humankind. The greater arc, running from God's creation to his final union with his creation in deification, is not to be sidelined, or ignored, in this way.

At the beginning of this essay, we explored the linguistic history of the word *atonement*, perhaps the only word in theological vocabulary that is native to English. We noted that very quickly the broader connotations of *atonement*—at-one-ment, that is, bringing the estranged into harmony or union—fall away, depriving the concept of atonement of any but a predominantly forensic meaning. We noticed too, however,

---

43. Archimandrite Sophrony (Sakharov), *Saint Silouan the Athonite*, trans. by Rosemary Edmonds (Essex: Stavropegic Monastery of St. John the Baptist, 1991), 48.

that although the verb associated with *atonement* is, surprisingly, secondary to the noun, there is a closely related verb in Middle English contemporary with the emergence of the word *atonement*, namely *to one*, used by the late Medieval English mystics, such as Julian of Norwich and the author of *The Cloud of Unknowing*, to designate the union of the soul with God. Perhaps awareness of that could lend to the word atonement a somewhat broader connotation, not limited to the forensic but embracing the at-one-ment, the union, with God, which is God's purpose in creating. Language is a living thing and not easy to legislate for (and in contrast to other countries, we English have made little attempt to legislate for the words of our language); nevertheless, the suggestion that the roots of the notion of atonement go deeper than might be suspected is worth bearing in mind.

Furthermore, atonement is the action of God, "whose mercy is without measure and whose love for mankind is beyond all telling," and from that perspective to consider the "extent of the atonement" is not to consider the limits of the atonement, as in traditional Western accounts, but to consider that, as an expression of the love and mercy of God, it is hard to put limits to the extent of the atonement, for God's love knows no limit. It is impossible—such is the burden of many of the Lord's parables—to find oneself outside his love. As Vladimir Lossky put it,

In the parousia, and the eschatological fulfilment of history, the whole created universe will enter into perfect union with God. This union will be realized, or rather will be made manifest, differently in each of the human persons who have acquired the grace of the Holy Spirit in the Church. But the limits of the Church beyond death and the possibilities of salvation for those who have not known the light in this life, remain a mystery of the divine mercy for us, on which we dare not count, but to which we cannot place any human bounds.[44]

44. Vladimir Lossky, *The Mystical Theology of the Eastern Church* (London: James Clarke, 1957), 235.

MATTHEW LEVERING

From his long ecumenical experience, Professor Louth knows well the depths of misunderstanding that can arise between East and West, especially regarding the charge of Western rationalism and legalism. For me, this issue is particularly pressing because I fear that my full-length essay, by concentrating too narrowly on what I took to be the theme of the present book, may have contributed to such misunderstanding. Here is not the place to take up the defense of Saint Anselm, which has been done by many scholars, most recently Fleming Rutledge.[1]

Instead, let me begin by concurring with Louth's emphasis on "at-one-ment" and with his highlighting of the Eucharist "along with Paul's reflection on his own transforming experience of God's grace" (p. 23). Louth observes that Christian Scripture and theology have used numerous metaphors or images to describe what God has accomplished in Christ, including "judgment and acquittal," "Christ as victor," "Christ as sacrificial victim, making expiation for the sins of humanity but also as priest offering sacrifice," "Christ as healer," "Christ as teacher," and "Christ as perfect example of what it is to be human" (p. 23). As Louth indicates, it would be easy to locate all of these in the writings of the fathers, including Augustine.

In post-Anselmian Catholic theology and piety, these images have retained their power and place, and other images have arisen as well. For example, Saint Catherine of Siena, building upon Gregory the Great, describes Christ as a bridge who functions to unite humanity and divinity. She also describes the cross as an anvil. Through his sufferings on the cross, she says, Christ is "hammered into an instrument to release

---

1. See Fleming Rutledge, *The Crucifixion: Understanding the Death of Jesus Christ* (Grand Rapids: Eerdmans, 2015).

humankind from death and restore it to the life of grace."[2] As Catherine remarks, Christ on the cross "drew everything to himself: for he proved his unspeakable love, and the human heart is always drawn by love."[3] Rejoicing in the divine attributes—among which she names wisdom, infinite being, beauty, goodness, mercy, generosity, and joy—she urges us to embrace God's "furnace of charity" in Christ.[4] Catherine proclaims, "You, eternal Trinity, are the craftsman; and I your handiwork have come to know that you are in love with the beauty of what you have made, since you made of me a new creation in the blood of your Son. O abyss! O eternal Godhead! O deep sea! What more could you have given me than the gift of your very self?"[5] Far from being in the grip of a rationalism, Catherine knows that she cannot plumb the depths of the wisdom and love of Christ. Indeed, she cries out to God: "You, eternal Trinity, are a deep sea: The more I enter you, the more I discover, and the more I discover, the more I seek you."[6]

Yet Catherine is not insensate to the question of why God would permit some persons to fail to be united to him due to their choosing to remain in their sins rather than to embrace his love in Christ. This is the question of the extent of the atonement. Catherine knows, however, that it is not the kind of question for which we can expect an answer. It belongs to God's own will, which is infinite love, and whose depths we cannot plumb. Still Catherine dares to urge God that it would be more fitting for God if, by his grace, he converted every human being away from sin and enabled every human being to share in the divine life. She tells God, "It would seem you would receive more glory and praise by saving so many people than by letting them stubbornly persist in their hardness. To you, eternal Father, everything is possible. Though you created us without our help, it is not your will to save us without our help. So I beg you to force their wills and dispose them to want what they do not want."[7] To put it simply, this is the issue that the question of the extent of the atonement hits upon. God answers that

---

2. Catherine of Siena, *The Dialogue*, trans. Suzanne Noffke, OP (New York: Paulist, 1980), 65.

3. Catherine, *The Dialogue*, 65.

4. Catherine, *The Dialogue*, 360; cf. 290.

5. Catherine, *The Dialogue*, 365.

6. Catherine, *The Dialogue*, 364.

7. Catherine, *The Dialogue*, 276.

he provides everything possible for the conversion and deification of every sinner—as can already be seen by contemplating the lengths to which God goes in Christ. Of course, this does not answer Catherine's question directly because God does not say that he will save all.

Catherine is not legalistic or rationalistic, but what about theologians trained in Rome in the nineteenth century? The Rome-trained German seminary professor Matthias Joseph Scheeben places his entire theology of Christ's Pasch under the sign of deification. He states, "Through the God-man the fullness of the divinity, which dwells corporally in the head, also dwells in the race, of which the head forms part, in order to elevate and deify it in every respect."[8] Scheeben does not deny that the fall of humanity means that Christ pays our debt on the cross. Indeed, Christ came "to give his life as a ransom for many" (Mark 10:45); and "since all have sinned and fall short of the glory of God, they are justified by his grace as a gift, through the redemption which is in Christ Jesus, whom God put forward as an expiation by his blood" (Rom. 3:23–25). But Scheeben makes clear that Christ's purpose is the "absolutely supernatural elevation of mankind" to "an inexpressible, inconceivably intimate union of mankind with God."[9] Given that this is the purpose of the atonement, Scheeben examines the payment of the debt only after he has, in the first place, underscored the need for the "re-elevation" of the fallen human race to a state of grace and for the corresponding "reunion of the race with God."[10] Certainly, in Christ's "infinite might He frees man from his guilt, and takes away the unworthiness and helplessness which resulted from sin."[11] But Christ does so as the one who deifies human beings, and this always has a primacy for Scheeben: Christ "introduces man into the presence of God, indeed into God's very bosom," and it is for this reason that Christ "is able to fill up the bottomless chasm that sin had blasted open between God and man."[12]

Perhaps it may be said that the problem with the Western view is that it fails to see the *cosmic* purpose of Christ's saving work, what Professor

---

8. Matthias Joseph Scheeben, *The Mysteries of Christianity*, trans. Cyril Vollert, SJ (New York: Crossroad, 2006), 398.

9. Scheeben, *The Mysteries of Christianity*, 399.

10. Scheeben, *The Mysteries of Christianity*, 399.

11. Scheeben, *The Mysteries of Christianity*, 400.

12. Scheeben, *The Mysteries of Christianity*, 400.

Louth calls God's aim from the outset, "to bring the whole of creation to union with God, to deification" (p. 35). Louth comments, "This sense that the goal of God's love is not just the redemption of the human but the deification of the whole cosmos is found in all the major Orthodox theologians of the last century" (p. 37). Scheeben makes precisely the same point. Citing Saint John of Damascus and Colossians 1–2, Scheeben states, "Although the God-man primarily enters into union with the human race, through His humanity as the microcosm, He is placed in relationship with the entire cosmos."[13] Indeed, Scheeben feels free to say that "by His hypostatic union with a created nature He is become the hypostasis of all creation and bears it upon His shoulders."[14] Scheeben insists that "the whole of creation is joined" to Christ and that "creation in its entirety becomes a temple of the Holy Spirit in a unique manner."[15]

When he turns to the work of satisfaction—payment of the penalty of sin—Scheeben highlights Christ's love. The cross was not necessary. Rather, God glorifies the cross, and dignifies the human race, by accomplishing the most sublime act of love and humility upon it. Far from perceiving a merely forensic transaction, Scheeben perceives that love has overcome rebellion from within: "Sin celebrated its triumph when it strove and actually contrived to slay God's Anointed. But at the very moment that Christ seemed to succumb to it, He performed the supreme act of adoration and glorification of God."[16] This perfect act of love was "the most precious honey" and the very opposite of the venom proper to sin.[17] Again, however, the purpose of the whole—the purpose that Scheeben cannot emphasize enough—is the "most extraordinary communication and glorification of God" in cosmic deification.[18] God created the world for Christ and "Christ is the ultimate end [or purpose] of the world."[19] This is how Scheeben, citing Anselm, answers Anselm's question *Cur deus homo?*

Professor Louth observes, "There is a danger in limiting the range of imagery in interpreting Christ's saving work, as one of the great

---

13. Scheeben, *The Mysteries of Christianity*, 401.
14. Scheeben, *The Mysteries of Christianity*, 401.
15. Scheeben, *The Mysteries of Christianity*, 402.
16. Scheeben, *The Mysteries of Christianity*, 427.
17. Scheeben, *The Mysteries of Christianity*, 428.
18. Scheeben, *The Mysteries of Christianity*, 429.
19. Scheeben, *The Mysteries of Christianity*, 429.

Orthodox theologians of the last century, Vladimir Lossky, warned"
(p. 24). This is the view of Thomas Aquinas as well. Aquinas observes,
for example, that the cross can be said to cause our reconciliation to
God in five ways: by the merit of his supreme love; by his satisfaction
for sin, undertaken in supreme love; by his sacrifice, which he offers
through his supreme love; by redemption from slavery to the devil; and
by the divine power.[20] Sometimes scholars assume that Aquinas rejects
the patristic account of the conquest of the devil, but the opposite is
the case.[21] Aquinas also argues that the fittingness of Christ's cross can
be seen from its connection to the many images or figures of the Old
Testament. For example, the cross answers to the tree from which Adam
and Eve rebelliously ate; the cross reveals the breadth, height, length,
and depth of God's work of salvation; the cross points to Noah's ark, to
Moses's rod on the exodus, and to the wood of the ark of the covenant;
and the cross shows that Christ purifies not only humankind but also
the air and the earth since he died in the open air and his blood and
water spilled upon the earth.[22]

  Aquinas explains that Christ came to give us "the full participation
of the divinity, which is the true bliss of man and end [or goal] of human
life."[23] He suggests that for this purpose, the cross was the "most suitable"
or most fitting means since "in the first place, man knows thereby how
much God loves him, and is thereby stirred to love Him in return, and
herein lies the perfection of human salvation."[24] But Aquinas points out
that it was not necessary for God to redeem us through the cross.[25] God
could have redeemed us otherwise; we cannot impose necessity upon the
mystery of salvation.

  Professor Louth suggests that "Anselm and his successors"—among
whom Aquinas is certainly one—approached the atonement (or salvation) solely in terms of "making amends, satisfaction, and expiation"
and offered a "forensic and quantitative" account of salvation that
sought to enable us to understand "the *ratio* (the inner logic) of God's

---

20. See Thomas Aquinas, *Summa theologiae*, trans. the Fathers of the English Dominican
Province (Westminister, MD: Christian Classics, 1981), III, q. 48.
21. See Aquinas, *Summa theologiae* III, q. 48, a. 2.
22. See Aquinas, *Summa theologiae* III, q. 46, a. 4.
23. Aquinas, *Summa theologiae* III, q. 1, a. 2.
24. Aquinas, *Summa theologiae* III, q. 46, a. 3.
25. See Aquinas, *Summa theologiae* III, q. 46, a. 2.

oikonomia, which might well be thought to be beyond human grasp" (p. 42). My purpose in this brief space has been to register agreement with Professor Louth in rejecting purely forensic, legalistic, and rationalistic approaches. At the same time, I think that his notion of "Anselm and his successors" needs to be revisited for the sake of better East-West understanding.

RESPONSE TO ANDREW LOUTH

MICHAEL HORTON

The Canons of Dort affirm that Christ's death "is of infinite value and worth, more than sufficient to atone for the sins of the whole world."[1] Hence, the gospel is "announced and declared without differentiation or discrimination to all nations and people."[2] Those who reject this free announcement perish "not because the sacrifice of Christ offered on the cross is deficient or insufficient but because they themselves are at fault."[3] "But all who genuinely believe and are delivered and saved by Christ's death from their sins and from destruction receive this favor solely from God's grace—which he owes to no one—given to them in Christ from eternity."[4]

According to the traditional Reformed view, the free announcement of Christ's saving work is for every person, and all the elect will freely embrace Christ through Spirit-given faith. From this perspective, then, I am honored to engage Christian scholars whom I hold in high esteem.

Noting important differences in both method and substance between Eastern and Latin approaches to the question, Andrew Louth helpfully identifies two broad areas of particular relevance.

Narrowing to a Forensic "Atonement"

Andrew Louth believes that Latin (including Protestant) theology tends to treat the cross in abstraction from the "greater arc" of creation and deification. In so doing, the Christian West focuses inordinately on the legal or forensic dimension, wedded to a rationalistic tendency and an

---

1. Canons of the Synod of Dort, 2nd Main Point, Art. 3, in *Liturgical Forms and Prayers of the United Reformed Churches in North America together with the Doctrinal Standards of the URCNA* (Wellandport, Canada: United Reformed Churches in North America [Canada], 2018), 267.
2. Canons of the Synod of Dort, Art. 5.
3. Canons of the Synod of Dort, Art. 6.
4. Canons of the Synod of Dort, Art. 7.

Anselmian theory of satisfaction that owes more to a feudal economy than to the economy of grace attested in Scripture and the patristic consensus. Consequently, the emphasis falls on a quantitative analysis of sin and justification (i.e., how much debt and how much satisfaction). By contrast, the Christian East indwells the "greater arc" of God's cosmic plan to unite all things in Christ and to deify humanity.[5]

First, and of less importance, I question his interpretation of Anselm (pp. 25–26), which is often taken for granted today, even in recent Reformed critiques.[6] At the beginning of his argument in *Cur Deus homo*, Anselm observes that an impassible God cannot be personally harmed—thus excluding at the outset the possibility that the atonement could be a satisfaction of God's personal dignity.[7] Thus, he argues, God's concern as loving, good, just, and righteous is to restore "the beauty and order of the universe" as its Lord and governor.[8] If Anselm thinks of God in feudal terms, is it far from the biblical conception of Yahweh as the suzerain who seeks the good of his realm? Satisfaction of justice is indeed essential to restoration, but the latter is clearly the goal.[9] The form indeed is deductive rather than exegetical; Anselm here assumes the scriptural support for his premises. I may quibble with bits and bobs, but Anselm's argument should be weighed on its own merits.[10] In any case, Anselm does not provide the definitive statement of Christ's saving work for Reformed theology. At the cross, God justifies himself as well as sinners.[11] Colin Gunton observes, "In face of a tendency to mythologize the metaphor of ransom, Anselm's achievement is immense."[12] But, as I've said, this is as much push-back against some traditional Reformed critiques of Anselm as others.

5. See Andrew Louth, "The Place of Theosis in Orthodox Theology," *Partakers of the Divine Nature: The History and Development of Deification in the Christian Traditions*, ed. Michael J. Christensen and Jeffery A. Wittung (Grand Rapids: Baker Academic, 2008), 33–35.

6. Louis Berkhof, *Systematic Theology* (Grand Rapids: Eerdmans, 1996), 385–86.

7. Anselm, *Cur Deus homo*, in *Basic Writings*, trans. S. N. Deane, 2nd ed. (Peru, IL: Open Court, 1962), 220, 223.

8. Anselm, *Cur Deus homo*, 223, 300.

9. Anselm, *Cur Deus homo*, 224.

10. See my exposition of Anselm's argument in *Justification*, vol. 2 (Grand Rapids: Zondervan, 2018), 249–51.

11. Referring to P. T. Forsyth's *The Justification of God*, Colin Gunton says, "The theme of the book is that the justice of God can be found only where he justifies himself, and that is in the act of atonement on the cross." Gunton, *The Actuality of Atonement: A Study of Metaphor, Rationality, and the Christian Tradition* (Edinburgh: T&T Clark, 1988), 106.

12. Gunton, *The Actuality of Atonement*, 87.

More important is Louth's suggestion that Western thinking focuses one-sidedly on the idea of *atonement*. Louth wisely reminds us of the "danger in limiting the range of imagery" (p. 24). In fact, the same warning appears in standard Reformed treatments. And that this range has been often limited in Western treatments I do not question. However, as on other points characterized as uniquely "Western," my greatest concern with Orthodox presentations is that while they affirm that ideas like substitution have been exaggerated, they end up dispensing with such concepts altogether.

At least with respect to classic Reformed confessions and expositions, the "greater arc" is fully legible, with the pattern (following the Nicene-Constantinopolitan Creed) of the triune God, creation, fall, redemption, and consummation. Christ's death itself is treated within the wider context of other aspects, with many terms other than *atonement* (viz., recapitulation, victory, redemption, reconciliation, propitiation, liberation, immortality, etc.).[13] Further, his saving work is identified not only with his passion but his incarnation and active obedience (recapitulation) as well as his resurrection, ascension, and parousia.

Like Basil and other patristic sources, confessional Reformed theology consistently places Christ's person and work within the larger category of his threefold office (*munus triplex*) as prophet, priest, and king. This rubric requires attentiveness to more than the discharge of a debt. Reformed theology draws heavily on the patristic (especially Irenaean) motif of recapitulation. Jesus Christ not only "undoes" Adam's treason but attains by his incarnation and active obedience the merit of the consummation—the Tree of Life—which our older theologians did not hesitate to celebrate under the name "deification." Calvin says that we find our purity in his conception, redemption in his passion, acquittal in his condemnation, remission of the curse in his cross, reconciliation in his descent into hell, mortification in his tomb, and newness of life and immortality in his resurrection.[14]

---

13. Reformed theology is placed within the "Irenaean" as opposed to "Origenist" stream of the patristic heritage. Justifying this distinction and the location of Reformed teaching in the former is my goal in "Atonement and Ascension," in *Locating Atonement: Explorations in Constructive Dogmatics*, ed. Oliver Crisp and Fred Sanders, (Grand Rapids: Zondervan, 2015), 226–50.

14. Calvin, *Institutes* 2.16.19.

His task was so to restore us to God's grace as to make of the children of men, children of God; of the heirs of Gehenna, heirs of the Heavenly Kingdom. Who could have done this had not the self-same Son of God become the Son of man, and had not so taken what was ours as to impart what was his to us, and to make what was his by nature ours by grace? Therefore, relying on this pledge, we trust that we are sons of God, for God's natural Son fashioned for himself a body from our body, flesh from our flesh, bones from our bones, that he might be one with us. Ungrudgingly he took our nature upon himself to impart to us what was his, and to become both Son of God and Son of man in common with us.[15]

Calvin says that "deification" is "the greatest possible blessing."[16] Our older theologians defended deification as well, often quoting patristic and Byzantine sources (especially the Cappadocians, Athanasius, and John of Damascus), although admittedly this topic (often treated under the heading "glorification") has not been as central in many modern Reformed treatments. Calvin offers this memorable reflection:

We see that our whole salvation and all its parts are comprehended in Christic. . . . If we seek any other gifts of the Spirit, they will be found in his anointing. If we seek strength, it lies in his dominion; if purity, in his conception; if gentleness, it appears in his birth. For by his birth he was made like us in all respects that he might learn to feel our pain. If we seek redemption, it lies in his passion; if acquittal, in his condemnation; if remission of the curse, in his cross; if satisfaction, in his sacrifice; if purification, in his blood; if reconciliation, in his descent into hell; if mortification of the flesh, in his tomb; if newness of life, in his resurrection; if immortality, in the same; if inheritance of all blessings, in his Kingdom; if untroubled expectation of judgment, in the power given to him to judge. In short, since rich

---

15. Calvin, *Institutes* 2.12.2.
16. Calvin, *Commentaries on the Catholic Epistles*, trans. John Owen (repr., Grand Rapids: Eerdmans, 1948), 371.

store of every kind of good abounds in him, let us drink our fill from this fountain, and from no other.[17]

In union with Christ, the archetypal εἰκὼν τοῦ Θεοῦ, we are being restored—and will be fully restored to God's image beyond anything experienced by Adam and Eve before the fall.

Still, the legal aspect of Christ's work remains the basis for all the other aspects of his achievement. The key biblical passages for *Christus Victor* confirm this point. For example, Christ's triumph over the "rulers and authorities" in Colossian 2:13–15 is credited to the fact that he forgave our sins "by canceling the record of debt that stood against us with its legal demands. This he set aside, nailing it to the cross." Death has lost its sting, but only because "the sting of death is sin, and the power of sin is the law," and by removing the *condemnation*, the sentence of death is lifted (1 Cor. 15:56). Satan has lost his kingdom because his accusations fall on deaf ears. "There is therefore no condemnation for those who are in Christ Jesus" (Rom. 8:1).

I find the Orthodox tradition helpful in reminding me that I need not only to understand what we are redeemed *from* (viz., guilt, death, condemnation, Satan's rule, etc.) but what we are redeemed *for* (deification). But where traditional Reformed theology encompasses both, my concern is that Eastern Orthodox expositions typically marginalize or ignore the former. If this is so, then Reformed interpretations are actually *less* reductionistic. More significantly, the marginalization or even absence of categories often dismissed as Western (e.g., original sin, propitiation, justification) leaves the other crucial aspects (e.g., evil powers and death, release from disordered passions, and immortality) without any legal foundation. The legal aspect is not the *whole* story, but without it there is no story.

Narrowing the Scope to the "Elect"

If the first area of broad difference narrows Christ's work to "atonement," then the second, according to Louth, is a narrowing of God's saving love and grace to the "elect." The very subject—"the extent of the atonement"—says Louth, "is a notion that arises from the cast of mind

---

17. Calvin, *Institutes* 2.16.19.

that is confident of success in exploring the ways of God with humans" (p. 26). Is this to suggest that Scripture sheds no light on the question? Or that even if it does, one would transgress the apophatic posture by presuming to interpret it faithfully?

We all acknowledge that there are passages that seem to favor particular grace. Louth even acknowledges, "The idea of salvation as election is a fundamental notion: 'you have not chosen me, but I have chosen you,' as the Lord says to his disciples (John 15:16)." Nevertheless, as with other doctrines deemed inordinately Latin, this is the last we hear of election; it seems to play no substantive role in theological exegesis. "The Western notion of predestination finds support in several passages from the New Testament," he mentions, but only to turn to a defense of a libertarian account of the moral liberty of fallen human beings (p. 29). In fact, "Human freewill remains sovereign in all this" (p. 31). Though he says that it is a "fundamental notion" in Scripture, electing grace is not "made much of in the theology of the Greek East" (p. 29). "The notion of election, of being chosen, was radicalized in the Pelagian controversy," he asserts (p. 27), although I would suggest that the notion of election was merely *defended* in the Pelagian controversy, since Pelagius and his disciples rejected it.

Louth also points to important differences over the extent of the fall. According to Eastern churches, "Losing one's freedom was not a consequence of the fall; only the further step of surrendering the passions could lead to such slavery, which would deprive one of humanity" (p. 30). Once more the argument fails to recognize that death is the consequence of guilt ("in Adam" and incurred by us) and also that in the fall humans did not lose their freedom to choose (natural ability) but rather their freedom to choose well (moral ability). The Reformed have always rejected *utter* depravity. It is not that we are by birth as bad as we can possibly be but that the inherited guilt and corruption affect the whole self (totally) such that one cannot (will not) seek God and his righteousness apart from the liberation that comes with regenerating grace. Yet, as image-bearers and by God's common grace, unbelievers can do many good things as far as common society is concerned. Like the ancient Christian teachers, Reformed theology is alert to the danger of pagan determinism and its denial of human responsibility.[18]

18. See Richard Muller, *Divine Will and Human Choice: Freedom, Contingency and Necessity in Early Modern Reformed Thought* (Grand Rapids: Baker Academic, 2017).

Louth suggests that the Western view correlates between viewing the *nature* of the atonement "in quantitative terms" and its *extent* in the same way: "in terms of a defined number of the elect" (pp. 26–27). His examples of Western arguments for election are intriguing (the 144,000 in the Apocalypse and the idea of a specific number of elect souls filling up the number of fallen angels to complete the cosmic hierarchy; p. 28), but I am not aware of any Reformed system that even mentions these passages (especially the speculative one based on the chain of being).

According to Orthodox teaching, "The suggestion is *less that* few are chosen and *more* what limit could there be to God's love—who could possibly fall outside such overwhelming love?" (p. 34, emphasis mine). "Less that . . . and more what . . ." suggests merely greater emphasis, but "more what" seems to *negate* the former entirely. If no one could possibly fall outside such overwhelming love, then of course it could not be that few are chosen, although he has affirmed this as "a fundamental notion" accepted by Orthodoxy (based on Matt. 22:14 and other passages). He concludes that everyone will experience God and his grace in differing degrees according to their response to his commands.

Passages on election as well as final separation, says Louth, "have prevented any unqualified endorsement of universalism in the Orthodox tradition, although pressure to affirm universal salvation (the restoration of all: ἀποκατάστασις πάντων) is not uncommonly manifest" (p. 34). Louth appears sympathetic to this position, suggesting the possibility that such passages could be simply "a kind of homiletic warning" (p. 34). Like Greggs (see below), it strikes me that Louth's position reflects a growing attraction to universalism in Orthodox (as in Roman Catholic and Protestant) circles that is distinctly modern. In any case, the Neoplatonic pattern of dispersion from a primal unity and return (*exitus-reditus*) appears to tilt toward Origen's ἀποκατάστασις πάντων. In contrast, Reformed theology is focused on the pattern of creation, fall, redemption, and the consummation (a more "Irenaean" emphasis on Christ's descent and ascent in the flesh). Reformed theology affirms quite strongly the breadth of redemption, including angels and humans as well as bringing the whole creation in its sweep—"as far the curse is found," in the words of the Calvinist hymn-writer Isaac Watts ("Joy to the World"). But "all creation" redeemed does not mean "every creature" redeemed.

FRED SANDERS

H ow would you say that in Greek?" is a salutary question in Christian doctrine and one that I think all theologians ought to keep in the back of their minds. It's a question that holds our theological ways of putting things, whatever language we may be using, a little closer to a shared home base in the linguistic matrix of the New Testament. From this position of apostolic textual privilege, theological Greek also looks back and forth over several centuries of usage, from the Septuagint's rendering of crucial Old Testament terms, to the early tradition of those church fathers who had the advantage of reading and writing with the same Hellenic terms and structures. Often, recourse to theological Greek clarifies and simplifies a discussion that is drifting into abstraction and overcomplexity, as when the modern formulation "the economic Trinity and the immanent Trinity" is redescribed as *oikonomia* and *theologia*. Recourse to theological Greek also materially enriches theological understanding. I remember the shock of illumination when I first learned that when we say the Son of God assumed human nature, we are alluding to a verb from Hebrews 2:16: the founder of salvation does not *epilambanetai* angels, but rather takes on, takes hold of, or assumes the seed of Abraham. All of this is clearest in Greek, where the connections were first drawn.

So there is something auspicious in Andrew Louth's oblique approach to the question of the extent of the atonement, starting as it does from the observation that there would be no perfect way to ask the question in Greek, or in directly New Testament phraseology, or, more to the point, in terms used by the Greek Orthodox patristic tradition. Louth's standoffishness about even entering the discussion is, I confess, bracing. It must be tempting to invoke Orthodox otherness, hover above the fray, and simply decline the invitation to make use of the terminology offered.

But Louth does in fact engage the question of the extent of the atonement, and he does so by locating it, with some admitted slippage, in the broad context of Orthodox theology. The immediate result is, in my opinion, beneficial: it elevates the discussion, introduces some helpful perspective, and expands the range of issues to be discussed. The story arc that runs from human fall to human redemption, Louth points out, is the arc traced by atonement theology. He directs our attention from this lesser arc to the greater one, which starts at creation and ends with cosmic deification. The point is not to deny the importance, or even the centrality, of this lesser arc. The point is rather to show its presuppositions and implications by reminding us that God's plan is to bring creation into being and then into union with himself. The purpose of the lesser arc of atonement is to restore the greater arc of union, or the deification of the creature.

This is the right context in which to do atonement theology. God's ultimate purposes with regard to the creature need to be invoked and held steadily in mind throughout the entire doctrine, or atonement theology itself will be distorted, cramped, and impoverished. What Louth's approach summons us to in particular is a dogmatic ordering of atonement and incarnation to each other: Did the Son become incarnate to make the sacrifice of reconciliation possible, or did he die and rise as a necessary step along the way to carrying out the real goal, which was joining divinity and humanity in himself? This delicate question requires balance and precision to get right. Readers of T. F. Torrance will recognize the question as central to the structure of his theology. In fact, Torrance's students report that he routinely assigned the essay topic, "The Interrelationship between the Incarnation and the Atonement." Less capable theologians sometimes make a mess of the relation between incarnation and atonement. Only a disfigured portrayal of the Christian message pits the two against each other: a supposedly life-affirming "incarnation instead of atonement" in particular fits modern sensibilities. But Louth's two-arc model holds open at least the possibility of rightly relating the two. The crucial move that he commends is to identify the creation-deification arc as the comprehensive one within which the sin-atonement arc is contextualized, not vice versa. That is true, but it is not all that needs to be said. The cross may be a means to the end of the incarnation's larger purposes, but the incarnation is also ordered to the cross in a quite direct way. The biblical message is never about any incarnation except the Paschal incarnation. The biblical incarnation moves directly to atonement by death and resurrection. Western advocates of the so-called Franciscan view of the incarnation, or "incarnation anyway," have usually acknowledged the way the actual biblical narrative, so focused on the death of Jesus, chastens or restricts a metanarrative that would give too much weight to speculative possibilities.

Louth affirms Lossky's argument that in the "constricting perspectives of a theology dominated by the idea of redemption, the patristic sentence, 'God made Himself man that man might become God,' seems to be strange and abnormal" (p. 24). That great patristic formula of exchange does sometimes land oddly on the sensibilities of, for instance, evangelical Protestants, and sometimes it has the beneficent effect of jolting their sensibilities into a larger framework. But another reason it makes a "strange and abnormal" sound in evangelical ears is that the sentence quoted in isolation simply fails to allude to redemption. In most contexts where the sentence appears among the Greek fathers, it is a ringing statement of the larger arc that is never far away from an evocation of the smaller arc. In *On the Incarnation*, for instance, Athanasius freely uses the vocabulary of debt, ransom, self-offering, sacrifice, and ending the law of sin and death. The larger arc enshrines the smaller, even in a work whose title and opening paragraphs signal its intent to speak comprehensively of the incarnation. This, I would say, is the patristic norm, and today we should seek ways to affirm it without imbalance or distortion of either arc.

A major task of theologizing about the extent of the atonement is the task of doing justice to the universal language used by Scripture. Louth offers a couple of ways to do this. First, he speaks of the deification of the whole cosmos, which has the advantage of directing our attention to the way the work of Christ changed something objective about the world. You can't get much more universal than the universe, so this is an interesting path to consider.

The second way Louth seeks to do justice to the universal language of Scripture is looser and less instructive: he shifts to a meditation on the unlimitedness of God's redeeming love. If we jump from the "all" passages of Scripture to a query about the extent of divine love, we are bound to suffer the thrilling vertigo of astonishment at God's great love.

It sounds inviting, but it is simply not the way Scripture or the great lines of the Christian tradition have approached the question. It is rhetorically powerful to ask "who could possibly fall outside such overwhelming love," but if the answer is flatly "nobody," then in our attempt to do justice to Scripture's universal language we have only ended by dogmatically affirming universal salvation. To use for once the much-maligned language of calculation, I always take soteriological universalism to be a sign that I should go back and check my work since I must have divided by zero at some point in the equation.

Louth's essay makes much of the tension between forensic and transformative motifs in soteriology. The oft-noted fact that the word atonement is uniquely aboriginal to the English language becomes, for Louth, an index to its potential as a bearer of theological meaning in either of these directions. Essentially, the word can point toward the forensic (as it usually does, aligning with justification) or else toward the mystical (ultimately, to deification). At some points, Louth seems to presuppose a dichotomy between the forensic and the transformative, as if we had to choose between the legal and the actual. But if the intention is to dichotomize, then we begin to run afoul of an important dynamic in Scripture: the inner relationship between the forensic and transformational is part of the substructure of biblical soteriology. Consider how Romans begins with a mostly juridical set of categories in its first five chapters before shifting to mostly transformational categories of experiential appropriation in chapters six through eight. Similar dynamics are evident in John's Gospel and Epistles. One of the constructive possibilities that I think Louth's etymological meditation on atoning versus oneing opens is that the uniquely English word *atonement* might be a fitting lexical receptacle for Scripture's own complex doctrine of salvation in both modes. Louth's own essay may contain some of these possibilities, as he is not consistent in treating the two quantities disjunctively.

The least helpful aspect of this Orthodox reflection on the extent of the atonement is not in its material content but in the rhetorical decision to handle classical proponents of Western theology with unnecessary roughness. Anselm in particular, who is surely by this time inured to being uncharitably misread and unread, takes a real beating once again, at least in effigy. Anselm speaks sometimes *remoto Christo*, sometimes with the voice of faith, sometimes in mathematical terms, sometimes in terms redolent of his social setting. But always he speaks from an intuition, perhaps more but never less than aesthetic, of the divine order that flows from God's triune perfection and permeates all God's ways in the world. Deafness to this fundamental element of Anselmian theology diminishes any work of theological interpretation. To miss the note of awe at God's well-ordered perfection is to miss the point of his classic treatment of atonement. And that is to miss the opportunity for mutually enriching dialogue between East and West, which remains a possibility.

RESPONSE TO ANDREW LOUTH

TOM GREGGS

I find it difficult to disagree with huge swathes of Professor Louth's presentation. The sense of the cosmic nature of divine salvation and the broader arc of divine loving transformation within which God responds to human sin through the crucifixion and resurrection of Christ corresponds well to the narrative of Scripture. Scripture tells of the loving economy of God from creation to transformation in the *eschaton*, and Professor Louth's emphasis on this relates well to a universalistic hope that concerns God's omnipotent love for the whole creation.

Indeed, it is significant that Professor Louth leaves open the possibility of universal salvation. He writes in captivating terms:

> God's love is the love of One of boundless might, glory, and mercy. From such a perspective, what is perceived in God is his overwhelming love, and redemption is an expression of this love, which is not qualified by any impotence on God's part in manifesting this love. So, too, from such a perspective the "extent of the atonement" (an unnatural term in this context) is not so much about the limits of the atonement as it is about what is entailed by the *unlimitedness* of God's redeeming love. The suggestion is less that few are chosen and more what limit could there be to God's love—who could possibly fall outside such overwhelming love? (p. 34)

And he follows this with a recognition of the limitless of God's redeeming love to tend or suggest a universal scope for the atonement. This corresponds well with my own account of Christian universalism emerging from an account of the omnipotence of divine love in Jesus Christ. Indeed, arising from this point, three more material and nuanced matters need to be discussed in terms of the parallels to the approach outlined in my own chapter.

First, the instinct for and possibility of the hope of universal salvation produces a committed desire not to detach one locus of doctrine or dogma from the others. Professor Louth's commitment to considering salvation (and its extent) within the broader framework of Christian doctrine and to see this locus through the lens of the nature of the God of the gospel, creation, and the *eschaton* prevents distorted accounts of salvation that separate the will of God from the love of God, the love of God from creation, the person of Christ from the work of Christ, Christ as judge from Christ as *Pantokrator*, and so forth. Professor Louth's chapter recognizes the dynamic interactions of doctrines and that we cannot divorce speech about divine loving from salvation, speech about creation from transformation, speech about sacrificial death from resurrection, and speech about sin and judgement from grace and re-creation. The same doctrinal schematic concerns that lead me to dare to hope that the scope of salvation might be universal are those which similarly lead this presentation of the Eastern Orthodox view to leave open the possibility.

Second, and related to this, for Professor Louth as for my own presentation, the *possibility* of universal salvation is a *hope* and not a dogmatic principle. Although I find much to support the case for universalism, *personally* I cannot do more than dare to hope for it: there can be no dogma of universalism. The reason is that God's free loving cannot be bound by a principle external to the free divine, self-determining life: there is a degree of *apophasis* about this issue since God's love is "beyond all telling" (p. 33). Furthermore, as I discuss in my own chapter, the urgency of the gospel and the reality of sin and judgement (in the current world as well as in Scripture) determines that there cannot be, in Professor Louth's words, "unqualified endorsement of universalism" (p. 34). My own way of discussing this is to speak of the final victory of Christ—a victory in a person (who in his divine loving is free as well as constant), not in a principle of triumphant grace.[1]

Third, while it is vastly important to locate Christian accounts of salvation within broader systemic schemas, to ensure there is consistency

---

1. See Tom Greggs, "'Jesus Is Victor': Passing the Impasse of Barth on Universalism," *Scottish Journal of Theology* 60, no. 2 (May 2007): 196–212.

with one's accounts of the divine life, the creation, the person of Christ and so forth, as Professor Louth points out, it is impossible to avoid a recognition of those passages which speak in binarized terms about rejection and the centrality of choice. In this, he leaves open a possibility not vastly dissimilar to that of J. A. T. Robinson and Trevor Hart in their senses of homiletic or kerygmatic hell (pp. 41–42; cf. my own chapter, p. 207). Certainly, as I account in my own chapter, *both* images of the omnipotence of divine love and the possibility of universal salvation *and* images of judgement and hell exist in the Scriptures. The question is how we hold these two sets of images together. Do we allow them to stand side-by-side as different possibilities of understanding the extent of the atonement? Or do we try to explain one set or other away—as an existential expression of the reality of life without God, as hyperbole aimed at reminding the Christian of the grace of divine loving, or as meaningful only contextually (either within the text or the historical geographical locations)? Or do we read one set of images hermeneutically through the other? Whatever choice we make, there needs to be, as this chapter makes clear, a willingness to recognise the existence of both possibilities rather than a theological operational presumption of the unquestionable and undebatable reality of separationism.

A further area of agreement that I have with Professor Louth is his pointing to further modes of expressing God's economy of salvation beyond forensic language (pp. 20–22). We have, at times, reduced the captivating, powerful, life-changing, history-shaping reality of the salvific work of the God of the gospel to reductive, overly conceptualised, semicontractual, self-limiting models of the atonement that we espouse as if there were only one and as if the model itself—and not Jesus Christ in his self-sacrificial life, death, resurrection, and ascension—was the cause of salvation. The language and imagery of salvation in the New Testament is manifold. The reduction of the life, death, and resurrection of Jesus to a single-dimensional account of the atonement or of the imagery of salvation runs deeply contrary to classical, creedal Christianity (cf. p. 30–32). Technically speaking, there is no dogma of the atonement: the ecumenical councils never settled—nor found it necessary to consider—which account of the salvation was *the account* that should be adhered to by all Christians. Instead, the Nicene-Constantinopolitan creed *narrates* the broad contours of the life of Jesus (the salvific *events* of his life) within the context of the gracious incarnating of God's Son in creation and the life and being of God, the Holy Trinity:

> who for us, and for our salvation, came down from heaven, and was incarnate by the Holy Ghost and of the Virgin Mary, and was made human;
> he was crucified for us under Pontius Pilate, and suffered, and was buried, and the third day he rose again, according to the Scriptures, and ascended into heaven, and sitteth on the right hand of the Father;
> from thence he shall come again, with glory, to judge the quick and the dead;
> whose kingdom shall have no end.

While the Council of Chalcedon added greater reflection on the dogma of Christ's *person* (Jesus Christ as *one* person in *two* natures—the hypostatic union of God and humanity in the one person Jesus Christ) and states that the Son of God's becoming human is "for our salvation," there is no conceptual model enshrined in relation to the *work of salvation*.

However, I have three concerns about the description offered by Professor Louth. First, while I do not think that forensic imagery is the *only* imagery, it is nevertheless present as well. So, for example, in Romans 5:8, we are told that Christ died for us. This is explained in verse 9 in forensic language: we are justified by his blood (with its potential ideas of sacrifice) and saved from God's wrath. In verse 10, this is augmented and supplemented with a more subjective account of personal realisation: we are reconciled to God and now saved by *life* (which means the account is no longer just forensic since it is life and not blood that saves). Forensic language is still nevertheless part of the narrative and makes sense of the urgency of the gospel.

Second, I am unsure the Western tradition(s) singularly utilise forensic language. Within the Protestant traditions (even described in the most cursory manner), Calvin and Barth offer a strong emphasis in their account of salvation of being *in Christ*, Wesley's accounts of sanctification and salvation are heavily influenced by Eastern accounts of participation, Schleiermacher has a strongly subjectivist account, and the more liberal traditions emphasise pedagogical understandings of Christ's life. Furthermore, I have rarely if ever come across the discussion of the fallen angels (pp. 27–28) and would consider Augustine (the greatest theologian of *charitas*) to be protecting the manifold love of God in salvation in response to Pelagius when read in terms of salvation and not hamartiology or theodicy.

Third, and related, I am unsure that Anselm has quite as much influence in terms of his account of satisfaction as the essay suggests. Certainly, Anselm's insistence that the work and person of Christ cannot be separated has been core to the Western understanding. But Anselm's account of satisfaction is recognised as an attempt to narrate the gospel to his own context—a context of feudalism which makes language of rendering honour and making satisfaction contextually meaningful by way of illustration.

Perhaps inevitably as a Western theologian, I do wonder about the dangers of underemphasising the grace of God in saving us from sin. In this way, I would wish to speak not of *theosis* in the transformation God brings about but *anthroposis*. We are made in the image of God in that we share in Christ's humanity, but we are not yet fully human as Christ is fully human. Christ becomes human both to restore us in our relation to God and to transform our humanity into the likeness of his. After all, it is the temptation "to be like God" that the serpent offers in the fall narrative. In God's loving and reconciling grace, we are transformed into true humanity in a manner which reverses the fall *and* brings us into the full likeness of Christ. We become, therefore, not participants in divinity but *in Christ* participants in Christ's *humanity*. In Barth's account of the eternal, double predestination of Christ and of all humanity in him (cf. my own chapter, pp. 206–7), creation is not elected in part to damnation (p. 27) but—in a way that parallels accounts of *theosis* but with an emphasis on participation and being in Christ—to full participation in the humanity of Christ. This takes place in the present through the gracious work of the Spirit (something that could be further explored in Professor Louth's chapter; cf. p. 43), who in time enables the human to take the form of Christ and in him (*as* creatures) and through his work of reconciliation and redemption to *participate* in the eternal loving of the Father by the Son and the Son by the Father.

ROMAN CATHOLIC VIEW

MATTHEW LEVERING

The difficulty with arguing in favor of the universal extent of the atonement consists in how to handle the nonuniversal extent of predestination and how to understand Christ's knowledge of those who have permanently rejected him or will permanently reject him. Although Catholic theologians today sometimes downplay the fact, a significant number of biblical passages teach a strong doctrine of predestination. Ephesians 1:4–5, for example, teaches that God "chose us in [Christ] before the foundation of the world, that we should be holy and blameless before him. He destined us in love to be his sons through Jesus Christ, according to the purpose of his will, to the praise of his glorious grace which he freely bestowed on us in the Beloved."[1] The meaning of predestination here is that God chose some people "before the foundation of the world" to be adopted sons in the Son. Far from conveying the message that God chose all people in this way, Ephesians goes on to observe, "Be sure of this, that no fornicator or impure man, or one who is covetous (that is, an idolater), has any inheritance in the kingdom of Christ and of God" (Eph. 5:5).

Similarly, Jesus in John 6:44 states, "No one can come to me unless the Father who sent me draws him." He underscores this point by adding (in light of Isaiah 54:13), "Every one who has heard and learned from the Father comes to me" (John 6:45). The point here is a predestinarian one: God teaches interiorly, or draws, some people to Christ. Other people,

---

1. Unless otherwise indicated, Scripture quotations in this chapter come from the RSV.

however, are not taught or drawn by God. Thus Jesus goes on to warn: "You do not believe, because you do not belong to my sheep. My sheep hear my voice" (John 10:26–27). Lest we assert that our own choice is the ultimate source of why we believe, Jesus instructs his disciples: "You did not choose me, but I chose you and appointed you" (John 15:16). God's (and Jesus's) choice is determinative; no one can ultimately frustrate God's will by his or her free actions.

Likewise, a variety of biblical texts teach that Jesus knows that his atoning death will not bring about the salvation of all persons. In the Gospel of John, Jesus has complete assurance that all whom God the Father has given him have been preserved in faith: "I have guarded them, and none of them is lost but the son of perdition" (John 17:12). Thus Jesus must have known that the "son of perdition," Judas, had in fact not been drawn by God. The Evangelist explains, "For Jesus knew from the first who those were that did not believe, and who it was that would betray him" (John 6:64). If Judas was the "son of perdition," then it makes sense to conclude that Judas was one of those whom Paul calls "the vessels of wrath made for destruction," so that Judas's betrayal of Jesus served "to make known the riches of [God's] glory for the vessels of mercy, which he has prepared beforehand for glory" (Rom. 9:22–23).

The other gospels are not as explicit as the Gospel of John, but they make clear that Jesus is not taken by surprise with respect to God's plan. He knows that "one of you [the twelve disciples] will betray me" (Mark 14:18). He knows that Peter will deny him three times before cockcrow but will not reject him in a definitive way. He tells Peter that "you are Peter, and on this rock I will build my church, and the powers of death shall not prevail against it" (Matt. 16:18). He knows that "Elijah [John the Baptist] has already come, and they did not know him, but did to him whatever they pleased. So also the Son of man will suffer at their hands" (Matt. 17:12). He knows the thoughts of those who accept him and of those who reject him (see Mark 2:8; Luke 9:47). On the cross, he knows that the good thief, who rebukes the bad thief for mocking Jesus, will "today . . . be with me in Paradise" (Luke 23:43), and he tellingly does not say the same about the bad thief.

The theological question, therefore, is whether when Jesus died on the cross he died for Judas and for the thief who mocked him (as well as all other humans). This question, it should be noted at the outset, differs sharply from the question of whether Jesus's cross has the power to save everyone. No Christian denies that Jesus's death is sufficient "expiation" (Rom. 3:25) for the sins of the whole human race. As Colossians 1:19–20 remarks, "For in him all the fulness of God was pleased to dwell, and through him to reconcile to himself all things, whether on earth or in heaven, making peace by the blood of his cross." All things are reconciled "by the blood of his cross." Yet, for whatever reason, not all humans accept the reconciliation, and at the judgment God's condemnation of unrepentant sinners will be evident. Thus Colossians 3:5–6 exhorts, "Put to death therefore what is earthly in you: fornication, impurity, passion, evil desire, and covetousness, which is idolatry. On account of these the wrath of God is coming." The books of the New Testament consistently refer to a coming "eternal punishment" (Matt. 25:46).

In Galatians 2:20, Paul rejoices that Christ "loved me and gave himself for me." Like other biblical texts, this text implies that Christ knows for whom he suffers. Did Christ love Judas and give himself on the cross for Judas, even if he knew that Judas was not among the elect? Or did Christ on the cross not die for Judas, even though technically speaking Christ's passion atoned for Judas's sin? In what follows, I respond to this question by engaging the Catholic Church's magisterial and theological tradition about the extent of the atonement. My essay has three steps: a survey of Catholic magisterial teaching, a section focused on the influential figures of Augustine and Aquinas, and an account of my own position that draws upon biblical texts and Francis de Sales.

Catholic Magisterial Teaching

The Catholic Church has responded formally and dogmatically to the proposition that Christ did not die for all humans. In 1640, a posthumous three-volume book by Cornelius Jansen, bishop of Ypres, appeared under the title *Augustinus*.[2] In Jansen's view, the renewal of

---

2. For the details in this paragraph, see Marguerite Tollemache, *French Jansenists* (London: Kegan Paul, Trench, Trübner & Co., 1893). Tollemache's book is an expression of nineteenth-century nostalgic Jansenism, as can be seen from its final paragraph describing her visit to the Jansenist hotbed of Port-Royal: "Ruined, desolate, and forlorn, the aspect of Port-Royal is very melancholy. It seems haunted by the remembrance of a great crime, but, on the other hand, it teems with holy associations and hallowed memories. We left the place with regret, touched and subdued by the thought of the saints of God, whose lives have made Port-Royal famous, and who being found 'faithful unto death,' have received the promised 'Crown of Life'" (256).

the church depended upon the full retrieval of Augustine's theology of grace. In an appendix to his book, Jansen argues that the Pelagian and semi-Pelagian heresies of the fifth century, which he explores in his book, have now returned in the thought of some leading sixteenth- and seventeenth-century Jesuit theologians, such as Leonard Lessius (1554–1623) and Luis de Molina (1535–1600). This charge, in addition to the intrinsically controversial elements of Augustine's theology of grace, roused significant concerns and led the Parisian theologian Nicolas Cornet, a Jesuit, to derive a set of propositions from Jansen's book, which Cornet then presented to Pope Innocent X for theological evaluation. Antoine Arnauld and other followers of Jansen denied that these propositions—which in fact (other than the first) are not literally found in *Augustinus*—succeed in accurately reflecting Jansen's thought. All the propositions, however, were formally condemned as heretical by the constitution *Cum occasione* in 1653. The fifth proposition reads, "It is Semipelagian to say that Christ died or shed his blood for all men without exception."[3] Pope Innocent condemns this proposition, "understood in the sense that Christ died only to save the predestined," as "impious, blasphemous, disgraceful, derogatory to divine piety, and heretical."[4]

The controversy did not end there. Responding to the ongoing significant presence of Jansenism especially in France, Pope Clement XI issued the Constitution *Vineam Domini Sabaoth* in 1705, which insisted that "the meaning condemned in the above-mentioned five propositions of Jansen's book, whose [meaning] the words express as they are expressed, must be rejected and condemned as heretical by all the faithful of Christ, not only by mouth but also in the heart; and the above-mentioned formulae cannot be licitly subscribed to with any other intention."[5]

Again, in his 1713 Constitution *Unigenitus Dei Filius*, Pope Clement XI specifically addressed the Jansenist theologian Pasquier Quesnel's 1693 *Le Nouveau Testament en françois avec des réflexions morales sur chaque verset*. Quesnel emphasized the absolute efficacy and irresistibility of

---

3. DH 2005, in Heinrich Denzinger, *Compendium of Creeds, Definitions, and Declarations on Matters of Faith and Morals*, 43rd ed., Latin-German ed. Peter Hünermann and Helmut Hoping; Latin-English ed. Robert Fastiggi and Anne Englund Nash (San Francisco: Ignatius, 2012); hereafter simply DH.

4. DH 2006.

5. DH 2390.

God's grace, and he insisted that grace is necessary for any good act whatsoever and that charity is required for our action not to be sinful. To name a few of the condemned propositions found in Quesnel's book: "Grace is the working of the omnipotent hand of God, which nothing can hinder or retard"; "All whom God wishes to save through Christ are infallibly saved"; and "What else can we be except darkness, except aberration, and except sin, without the light of faith, without Christ, and without charity?"[6] Among Quesnel's statements condemned by Pope Clement XI is the claim that Christ died solely for the predestined rather than for all people: "Jesus Christ handed himself over to death to liberate by his blood for all time the firstborn, that is, the elect, from the hand of the exterminating angel."[7] Another of Quesnel's condemned opinions is that the church is composed solely of "all the elect and the just of all ages," and includes no one else in any way.[8]

Already in response to certain reactions to Augustine's theology of grace, the Second Synod of Orange in 529 had set forth canons for orthodox belief about the relationship of grace and free will. These canons firmly support Augustine in the rejection of the view that "the fall harmed Adam alone and not his descendants."[9] In these canons too, the priority of the Holy Spirit's work vis-à-vis the movement of the will is affirmed. Even the desire for faith and the beginning of faith come from grace rather than from fallen human nature. Our natural strength cannot bring about, by its own resources, assent to the gospel. Against the semi-Pelagians, the Second Synod of Orange affirms that "to love God

---

6. DH 2410, DH 2430, and DH 2448.

7. DH 2432.

8. DH 2476. Likewise condemned, however, are some statements whose problematic character is far from clear, such as "The Lord's Day ought to be sanctified by Christians with readings of pious works and above all of the Holy Scriptures. It is harmful to wish to restrain a Christian from this reading" (DH 2482). Quesnel also treats such topics as penance, excommunication, and true preaching—all topics favored by the Jansenists. Not all the condemned statements are condemned in the same way. Thus Pope Clement XI remarks in conclusion: "We declare, condemn, and reject . . . the preceding propositions, as the case may be, as false, fraudulent, offensive to pious ears, scandalous, pernicious, rash, injurious to the Church and her practice, insulting not only to the Church but also the secular powers, seditious, impious, blasphemous, suspect of heresy, and having the flavor of heresy itself, and, besides, favoring heretics and heresies and also schisms, erroneous, close to heresy, many times condemned, and finally heretical, clearly renewing many heresies respectively and most especially those that are contained in the infamous propositions of Jansen and, indeed, accepted in that sense in which these have been condemned" (DH 2502).

9. DH 372.

is completely a gift of God."[10] Authoritatively summarizing these canons in 529, Bishop Caesarius of Arles adduces numerous scriptural passages confirming the utter priority of grace in matters of faith and salvation.

At the same time, however, Caesarius insists that "all the baptized, if they are willing to labor faithfully, can and ought to accomplish with Christ's help and cooperation what pertains to the salvation of their souls."[11] He rejects making a distinction here between the elect or predestined members of the baptized and those baptized persons who are not elect or predestined. He emphasizes this point by affirming strongly that no one is "predestined to evil" by God.[12] Indeed, he anathematizes such a viewpoint. He argues that everyone who has received the grace of baptism can and should be thought to be on the path of salvation since they have received the gift of God's help. When, in his letter *Per filium nostrum* of January 25, 531, Pope Boniface II responded to Caesarius and to the decisions of the Second Council of Orange, he confirmed the council's teachings about the priority of grace. Citing John 15:5 and Romans 11:35, Pope Boniface underscores that "the faith by which we believe in Christ, just as all blessings, comes to each man from the gift of celestial grace, not from the power of human nature."[13]

Two further magisterial texts should be mentioned here. First, Pope Paul V's July 26, 1611, Address to the Legate of King Philip III of Spain has significance, at least broadly speaking, for its effects upon Catholic predestinarian teaching. In this address, Paul V defended his decision to defer a conclusive response to the issues raised by the Molinist controversy that placed Jesuit and Dominican theologians at odds in the late sixteenth and early seventeenth centuries (and even to the present day). Paul V argues that both parties advocate a nonheretical position since both affirm "that God causes us to act with the efficacy of his grace, that he makes those to will who are unwilling, and he bends and changes the wills of men."[14] According to Paul V, there is no real problem because the two parties are divided solely about the manner in which God moves us. He explains, "The Dominicans say he predetermines our will physically,

---

10. DH 395.
11. DH 397.
12. DH 397.
13. DH 399.
14. DH 1997a.

that is, really and efficiently, while the Jesuits maintain that he does so congruently and morally."[15] The disputants in the Molinist controversy did indeed disagree on the matter of how God moves us, but, just as significantly, they disagreed about the very root of God's predestining will. The fundamental issue—left deliberately unresolved by Pope Paul V—was whether God predestines the elect because he *foresees* their good acts, or whether his predestination has no reason other than his own will so that his predestining will is the *cause* of their good acts.

Second, the Council of Trent's Decree on Justification (January 13, 1547) contributes to our topic. In this decree, the council first makes clear that Christ died for all, citing 1 John 2:2 as the definitive text in this regard: "God has 'put him forward as an expiation by his blood, to be received by faith' [Rom. 3:25], for our sins and 'not for our sins only, but also for the sins of the whole world' [1 John 2:2]."[16] The council adds, however, that not all humans receive the salvation won by Christ since humans must be "reborn in Christ" through faith and baptism.[17] Citing John 3:5, the council notes that being united to Christ's saving passion requires faith and baptism, and furthermore in this journey of salvation, at every step "God's grace precedes us" since only through God's unmerited grace can a person freely "move toward justice in God's sight."[18] All justified persons enjoy the ability to follow God's commandments; according to the council, this ability is not reserved to the elect.[19] Regarding predestination, the council says simply that no one can know "with certainty that he is definitely among the number of the predestined," or at least no one can know this without receiving a "special revelation" of the fact.[20] Thus no one should be certain that he or she will persevere in faith and charity until the end of life. Final perseverance is itself a grace—even though believers can be sure that "unless they themselves are unfaithful to his grace, God, who began the good work [cf. Phil. 1:6], will bring it to completion, effecting both the will and the execution [cf. Phil. 2:13]."[21]

---

15. DH 1997a.
16. DH 1522.
17. DH 1523.
18. DH 1525.
19. See DH 1536.
20. DH 1540.
21. DH 1541.

Thomas Aquinas and Augustine

In the theological tradition, the question of whether Christ died for all is often specified with regard to whether, on the cross, Christ loved all people or truly wished to save all sinners or prayed for all people that they might be saved. For example, in Luke 23:34, Jesus prays during his crucifixion: "Father, forgive them; for they know not what they do." Is this evidence that Jesus asks his Father to forgive all sinners? If so, then if any human is damned, is it the case that Jesus's prayer has not been heard, so that Jesus's will differed (on the most central matter) from the will of the Father? In answer, Thomas Aquinas reasons that in fact, "Our Lord did not pray for all those who crucified him, as neither did he for all those who would believe in him; but for those only who were predestinated to obtain eternal life through him."[22] In *Catena Aurea*, in which he collects patristic commentaries upon the Gospels, Aquinas notes with regard to Luke 23:34 that the Venerable Bede teaches that Christ did not pray in vain, and so Christ here did not pray for those who crucified him despite knowing who he was. Instead, Christ solely prayed for those who did not know what they were doing, who were misled by their zeal.[23] According to Aquinas, Jesus, in his human soul, "knows in the Word all things existing in whatever time, and the thoughts of men."[24] He has this knowledge because his soul enjoyed beatific vision even during his earthly life. Furthermore, in Aquinas's view, Christ also has infused (as distinct from beatific) knowledge of all "present, past, and future things."[25] Christ therefore can truly take upon himself all human sins. Yet in dying for all sins, Christ knows who will accept him (by the grace given by God's predestining will) and who will reject him. Since God's will is good, Christ on the cross does not pray in opposition to God's will, and therefore Christ on the cross prays only for the salvation of the elect.

Aquinas affirms, of course, that Christ's passion is a "universal cause of the forgiveness of sins."[26] The universal sufficiency of Christ's

---

22. Thomas Aquinas, *Summa Theologica*, trans. Fathers of the English Dominican Province (New York: Benziger, 1947–48), III, q. 21, a. 4, ad. 2; hereafter *ST*.
23. See Thomas Aquinas, *Catena Aurea*, vol. III, part 2 (Albany, NY: Preserving Christian, 1995), 752.
24. *ST* III, q. 10, a. 2.
25. *ST* III, q. 11, a. 1, ad. 3.
26. *ST* III, q. 49, a. 1, ad. 4.

passion to satisfy for all sins is never in doubt. Aquinas underscores that "Christ's Passion was sufficient and superabundant satisfaction for the sins of the whole human race."[27] The difficulty consists in the fact that despite its universal saving power, "Christ's Passion works its effect in them to whom it is applied, through faith and charity and the sacraments of faith."[28] This means that humans must attain at least implicit faith in order to be saved. Aquinas is generally generous in his account of implicit faith in Christ. He assures us, for example, that "men are brought to the glory of eternal beatitude by Christ,—not only those who lived after him, but also those who preceded him."[29] In his discussion of faith, he explains that even if some "were saved without receiving any revelation, they were not saved without faith in a Mediator, for, though they did not believe in him explicitly, they did, nevertheless, have implicit faith through believing in divine providence, since they believed that God would deliver mankind in whatever way was pleasing to him."[30]

The connection between faith and predestination requires elucidation. Faith comes about through an assent to realities revealed by God, either directly or through preachers whom God sends; but the human mind cannot make this assent with certitude without the assistance of God. Aquinas explains in this regard that "since man, by assenting to matters of faith, is raised above his nature, this must needs accrue to him from some supernatural principle moving him inwardly; and this is God. Therefore faith, as regards the assent which is the chief act of faith, is from God moving man inwardly by grace."[31] Aquinas affirms that God can move the human will without doing violence to human freedom. Since God is the perfect good, he can move the human will as its object (so that the will freely moves), and God can also incline the will to incline freely toward himself. Here Aquinas remarks that "God, while moving the will, does not force it, because he gives the will its own natural inclination. . . . Its being moved by another does not prevent its being moved from within itself."[32] Since God is utterly transcendent,

---

27. *ST* III, q. 49, a. 3.
28. *ST* III, q. 49, a. 3, ad. 1.
29. *ST* III, q. 45, a. 3.
30. *ST* II-II, q. 2, a. 7, ad. 3.
31. *ST* II-II, q. 6, a. 1.
32. *ST* I, q. 105, a. 4, ad. 1 and ad. 3.

he is not a competitive cause of the will's motion, which remains free in its movement.[33]

In his discussion of whether God's will imposes necessity upon the things that he wills, Aquinas reasons that God, as a transcendent and noncompetitive cause, can will some things to be done freely by creatures. He states, "God wills some things to be done necessarily, some contingently, to the right ordering of things, for the building up of the universe."[34] Predestination, then, is simply God's will that some persons come to enjoy eternal beatitude with him through his grace. Human resources alone could not suffice for making us sharers in the divine life, and so God himself must elevate us to this beatitude. The term "predestination" simply signifies God's eternal "direction of a rational creature toward the end of life eternal."[35] Predestination is God's eternal plan to give grace and glory to particular creatures. Aquinas observes that predestination is rooted in God's love, or, to put it another way, in God's free will to communicate his goodness in a special way.[36] He denies that any foreknown good acts or foreknown merits of the creature can influence God's predestining or not predestining any creature, since in fact "whatsoever is in man disposing him towards salvation, is all included under the effect of predestination; even the preparation for grace."[37] The priority of God's plan of predestination is absolute.

For Aquinas, God's love is causal: God's love "infuses and creates goodness," and "God's loving one thing more than another is nothing else than his willing for that thing a greater good."[38] When Christ, whose human will is perfectly united to his divine will, loves the elect on the cross, he loves them more than he loves the nonelect, because he knows and embraces the divine plan of predestination. This explains why he prays for the elect in a manner that he does not pray for the nonelect. If Christ is not praying for the nonelect on the cross, however, how can he be said to shed his blood for them and for their salvation?

Near the very end of his life, Augustine wrote *On the Predestination of the Saints* in response to a position taken by monks of Marseille

---

33. See *ST* I, q. 105, a. 5, including ad. 1 and ad. 2.
34. *ST* I, q. 19, a. 8.
35. *ST* I, q. 23, a. 1.
36. See *ST* I, q. 23, aa. 4–5.
37. *ST* I, q. 23, a. 5.
38. *ST* I, q. 20, a. 2 and a. 4.

against Augustine's anti-Pelagian writings. Specifically, in the words of Augustine's friend Prosper of Aquitaine, these monks emphasized against Augustine that "God foresaw before the foundation of the world those who would believe or who would stand firm in the faith, which thereafter would be seconded by grace; and he predestined to his kingdom those whom he called freely, of whom he foresaw that they would be worth of election and would depart from this life by a good death."[39] Notably for our topic, the monks of Marseille argued in favor of pre-destination by foreseen merits precisely because they saw no other way to defend the claim that "the propitiation which is found in the mystery of the blood of Christ was offered for all men without exception; hence, all who are willing to approach to faith and baptism can be saved."[40] This claim, as we saw above, was authoritatively reiterated by Caesarius of Arles in the sixth century. Recall that in otherwise defending Augustine's position, Caesarius affirmed that "all the baptized, if they are willing to labor faithfully, can and ought to accomplish with Christ's help and cooperation what pertains to the salvation of their souls."[41]

Augustine answers the monks of Marseille by means of an extensive biblical argument. For our purposes here, it suffices to consider Augustine's reading of John 6, in which Jesus states that "all that the Father gives me will come to me" (John 6:37) and "no one can come to me unless the Father who sent me draws him. . . . Every one who has heard and learned from the Father comes to me" (John 6:44–45). Interpreting the latter text, Augustine notes that if everyone who hears and learns from the Father comes to Jesus, then logically "it follows that everyone who does not come has not heard from the Father and learned, for if he had heard and learned he would have come."[42] How, asks Augustine, do we hear and learn from the Father? It must be that the Father teaches us interiorly, and does so by converting us and giving us a "heart of flesh" (Ezek. 11:19) rather than a heart of stone.

---

39. St. Augustine, "Letter 225: Prosper to Augustine," in *Four Anti-Pelagian Writings*, trans. John A. Mourant and William J. Collinge (Washington, DC: Catholic University of America Press, 1992), 200–8, at 201–2.

40. Augustine, "Letter 225: Prosper to Augustine," 201.

41. DH 397.

42. Augustine, *On the Predestination of the Saints* 8.13, in *Four Anti-Pelagian Writings*, trans. John A. Mourant and William J. Collinge (Washington, DC: Catholic University of America Press, 1992), 218–70, at 233.

The Father's teaching, in order words, consists in moving us by grace to assent freely to Christ. Since grace changes our heart, it is grace (the Father's teaching, which is also the teaching of the Son and Spirit) that ensures that we truly hear and learn. The logical conclusion is that this grace in fact "is rejected by no one, no matter how hard-hearted he may be. For it is given so that hardness of the heart may first be taken away."[43]

If the Father's teaching does its work so easily and efficaciously, why does the Father not teach everyone, so that everyone learns and all are saved? Augustine argues on the basis of Romans 9:14–24 that the answer consists in God's will to show both his mercy and his justice. After all, those who freely sin are not compelled to do so by God, and so God is free to have "mercy upon whomever he wills" (Rom. 9:18). There is no requirement of justice that God have mercy upon all human sinners by saving them.

Even so, in John 6:45, Jesus cites Isaiah 54:13, which he renders as "they shall all be taught by God." Augustine has to consider, therefore, whether this text requires that *all* humans will indeed learn from God and come to Jesus. Rather than denying that all humans are taught by God, Augustine affirms a sense in which it is the case. According to Augustine, all humans are taught by God in the sense that all humans who come to Jesus are taught by God. On this interpretation, Jesus's meaning is that "no one comes in any other way."[44] Aware that this interpretation seems a bit lame, Augustine emphasizes that Scripture does not allow for an interpretation that would require universal salvation. Scripture is clear both that God predestines the elect by his powerful grace and that God allows some to turn away permanently from Christ. Augustine quotes 1 Corinthians 1:18, where this tension is on display: "For the word of the cross is folly to those who are perishing, but to us who are being saved it is the power of God." In this context, Augustine similarly argues that 1 Timothy 2:4 is about God's will for all *the elect* to be saved. Augustine emphasizes God's power to save: "For if God had willed to teach even those to whom the word of the cross is foolishness, so that they would come to Christ, undoubtedly they too would have come."[45]

---

43. Augustine, *On the Predestination of the Saints*, 234.
44. Augustine, *On the Predestination of the Saints*, 235.
45. Augustine, *On the Predestination of the Saints*, 236.

Having argued that when the Father teaches, humans come to Jesus without fail, Augustine adds that we cannot turn this around by asserting that the Father chooses not to teach some because he foreknows that they will not listen. At stake here is God's power to save his people. After all, faith is a divine gift; God converts us by giving us faith. If we do not wish to assent to the realities of faith, this means that God has not converted us or yet given us the gift. Interpreting John 6:44, Augustine makes clear that God draws some by giving them faith, and God does not draw or give faith to others. Augustine makes much of John 6:63–64, where Jesus notes that some of his hearers do not believe and where the evangelist John comments that "Jesus knew from the first who those were that did not believe, and who it was that would betray him" (John 6:64). Augustine concludes that "to be drawn toward Christ by the Father, and to hear and learn from the Father that one might come to Christ, is nothing other than to receive from the Father the gift by which one believes in Christ."[46] We cannot give ourselves this gift; and when God gives it to us, we believe and come to Christ. So long as the Father wills for us to come to Christ, we cannot be separated from Christ, because we freely choose Christ in accordance with God's merciful plan and work of grace. Augustine adds in conclusion that we simply cannot know "why God delivers this person rather than that one," although we can know that God wills nothing unjustly.[47]

Aquinas, in his *Commentary on the Gospel of John*, cites Augustine's interpretation of John 6:45, but Aquinas also includes two other possible interpretations. The first comes from John Chrysostom, who argues that "all" here means "many." The second is particularly significant for our purposes. Aquinas states that "it could mean, *all*, so far as God is concerned, shall be taught, but if some are not taught, that is due to themselves. For the sun, on its part, shines on all, but some are unable to see it if they close their eyes, or are blind."[48] This interpretation, which Aquinas allows (he does not choose between the three interpretations), indicates that God gives grace to all and emphasizes that God is not

---

46. Augustine, *On the Predestination of the Saints*, 237.
47. Augustine, *On the Predestination of the Saints*, 238.
48. Saint Thomas Aquinas, *Commentary on the Gospel of John: Chapters 6–12* §943, ed. Daniel Keating and Matthew Levering, trans. Fabian Larcher, OP, and James A. Weisheipl, OP (Washington, DC: Catholic University of America Press, 2010), 36.

responsible for some persons failing to respond to grace. Earlier, discussing John 6:44, Aquinas emphasizes that God is not to blame for our failing to come to God, even though it is true that "no one can come to me [Jesus] unless the Father who sent me draws him." Aquinas observes that if a sinful heart cannot rise up to God, "this is not due to the failure of the one lifting it, who, so far as lies in him, fails no one; rather, it is due to an obstacle in the one who is not drawn or lifted up."[49] Aquinas takes more care than does Augustine to absolve God from any blame, or at least Aquinas's remarks in this regard are clearer. Thus Aquinas goes on to say that "God, in so far as it depends on him, extends his hand to every one, to draw every one."[50] This is more than Augustine is willing to say in commenting on John 6 in *On the Predestination of the Saints*.

The question, of course, is what it means for God to extend "his hand to every one." In Aquinas's account in the *Summa theologiae* of God's predestination and God's love, it seems clear that God does not in fact will to communicate much goodness to some of his rational creatures. God allows them to fall permanently rather than extending his hand as much as would be needed to do them real good. Indeed, in discussing John 6:44 in his commentary, Aquinas affirms Augustine's fundamental position that "God, for the completion of the universe, draws certain ones in order that his mercy may appear in them; and others he does not draw in order that his justice may be shown in them."[51] But it is nonetheless noteworthy that in his *Commentary on John* Aquinas places a strong emphasis on God's offering grace to all.

In insisting that "God, in so far as it depends on him, extends his hand to every one, to draw every one," Aquinas points in his *Commentary on John* to the significance of 1 Timothy 2:4, which teaches that God "desires all men to be saved and to come to the knowledge of the truth." Recall that Augustine argues that 1 Timothy 2:4 refers to "all men" who have faith in Christ rather than to all men per se. When Aquinas treats 1 Timothy 2:4 in his *Commentary on the First Letter of Saint Paul to Timothy*, he supports this text by citing 2 Peter 3:9's assurance that God does not wish "that any should perish, but that all should reach repentance." Given that Scripture makes clear that some do perish,

---

49. Aquinas, *Commentary on the Gospel of John: Chapters 6–12* §937 (33).
50. Aquinas, *Commentary on the Gospel of John: Chapters 6–12* §937 (33–34).
51. Aquinas, *Commentary on the Gospel of John: Chapters 6–12* §938 (34).

however, does this fact mean that God's omnipotent and transcendent will is frustrated by the wills of his creatures?

In Aquinas's view, such an outcome is impossible; God cannot be taken by surprise or frustrated, since God ontologically transcends creatures and is eternal (meaning that nothing unfolds temporally for God, even if temporal things unfold temporally in themselves). Therefore, Aquinas looks for other interpretations of 1 Timothy 2:4. Interestingly, he observes at this stage that God "makes his saints will that all men be saved" since "this type of willing should be found in the saints, because they do not know who are predestined and who are not."[52] If saints should will or truly wish that all humans be saved, then it is no wonder that many saints have indeed wished this. Aquinas adds that it is also the case that God in fact "offers to all the precepts, counsels and remedies required for salvation."[53] Here again the emphasis falls upon the fact that there is nothing deficient in what God does for everyone: God "extends his hand" salvifically to everyone.

When Aquinas arrives at his solution, he draws primarily not upon Augustine—though he mentions Augustine's view that "all men" refers to all who are elect—but rather upon John of Damascus, who feared that predestination involved determinism (something that Aquinas eschews too).[54] John of Damascus distinguishes between God's "antecedent" will and God's "consequent" will. This distinction, Aquinas states, does not import temporality into God. It merely makes clear that God's general ("antecedent") will, abstracted from any particular circumstances, is always for salvation, even if in particular circumstances God, in his "consequent" will, permits some to be lost. Aquinas explains the distinction using the example of "a merchant who absolutely wills to save all his goods, and this by his antecedent will; but if he considers the safety factor, he does not will all his goods to be saved, through comparison to others, namely, when the sinking of his ship follows the saving of all

52. Thomas Aquinas, *Commentary on the First Letter of Saint Paul to Timothy* §62, trans. Fabian Larcher, O.P., in *Commentary on the Letters of Saint Paul to the Philippians, Colossians, Thessalonians, Timothy, Titus, and Philemon*, ed. J. Mortensen and E. Alarcón (Lander, WY: Aquinas Institute for the Study of Sacred Doctrine, 2012), 241–341, at 264.

53. Aquinas, *Commentary on the First Letter of Saint Paul to Timothy* §62 (264).

54. For Aquinas on John of Damascus's view of predestination, see *ST* I, q. 23, a. 1, obj. 1 and ad. 1. For fuller discussion of John of Damascus's view, see my *Predestination: Biblical and Theological Paths* (Oxford: Oxford University Press, 2011).

his goods."[55] In particular circumstances ("consequent" will), a merchant would find it wise to allow some of his goods to be lost rather than to ensure that no goods make it to port. But could not God simply ensure that his "antecedent" will makes the circumstances such that his "consequent" will squares perfectly with his antecedent will? In other words, could not God simply convert all people? In his *Commentary on First Timothy*, Aquinas does not consider this possibility. Rather, he assumes that God has a good reason for making a world in which some sinners refuse God's help, despite the sincere offer of that help.

In his discussion of 1 Timothy 2:4 in the *Summa theologiae*, Aquinas takes the same approach, mentioning Augustine but settling upon John of Damascus's distinction between antecedent and consequent will. Rather than giving the example of the merchant, Aquinas in the *Summa* gives the example of a murderer: antecedently, a judge wills that no one be killed, but in his consequent will, given the fact that the man is a murderer, a judge wills the death penalty. What takes place is what the judge wills absolutely rather than what he wills in an indeterminate manner. God absolutely wills that not all be saved, given the particular circumstances (namely unrepentant sin) that exist. As in his commentary, Aquinas does not explain why God does not will to overcome the particular circumstances. It would seem that God, having died for the murderer, could convert the murderer with the aim of saving all. This possibility would seem especially appealing given Aquinas's denial that evil operates "towards the perfection and beauty of the universe," although of course God can use evil to accomplish good.[56] Admittedly, Aquinas elsewhere argues (much like Augustine) that God permits the damnation of some humans in order to ensure that the divine goodness is represented not only in mercy but also in justice, so that all "grades of being" (and thus all grades of goodness) are present in "the completion of the universe."[57]

The God of Election

In my view, the above survey of Augustine and Aquinas reflects tensions that are found in Scripture itself. On the one hand, it seems impossible, biblically, to deny God's power both to save us by his grace and to move

---

55. Aquinas, *Commentary on the First Letter of Saint Paul to Timothy* §62 (264).
56. *ST* I, q. 19, a. 9.
57. *ST* I, q. 23, a. 5, ad. 3.

our will by grace so that we freely respond positively to grace. The Gospel of John and the Letters of Paul, in particular, make clear that God draws us by his grace and that those whom God draws come to God. The Gospel of John and the Letters of Paul also make clear that some reject and resist God permanently. But this rejection is not due to a deficiency of saving power on the part of God's grace since all that the Father has eternally given to the incarnate Son will indeed be saved. Augustine rightly emphasizes these points. On the other hand, such texts as 1 Timothy 2:4 and 2 Peter 3:9 (linked to Old Testament texts such as Ezekiel 18:32 and 33:11) are not mere outliers in the biblical testimony to God's will. It does not seem consistent with the biblical testimony to God or to Christ if we suppose that God "extends his hand" (to use Aquinas's image) but does not extend it in a full way. The same holds for supposing that Christ, on the cross, really is praying only for those whom he knows to be elect and does not superabundantly love those whom he knows will not repent. Furthermore, if sinners are responsible for their permanent rebellion, and yet God could have saved them if God had but lifted a finger to do so, then one need not to accuse God of injustice to be horror-struck at God not lifting a finger to save so many humans. Such a God is less than a father; he is kind to some and to others he turns away his face as though he were a mere bystander.

Fortunately, the God of election is not a two-faced God in this way. The Gospel of John testifies that "God so loved the world that he gave his only Son. . . . For God sent the Son into the world, not to condemn the world, but that the world might be saved through him" (John 3:16–17). God enters the world truly to save it, not merely to act and pray for the elect. God loves the world; he truly does not love the spiritual death of sinners or wish for their death. After all, as 1 John 4 makes clear, God is love itself, and God loves more fully than we sinners can imagine: "Beloved, let us love one another; for love is of God, and he who loves is born of God and knows God. He who does not love does not know God; for God is love. In this the love of God was made manifest among us, that God sent his only Son into the world, so that we might live through him" (1 John 4:7–9). If we love, we must love sinners, since God loves us who are sinners. We must love our sinful brother, "for he who does not love his brother whom he has seen, cannot love God whom he has not seen" (1 John 4:20). We must love without limits, without counting the cost or excluding anyone, since "in this is love, not that we loved God but that he loved us and sent his Son to be the expiation for our sins" (1 Jonn 4:10). God's love is not narrow or restricted to an elite. God's love breaks through all our efforts to construct a spiritual elite; Christ goes forth to sinners and eats with them, calling them, and all of us, to repentance and faith.

Certainly, God's love does not countenance sin or leave it unjudged. The point rather is that God loves sinners and does not show himself to be a God whose love for sinners is limited or constricted. God's fatherly love is manifested by the parable of the prodigal son in which God rejoices over the return of the lost son and firmly corrects the elder son who asks why God cares so much for the lost son: "Son, you are always with me, and all that is mine is yours. It was fitting to make merry and be glad, for this your brother was dead, and is alive; he was lost, and is found" (Luke 15:31–32). Far from superabundantly loving only the elect, or seeking and truly caring for only the elect, God seeks the lost sheep. Jesus promises that "there will be more joy in heaven over one sinner who repents than over ninety-nine righteous persons who need no repentance" (Luke 15:7). Simply put, the God who truly cares only for the elect does not fit the description of the prodigal father, nor does the God who truly cares only for the elect fit the description of one who cares profoundly for each and every sinner and rejoices greatly when even one sinner repents. The true Father loves everyone in a superabundant manner: "He makes his sun rise on the evil and on the good, and sends rain on the just and on the unjust. For if you love those who love you, what reward have you? Do not even the tax collectors do the same?" (Matt. 5:45–46). God is not like a tax collector; God truly and superabundantly loves even those who do not love him and never will love him.

Jesus puts the point even more sharply: "What father among you, if his son asks for a fish, will instead of a fish give him a serpent; or if he asks for an egg, will give him a scorpion? If you then, who are evil, know how to give good gifts to your children, how much more will the heavenly Father give the Holy Spirit to those who ask him!" (Luke 11:11–13). The Father gives good gifts; he cares for and loves all the humans that he has created. From eternity, he does not lovingly give a fish to one and leave the other to starve for lack of love. Election and predestination would therefore be profoundly misconstrued if they were interpreted along the lines of God loving some greatly and not really loving others much (or giving them solely the amount of goodness needed for them to freely choose to rot in hellish torment forever). Right from the outset, the covenantal election of Abraham has "all the families of the earth" (Gen. 12:3) in view: the elect people are to serve all nations. As God works out his covenantal plan, he has the outsiders in view, since he loves all the humans he has created. Through the prophet Isaiah, just to give one example, God promises that "I am coming to gather all nations and tongues; and they shall come and shall see my glory" (Isa. 66:18). Election is not exclusionary in the sense of meaning that God loves some humans superabundantly and leaves other sinful humans to fend for themselves, knowing they cannot do so.

This wondrous portrait of God's love, found in numerous biblical texts and impossible to dismiss by arguments from the logical implications of other texts, helps us see the significance of Aquinas's point that "God, in so far as it depends on him, extends his hand to every one, to draw every one."[58] Although Aquinas does not say so, those who are not predestined to grace and glory must reject God's love in a way that, while not thwarting the primacy of God's will or rendering a creature autonomous from God, nonetheless constitutes an exercise of free resistance that God, without any deficiency in the active outpouring of his love for the resistant creature, mysteriously (and impenetrably in this life) allows to stand. Jacques Maritain attempts to describe just such rebellion in his *God and the Permission of Evil* and *Existence and the Existent*, and although Maritain's solution (rooted in the philosophy of action) does not seem to me to work, something like it must be true.[59] The biblical tension between two portraits of God—the eternal God

---

58. Aquinas, *Commentary on the Gospel of John: Chapters 6–12* §937 (33–34).

59. Jacques Maritain, *God and the Permission of Evil*, trans. Joseph W. Evans (Milwaukee, WI: Bruce, 1966); Maritain, *Existence and the Existent: An Essay on Christian Existentialism*, trans. Lewis Galantiere and Gerald B. Phelan (Garden City, NY: Image, 1957). For another significant effort along these lines—drawing upon an array of Baroque Catholic thinkers who had engaged with this problem—see the three articles by Francisco Marín-Sola, OP, as well as the interpretive essays by Michael D. Torre, in *Do Not Resist the Spirit's Call: Francisco Marín-Sola on Sufficient Grace*, trans. and ed. Michael D. Torre (Washington, DC: Catholic University of America Press, 2013). On pages 250–51, Torre responds to the doubts about Maritain's position that I express in my *Predestination*. Torre notes that for Marín-Sola "the creature fails on its own, just when there is no need to fail, no ground or explanation of failure beyond its own will. . . . Sin is permitted to be *possible*—a creature being moved according to, and not specially protected from, its defectibility—and it is permitted to be *actual*—the creature's defective judgment being *supposed*, and not prevented from causing" (251).

efficaciously predestining and causing the unmerited salvation of some while allowing others to remain permanently in their sins, on the one hand, and the eternal God actively and superabundantly working for the salvation in Christ of all his human creatures, on the other—must be held together in tension rather than choosing either pole of the tension as a standard for measuring and limiting the other pole.

For our purposes here, it suffices to note that Francis de Sales (in 1616), deeply mortified by the Molinist controversy, is quite right to emphasize "the abundance of the means of salvation, since we have so great a Saviour, in consideration of whom we have been made, and by whose merits we have been ransomed."[60] De Sales insists that Christ died for all humans and that all humans have received a "most abundant sufficiency of grace."[61] According to de Sales, there can be no limit to Christ's active love for each human being. As he says, "The sweet Jesus who bought us with his blood, is infinitely desirous that we should love him that we may eternally be saved, and desires we may be saved that we may love him eternally."[62] Far from coldly dividing the elect and the nonelect, God—as represented by de Sales—has infinite desire that each of us be saved. De Sales confesses with wonder and admiration, "how amorous the divine heart is of our love," and de Sales goes on to observe of God: "he is not content with announcing thus publicly his extreme desire to be loved, so that every one may have a share in his sweet invitation, but he goes even from door to door, knocking."[63] Put in more technical theological terms, "God does not only give us a simple sufficiency of means to love him, and in loving him to save ourselves, but also a rich, ample and magnificent sufficiency, and such as ought to be expected from so great a bounty as his."[64]

In my view, this observation of de Sales's corresponds to the biblical portrait of God's bountiful love for all sinners. De Sales supports his claim by numerous biblical citations, including from Song of Songs 2, Ezekiel 18, 1 Timothy 2, Jeremiah 31, and others. He notes that we nonetheless often resist God's love. In this regard, he emphasizes that

---

60. Francis de Sales, *Treatise on the Love of God*, trans. Henry Benedict Mackey, OSB (Rockford, IL: Tan Books, 1997), 77.
61. De Sales, *Treatise on the Love of God*, 81.
62. De Sales, *Treatise on the Love of God*, 83.
63. De Sales, *Treatise on the Love of God*, 84–85.
64. De Sales, *Treatise on the Love of God*, 85.

we cannot blame a lack of grace, and he gives the example of the fall of the angels: "Grace did not fail thee [Lucifer], for thou hadst it, like thy nature, the most excellent of all, but thou wast wanting to grace. God did not deprive thee of the operation of his love, but thou didst deprive his love of thy co-operation."[65] He concludes by insisting that God superabundantly loves each rational creature and that God gives each creature more than enough grace for them to be saved. He proclaims, "O all-good God! thou dost not forsake unless forsaken, thou never takest away thy gifts till we take away our hearts."[66] Lest his point be unclear, he underscores the fact that no deficiency in grace is to blame for any failure of a rational creature to move from a state of sinfulness to a state of justice or to blame for any movement from a state of justice to a state of sinfulness. He gladly admits that God alone is the cause of our salvation since only grace can heal and elevate us. But when we are not healed and elevated, we cannot claim that we must have lacked sufficient grace to be able to move from sin. As de Sales states, "If we do not confess his benefits we wrong his liberality, but we blaspheme his goodness if we deny that he has assisted and succoured us."[67]

Here we should recall the Catholic magisterial teaching on the topic of the extent of the atonement. The most important and explicit teaching, of course, appears in the constitution *Cum occasione* (1653), which condemns the proposition that "it is Semipelagian to say that Christ died or shed his blood for all men without exception."[68] According to Pope Innocent X, the assertion or implication that "Christ died only to save the predestined" is "impious, blasphemous, disgraceful, derogatory to divine piety, and heretical."[69] Less clear, but still significant, statements of the Catholic Magisterium on the topic of the extent of the atonement include Caesarius of Arles's insistence that "all the baptized, if they are willing to labor faithfully, can and ought to accomplish with Christ's help and cooperation what pertains to the salvation of their souls."[70] In Pope Paul V's 1611 Address to the Legate of the King of Spain, similarly, we find the affirmation (presented as an authoritative

---

65. De Sales, *Treatise on the Love of God*, 91.
66. De Sales, *Treatise on the Love of God*, 91.
67. De Sales, *Treatise on the Love of God*, 91.
68. DH 2005.
69. DH 2006.
70. DH 397.

interpretation of the Council of Trent's Decree on Justification) that the free will, when "moved, stirred up, and assisted by the grace of God" can in fact "freely assent and dissent" so that grace is not irresistible.[71]

More recently, the 1997 *Catechism of the Catholic Church* has weighed in on the issue. Quoting 2 Corinthians 5:14, "the love of Christ controls us, because we are convinced that one has died for all" (and referencing Gal. 2:20 and Eph. 5:2, 25), the catechism states that Christ "knew and loved us all when he offered his life" on the cross.[72] The crucial point here is that not only did he die for all humans, but he actively loved all humans in dying. He did not simply love the elect, nor was his love restricted vis-à-vis those whom he knew would not accept his love (the catechism professes "the existence of hell and its eternity," and so if Christ knew all persons on the cross, he would have known some rational creatures who permanently reject him).[73] The catechism adds that Christ can die for all because he is the incarnate Son: "The existence in Christ of the divine person of the Son, who at once surpasses and embraces all human persons and constitutes himself as the Head of all mankind, makes possible his redemptive sacrifice *for all*."[74] The catechism also traces Christ's love for all humans to the Father's love for all humans and desire for the salvation of all. Christ's humanity serves as "the free and perfect instrument of his divine love which desires the salvation of men."[75]

Conclusion

The Catholic Church, therefore, teaches that predestinarian biblical texts such as Romans 9:21–24, John 6:44–45, and John 17:9 cannot be taken to mean that Christ loved only the elect on the cross, let alone died only for the elect. In making satisfaction on the cross for all sins, Jesus died out of love for all humans and desired the salvation of all humans. As I made clear above, this is my position as well. I recognize that there is a tension in Scripture's portrait of God's love. Some passages indicate that God abundantly loves only the elect (while permitting others to

---

71. DH 1997a.
72. *Catechism of the Catholic Church*, 2nd ed. (Vatican City: Libreria Editrice Vaticana, 1997), §616.
73. *Catechism of the Catholic Church*, §1035.
74. *Catechism of the Catholic Church*, §616.
75. *Catechism of the Catholic Church*, §609.

fall away due to their own free sin), while other passages indicate that God loves all humans and desires the salvation of all. Certainly, God is eternal—utterly transcending temporality of any kind—and God's plan of grace is not an eternal response to his foreknowledge of how humans will exercise their free will. I affirm the priority, efficacious causality (not merely as efficient cause), and goodness of God, and I accept that the incarnate Son loved and died for some whom he knew would reject him. I doubt that the problem of predestination and the resistibility of grace has a philosophical solution. Most importantly, the two biblical portraits of God cannot be squared by subordinating one to the other, as theologians throughout the centuries have tried to do. It seems to me, instead, that we must hold two affirmations in tension without being yet able to see how they can be integrated: from eternity God efficaciously predestines some rational creatures to salvation and permits the free everlasting rebellion of others, and from eternity God superabundantly loves without any constriction or narrowness each and every rational creature. What is at stake here is allowing ourselves to be guided and instructed by the full breadth of the biblical testimony.[76]

I agree strongly with Aquinas that "God, in so far as it depends on him, extends his hand to every one, to draw every one." This extension of God's "hand" includes Christ dying for the salvation of each and every human. With de Sales, I hold that "God does not only give us a simple sufficiency of means to love him, and in loving him to save ourselves, but also a rich, ample and magnificent sufficiency." The old joke runs, Question: How do you distinguish sufficient grace and efficacious grace? Answer: Sufficient grace is insufficient. Against such a viewpoint, de Sales is certainly right that God's grace is never insufficient but rather is always superabundantly and magnificently sufficient, just as God's (and Christ's) love is superabundantly sufficient for the salvation of every human. The idea that Christ loves all humans on the cross, but loves some in a highly restricted and limited way or does not really pray for them, is not acceptable as a full biblical portrait.

---

76. I think that my position accords with that of the Reformed biblical scholar D. A. Carson, who argues that God's love appears in a fivefold way in Scripture and that we cannot make any of these ways absolute over against the other ways unless we wish to distort the biblical testimony to God. See Carson, *The Difficult Doctrine of the Love of God* (Wheaton, IL: Crossway, 2000).

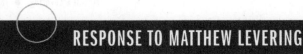

ANDREW LOUTH

Not entirely to my surprise, I find that the four "other" views on the extent of the atonement, for all their differences, have a great deal in common. First of all, none of them has any difficulty in engaging with the topic: it occupies a clear area of their doctrinal landscape, whether Catholic, traditional Reformed, Wesleyan, or Christian Universalist. The differences between these (Western) positions are well-aired and the arguments familiar; there is a whole history of argument over the topic from Augustine to the present day.

In contrast, I had to begin my piece by trying to find my way into a subject that does not fit at all well on the doctrinal landscape of Orthodox theology. (This is not just a personal whim of mine. It finds some support from Marcus Plested, who in his introduction to a recent symposium on Fr. Georges Florovsky and the "patristic doctrine of the atonement" also begins by teasing out the meaning of that peculiarly English theological term, atonement.)[1] Reading the four essays, I found myself entering territory largely unknown to me (save for Matthew Levering's essay), populated by learned and respected theologians, many of whose names, even of those still living, I had scarcely heard of—certainly my fault and to my detriment.

I have, however, an excuse, for unlike my fellow symposiasts, I am not a dogmatic theologian by academic training but rather a patristic scholar (and something, perhaps, of a historian). My approach is different from theirs not just because I am Orthodox but perhaps just as much because my academic background is significantly different (for all the importance attached to the fathers in Christian dogmatic theology). I fear my fellow symposiasts may have felt upon reading my essay a

---

1. Matthew Baker, Seraphim Danckaert, and Nicholas Marinides, eds., *On the Tree of the Cross: Georges Florovsky and the Patristic Doctrine of the Atonement* (Jordanville, NY: Holy Trinity Seminary Press, 2016), 19–23.

certain amateurishness about my venturing into the territory of the dogmatic theologian. I was certainly conscious of entering a realm of scholarship in which each of my fellow symposiasts moved with enviable familiarity, the fruit of long and patient study of the leading figures, and lesser though still significant figures of well-established traditions. Nevertheless, with all the essays, to one degree or another, I felt that the clear sense of the place of the atonement in the several traditions meant that little reflection needed to be given to how the doctrine of the atonement fitted alongside other doctrines of the Christian faith. The arguments rehearsed were well-honed and the product of much thought (and controversy), with the result that the *context* of the argument was (maybe, quite properly) taken for granted in ways that I sometimes found quite disconcerting. The major exception to this was the essay from the Wesleyan tradition by Fred Sanders, where I found myself on more familiar ground (though plotted with unfamiliar reference points).

The point of these introductory words is that, though asked to write four responses to my fellow symposiasts' essays, I find in my responses a good deal of commonality: they all seem to know where they are, but I find the territory, as I rather suspected might be the case, unfamiliar in significant ways. Nevertheless, I must seek to fulfil the task assigned me.

In many respects, Levering's essay was the one where I felt most at home, for though we treat the tradition differently, we share the same tradition in many respects. Nevertheless, from the beginning there was a certain accent that made me uncomfortable. The very first paragraph seemed to me to contain a non sequitur not untypical of what I was going to find as I proceeded. Ephesians 1:4–5 is certainly about election, about the fact that, in responding to Christ and seeking to be his disciples, we discover that we have been chosen, even from before the foundation of the world. Matthew Levering finds it necessary to qualify this by asserting that God's choosing means that some are chosen and others are *not*. I don't find this at all in the apostle Paul's lyrical celebration of God's plan "to unite all things in [Christ], things in heaven and things on earth . . . for the praise of his glory" (Eph. 1:10, 12). Election, even predestination here, embraces everything. As Hans Urs von Balthasar put it in his reflections on Elizabeth of the Trinity, whose heart opened to the vision of Paul's words in the early chapters of Ephesians so that she dedicated her life *in laudem gloriae*: "The Church, in her members both on earth and in heaven, prays and lives in a love and a hope not limited to a few, but open to all."[2] To qualify this vision by leaping to the paraenetic verses in chapter 5 seems most odd. These verses are not intended to qualify the range of God's calling but simply to clarify that all stand in need of conversion.

Furthermore, Saint Paul's vision in the opening passage of Ephesians is not just about God's election of those "destined in love to be his sons [and daughters] through Jesus Christ" but embraces the whole of creation (see Eph. 1:10; cf. 1:19–23), for election should not be separated from our confession of God as Creator, to which Paul returns in all his perorations in his long, and breathless, account of God's purpose; see, for example, Paul's summary of what he has to preach as an apostle: "to preach to the Gentiles the unsearchable riches of Christ, and to make visible what is the plan of the mystery hidden for ages in God who created all things" (Eph. 3:8–9). To take creation for granted and move directly to the doctrine of redemption and election seems to cut short the extent of God's love, which embraces the whole creation, not just human beings. Such a narrow vision, however, seems to happen all too easily in much Western theology.

But it is wrong to make so much of Levering's first page, for what follows is a feast of theological learning and careful argument? First, there is a brief account of the New Testament witness on the atonement and its extent, which is fair and even-handed (too even-handed to my taste, as Levering is keen to bring out the way in which the gospel of God's love, manifest in Christ's self-offering on the cross, is always qualified by the human need to respond).

The bulk of Levering's essay consists of a presentation of the Catholic Magisterial Teaching, followed by an expert discussion of Augustine and Aquinas, and ends with his own position, drawn from biblical texts and St François de Sales (I found it odd that a Catholic theologian should so clearly mark a distinction between the teaching of the *magisterium* and his own view).

The section on the Catholic Magisterial Teaching begins with the Jansenist controversy, which, without doubt, clarified Catholic teaching on grace and predestination. In a few paragraphs, Levering gives us an

---

2. Hans Urs von Balthasar, *Elizabeth of Dijon: An Interpretation of Her Mission* (London: Harvill, 1956), 41.

insight into the issues raised by this controversy, making it clear that the Catholic Church rejected the Jansenist view that Christ did not die for all human kind. He quickly moves back to an earlier controversy concerning the heritage of Augustine's teaching of grace culminating in the Second Synod of Orange of 529. Here Caesarius of Arles played a major role in securing the condemnation of what was much later called *semi-Pelagianism*, though it could well be thought that he was qualifying a strict Augustinianism by insisting that "all the baptized, if they are willing to labour faithfully, can and ought to accomplish with Christ's help and cooperation what pertains to the salvation of their souls." Levering comments that here Caesarius rejects making a distinction within the baptized between the elect and the nonelect. Certainly, but more significantly is Caesarius's concern not to let a theoretical doctrine of predestination undermine the sacramental economy of the Christian life. This is a point I shall return to. Other declarations of the Catholic magisterium are mentioned, which I shall pass over (as it is not my intention to summarize what can be read in this volume).

Let us move on to Levering's discussion of two key figures in the Western Catholic tradition, namely, Saint Augustine and Saint Thomas Aquinas. As a simple patristic scholar, I find Levering's discussion less than helpful (though I recognize that it is a fine piece of exegesis, at least of Saint Thomas), for it seems that Saint Thomas (and Levering following him) are asking the wrong questions and answering them with a logic all too confident of its ability to explore the mystery of God. The question, as Levering puts it, is this: "Whether, on the cross, Christ loved all people or truly wished to save all sinners or prayed for all people that they might be saved." He illustrates this by invoking Jesus's prayer for forgiveness for those who crucified him: "For example, in Luke 23:34, Jesus prays during his crucifixion: 'Father, forgive them; for they know not what they do.' Is this evidence that Jesus asks his Father to forgive all sinners? If so, then if any human is damned, is it the case that Jesus's prayer has not been heard, so that Jesus's will differed (on the most central matter) from the will of the Father?" (p. 74). I find these questions quite bizarre, betraying the mind of the lawyer trying to persuade someone that what they intended by their words really means something different. Are we to imagine that Christ on the cross had all these mental reservations in mind? To suppose so seems incredible.

I find the same sort of problem with Levering's exposition of Augustine (though I recognize that he is primarily concerned with what Thomas found in Augustine).

If I were to attempt to expound (in this context, inevitably very briefly) how Augustine came to his doctrine of predestination, I wouldn't start with his late works but rather try to present Augustine's thought as a whole, paying attention to its development. From the beginning, Augustine had a profound sense of election, a profound conviction that, as he looked back over his life, he could trace a thread that represented God's loving concern for him, a loving concern marked, not least, by his mother Monica's love . . . and her tears. (He quotes Ambrose's words to Monica: "As you live, it cannot be that the son of these tears should perish.")[3] Whatever he thought he was doing with his life—perfecting his rhetorical skills, seeking preferment, even joining the Manichees for nearly a decade—what *God* was doing with his life was far more important. This sense of election is fundamental to Augustine, at least once he becomes a Christian. Pelagius found this radical dependence on God intolerable, as it undermined his preaching of the importance of moral effort. As the controversy developed, Augustine begins to harden his presentation of God's electing will: it is solely on God's election that our salvation depends; good works may be a sign of salvation (though not infallibly), but they have no causal role. Under the pressure of controversy, Augustine pushes the question of election back into the mystery of God's will: salvation, or reprobation, has been settled in God's will "from before the foundation of the world." He even in some of his later writings speaks of those *quos praedestinavit [Deus] ad mortem*—those whom God predestined for [eternal] death.[4] From these hints one could accuse Augustine of belief in double predestination, *gemina praedestinatio*, a horrific doctrine, which was to be developed from Augustine's thought in the ninth century by Gottschalk of Orbais. Augustine, however, trembles on the brink of *gemina praedestinatio* rather than explicitly embracing the doctrine. And Augustine's error—one in which he is followed by

---

3. Augustine, *Confessions* 3.12.21, trans. Henry Chadwick (Oxford: Oxford University Press, 1991), 51.

4. Augustine, *The City of God* 22.24.

a whole procession of male theologians in the West[5]—is that he will not be satisfied with seeing the engagement between divine grace and human freewill as *itself* a fundamental mystery, well beyond our human capacity to comprehend, but insists on tracing this mystery back into the unfathomable depths of the divine will, to such an extent as to insert there a fundamental dualism.

A further point: Levering rightly points out that Thomas relies in his discussion of God's will on the distinction made by the Damascene between God's antecedent and consequent will, but this ignores the fact that John Damascene's doctrine fits into a very different context in his own philosophical thought than that presupposed by the largely Augustinian Aquinas. The Damascene nowhere pushes predestination into the forefront of his understanding of God's will in the way that Levering demonstrates Aquinas does.

Levering presents his own views in his section called "The God of Election." He begins by affirming that "in [his] view, the above survey of Augustine and Aquinas reflects tensions that are found in Scripture itself" (p. 82). That there is tension, perhaps paradox, in scriptural teaching on election one might well admit, but I find myself uneasy about the way this tension is represented. As Levering sees it,

> On the one hand, it seems impossible, biblically, to deny God's power both to save us by his grace and to move our will by grace so that we freely respond positively to grace . . . [the Scriptures] also make clear that some reject and resist God permanently. But this rejection is not due to a deficiency of saving power on the part of God's grace since all that the Father has eternally given to the incarnate Son will indeed be saved . . . On the other hand, such texts as 1 Timothy 2:4 and 2 Peter 3:9 . . . are not mere outliers in the biblical testimony to God's will. It does not seem consistent with the biblical testimony to God or to Christ if we suppose that God "extends his hand" (to use Aquinas's image) but does not extend it in a full way. (pp. 82–83)

---

5. Contrast Balthasar's "tout un cortège des saintes femmes," who were convinced that God's love could know no limit: Hans Urs von Balthasar, "Actualité de Lisieux," in *Thérèse de Lisieux: Conférences du Centenaire 1873–1973; Nouvelles de l'Institut Catholique de Paris*, numéro spéciale ([Paris: Institut catholique], 1973), 107–23, here 120–1.

In reality, there are several tensions here. The "on the one hand" section reveals a tension between God's will to save humankind and the possibility that human freedom, a freedom inherent in their creation in the image of God, may allow human beings to refuse God's offer of salvation. The "on the other hand" makes it clear that for Levering the real tension concerns God's power. If God's power is sufficient to save, does not even the possibility of refusal suggest that God's power is not adequate?

To recap what I have already suggested, for the Western theologians whom Levering interprets so well (and among whom he is rightly to be counted), the fundamental tension must be traced back to God's eternal will. This seems unnecessary and, given its implications, hazardous. The real tension here is between God's grace and human freedom. Better put, the engagement between God's grace and human freedom is a mystery—here human thought finds itself utterly out of its depth. Levering is right to counter this line of thought by saying that "the God of election is not a two-faced God in this way," but it seems to me that the attempt to make the paradox (or antinomy, to use Pavel Florensky's expression) of the engagement between God and human kind into something that reaches back into the unfathomable being of God—the attempt of *human thought* to do this—has led to the suggestion that the God who elects is two-faced by electing some to salvation and some to perdition. Levering eloquently disposes of such a horrific picture of God by drawing on Scripture itself (where, earlier, he had claimed they have their origin) and the gentle teaching of St François de Sales.

There is a further loss in tracing the "mystery" back to the unfathomable will of God rather than concentrating, like Scripture, on the engagement between God and humankind. While the former leads us into realms that we cannot expect to make sense of, the latter takes us directly to the divine economy of salvation, which is not just a matter of philosophical riddles but is concerned with the history of salvation and the sacramental economy of the church. Towards the end of his essay, Levering expresses doubt "that the problem of predestination and the irresistibility of grace has a philosophical solution" (p. 89), but why should it? Why does he find himself with such expectations in the first place? Levering ends, in his final paragraph, by rejecting notions of Christ's love for humankind that should never have been entertained in the first place.

RESPONSE TO MATTHEW LEVERING

MICHAEL HORTON

As Matthew Levering observes, "The difficulty with arguing in favor of the universal extent of the atonement consists in how to handle the nonuniversal extent of predestination and how to understand Christ's knowledge of those who have permanently rejected him or will permanently reject him" (p. 67). Especially illuminating is Levering's comparison of Augustine and Aquinas on the extent of the atonement. The general lines of Thomas's argument at least on predestination—the efficacy of grace and noncompetitive (analogical) construal of the relationship between divine and human agency, as well as the scope of redemption (sufficient for all and efficient for the elect)—are adopted by the formative Reformed theologians. We are closer than Pope Paul V to Thomas Aquinas when the former, as Levering relates, left open the question of whether election was based on anything foreseen in the saved (p. 73). From Aquinas's perspective, this was tantamount to Pelagianism, opening the door to the possibility that the elect merit final justification by their own works.[1] I should note in passing that arguments from the chain of being ("grades of being" for "the completion of the universe"; p. 82) play no role in Reformed defenses. Further, Luke 23:34 figures more prominently in Levering's summary of Augustine and Aquinas than it does in Reformed treatments of particular redemption. To my mind, Jesus's prayer is specific to the context: he is asking the Father not to hold them guilty *of his crucifixion*. A more germane prayer is John 17:9: "I pray not for the world, but for those you have given me, for they are yours and you gave them to me."

---

1. I develop this historical argument in *Justification*, vol. 1 (Grand Rapids: Zondervan, 2018), 100–124.

Levering says, "In my view, the above survey of Augustine and Aquinas reflects tensions that are found in Scripture itself" (p. 82).[2]

> The biblical tension between two portraits of God—the eternal God efficaciously predestining and causing the unmerited salvation of some while allowing others to remain permanently in their sins, on the one hand, and the eternal God actively and superabundantly working for the salvation in Christ of all his human creatures, on the other—must be held together in tension rather than choosing either pole of the tension as a standard for measuring and limiting the other pole. (pp. 85–86)

Levering adds, "I recognize that there is a tension in Scripture's portrait of God's love. Some passages indicate that God abundantly loves only the elect (while permitting others to fall away due to their own free sin), while other passages indicate that God loves all humans and desires the salvation of all" (pp. 88–89). These represent "two biblical portraits of God" that must be held in tension without "subordinating one to the other, as theologians throughout the centuries have tried to do" (p. 89).

I agree that we must affirm both groups of passages (universal and particular), but I would not characterize the former as Levering does. In fact, I do not see them as opposite (perhaps even contradictory) "poles" or "portraits" that we must hold in tension. Rather, I see two concentric circles. God's love for the whole world moves him to choose many from every nation, to send his Son to redeem them, and to send his Spirit to unite them to his Son. Beyond mere tension, it seems contradictory to say that there are "two portraits of God" in Scripture, one in which God is "actively and superabundantly working for the salvation in Christ of all his human creatures" and a second in which "the eternal God efficaciously predestining and causing the unmerited salvation of some while allowing others to remain permanently in their sins." Instead, I would say that God so loves the world that he determined to save a great church from condemned humanity as a remnant of his special love.

Further, how can it be said that God provides *sufficient* grace to all if in fact it requires God's *efficient* grace for anyone to believe? Levering

---

2. With Levering, I recommend D. A. Carson's *The Difficult Doctrine of the Love of God* (Wheaton: Crossway, 2000).

relates, "The old joke runs, Question: How do you distinguish sufficient grace and efficacious grace? Answer: Sufficient grace is insufficient" (p. 89). Exactly. This is where Reformed theology diverges from all the other options, by insisting that God the Father actually saves sinners by his Son and Spirit rather than making salvation merely possible. Only effectual grace can rescue and raise us from spiritual death.

At the outset, Levering affirms election and particular redemption from Scripture as well as from Augustine and Aquinas. "Certainly . . . God's plan of grace is not an eternal response to his foreknowledge of how humans will exercise their free will" (p. 89). Yet in his own argument he does appear to subordinate (or even surrender) one "pole" or "biblical portrait" to the other (pp. 88–89). He states passionately that "God's love is not narrow or restricted to an elite. . . . Christ goes forth to sinners and eats with them, calling them, and all of us, to repentance and faith" (p. 84). Yet the doctrine of election is hardly elitist (see 1 Cor. 1:26–27). Christ's deliberate movement toward the outcasts in the Gospels is evidence that many who considered themselves elite are excluded while the elect are the lost sheep, the sinners, the prodigal son. I do not see how election contradicts the testimony of Scripture that God "rejoices greatly when even one sinner repents" (p. 84). God's electing, redeeming, and effectual grace secures such repentance. Levering highlights the fact that the Abrahamic covenant all along had "all the families of the earth" in its sights, a remnant from all the nations streaming to Zion (p. 85).

But Reformed theology cheerfully embraces this realization of the Abrahamic promise in the new covenant. Far from restricting election to one people or nation, Reformed theology celebrates the fact that Christ "purchased with his blood people out of every tribe, kindred, people and nation" (Rev. 5:9). By saving a remnant from Israel and the nations, joined in one body as a new humanity, the triune God fulfills these prophecies of a truly global kingdom of peace and righteousness. Indeed, the whole cosmos will share in this glorious salvation (Rom. 8:18–25). In this way the world is truly saved. If the world was saved through Noah and a remnant of seven people (1 Peter 3:20; cf. 2 Peter 2:5), and Judah was preserved through an exiled remnant, then it is hardly improper to speak of the whole world being redeemed through an elect remnant (as the choir in Rev. 5:9 sings). Not only souls but bodies, not only individuals but the ecclesial body of Christ, not only Jews but gentiles, not only human beings but the whole creation—the extensiveness of redemption is emphasized in the many passages that speak of the salvation of "all people" and "the world."

From the confessional Reformed perspective, the question before us is not the sufficiency of Christ's work or even whether God loves the world. Rather, it is the revealed *purpose* of the triune God from creation to consummation. Election *includes* in Christ people from every nation who would otherwise have excluded themselves. Election ensures that God's Son will have a bride—composed of all those for whom the Father gave his Son and sent his Spirit to unite to Christ. When we read that God "desires all people to be saved and to come to the knowledge of the truth" (1 Tim. 2:4), it is in the context of the command in verses 1–3 to "pray for all people, *for kings and all who are in high positions.*" Not only should we pray for fellow believers but even for secular rulers—indeed, even for those who may be persecuting the church. Similarly, God sends his gospel out to "all people," irrespective of their station or current opposition to Christ. He adds that the "living God" is "the Savior of all people, especially of those who believe" (1 Tim. 4:10).

RESPONSE TO MATTHEW LEVERING

FRED SANDERS

Holy Scripture is clear, except when it isn't. To be more precise, one of the attributes of Holy Scripture is clarity, but its clarity shines forth in the main and central things it teaches about God and the gospel; that clarity does not extend all the way out to all the conjectural and speculative lengths we might hope for, nor into all the deducible implications and complications. It would be both impious and inaccurate to talk about contradictions in Scripture. But by common consent there are tensions. We encounter these tensions when some lines of scriptural teaching point vigorously in one direction, while other lines point just as vigorously in another. Matthew Levering's chapter is an essay par excellence on a soteriological tension. He presents one of the most significant tensions in the theology of atonement: God has the power and the desire to save all, yet not all are saved. Here is something for all theologians to grapple with because here is a tension in Scripture itself.

Levering writes from a Roman Catholic position, but here he writes not simply as an apologist for Roman Catholicism. A proselytizing theologian in that vein might emphasize the tension in Scripture only to resolve it by an appeal to magisterial teaching: the Bible is unclear, but the magisterium is clear, as the argument might go. Many Roman Catholic apologists offer such appeals to Protestants, holding out the promise that certainty on every subject awaits in the arms of the magisterium. But Levering knows the great tradition well enough to know that it has not attempted to rescue Scripture from itself, as it were, on this point. The tension in Scripture has been transmitted down through the tradition and is still with us today; carefully following the lead of the magisterium does not resolve it. Because Levering sees this clearly and reports it fairly, his essay provides a service for theologians from many confessions. We all stand in the field of this particular strange tension in the Word of God.

There are several ways to name and frame the tension, and much depends on the terms and contexts we choose in our description of it. Initially Levering describes it as the juxtaposition of the apparently nonuniversal extent of predestination and the universal extent of atonement. The latter position can be discerned as magisterial because 1653's papal bull *Cum occasione* condemned the proposition that "it is Semipelagian to say that Christ died or shed his blood for all men without exception." This way of reaching the conclusion of unlimited atonement leans heavily on an analysis of the intention of Jesus Christ in his self-offering. It asks whether Jesus intended his death to save only the particular people who would ultimately be saved or whether he intended it for all. The answer which Levering marshals from Scripture and tradition, as well as in his own meditations on whether Jesus died for Judas, is that Jesus intended his offering for all.

But several unacceptable alternatives immediately open up here. First, this focus on the intention of Jesus Christ might place him over against the particular predestining will of God. If we parsed that according to simple two-natures categories, we might be tempted to pit God against man, placing a particularly predestining deity over against a universally atoning humanity. That move is obviously unacceptable on a number of Christological fronts: it runs afoul of the third council (treating natures as willing agents or persons in a Nestorian manner) and makes nonsense of Trinitarian unity by putting Jesus Christ exclusively on the human side of the ledger. Warned away from this error by solid conciliar guidance, we might move in a second direction and place the Son of God, with his intention to die for all, over against God the Father, with his intention to elect some. But it would be hard to imagine a shallower way of reading the work of salvation. Such a reading treats the history of salvation as a work undertaken by different divine agents who needed to adjust their discrete projects in relation to each other, sometimes working at odds but ultimately coming to terms with one another. A rupture in the Trinity would be inevitable, with the Father apparently against and the Son apparently for universal salvation.

The division cannot fall between divinity and humanity on pain of bad Christology, and it cannot fall between Father and Son on pain of bad Trinitarianism. Where then? Levering considers locating the division between God's power to save, which must be absolutely unlimited, and his will to save, which seems to have a particular limitation. Indeed, to make explicit the claim that the power of the cross is sufficient for the salvation of all is already to tend in this direction. Levering clarifies these terms by listing side by side two things which we cannot deny: that God could move all to respond to grace and that some are not so moved and do not so respond. To draw the line this far down in the dogmatic sequence is to keep it away from the great, objective core of the doctrines of God and the incarnation. It preserves us from christological and Trinitarian error. It locates the tension somewhere in the doctrine of grace, or at least in the field of the human response to God's offer of salvation.

And that is where, if we are to follow the lead indicated by Levering's use of Francis de Sales, the tension must be settled. "God did not deprive thee of the operation of his love," counsels de Sales, "but thou didst deprive his love of thy co-operation" (p. 87). The work of divine love is sufficient and adequate for the salvation of each and of all; it is given and not withheld. That accounts for the universal element in soteriology. Levering quotes Aquinas similarly: "God, in so far as it depends on him, extends his hand to everyone, to draw everyone" (p. 89). But there remain those for whom it is not effective, and what makes the difference between salvation and nonsalvation is a cooperation that answers to the divine love.

It is no surprise that this is a characteristically Roman Catholic answer in the final analysis. Locating the tension within the doctrine of grace, Levering evokes, without explicating, all the issues that typically come to the fore in confessional arguments about salvation. This chapter stands in sharpest contrast to a characteristically Reformed answer that would go ahead and locate the tension in the doctrine of God (or at least the ordering of his eternal decrees). But it also stands in contrast to a characteristically Wesleyan answer that would locate the tension in prevenient grace, focusing on the grace-enabled and grace-empowered human response to the gospel. The Roman Catholic answer is traditionally framed in terms of cooperation and rounded out with the notion of supernaturally enabled merit. The result, given due elaboration in the theology of Thomas Aquinas and sharpened in the Tridentine theology, is that the gap between God's universal intention to save and the mixed results in which some humans remain unsaved is filled in with the mechanics of merit and cooperation. This was the soteriological complex against which Calvin protested, insisting that it relativized redemption and salvation and stripped them of their spiritual force.

"True," Calvin admitted, Jesus is "called a Redeemer" in the Catholic system "but in a manner which implies that men also, by their own free will, redeem themselves from the bondage of sin and death. True, he is called righteousness and salvation, but so that men still pursue salvation for themselves, by the merit of their works."[1] Stepping back a bit from the sharpness of Calvin's polemic, we can agree that any system, Catholic or Protestant, theoretical or practical, that blunts the force of redemption in this way is a spiritual disaster.

Levering's treatment of the extent of the atonement does not simply provide a platform on which to restage Roman Catholic and Protestant doctrinal disagreement. He has succeeded in keeping the discussion in shared, interconfessional space because he has approached the question as fundamentally one of understanding the biblical message. The tension he identifies is one that all theologians who seek to submit to the authority of Scripture must face.

Perhaps we can glimpse another Protestant-Catholic difference here, one almost resulting from different doctrinal temperaments. Broadly speaking, there are two major strategies for dealing with major biblical tensions. The theologian can either smooth them out or play them up. To smooth out the biblical tension would be to fill in the gap with the sort of explanatory material that makes it possible to see how the two sides of the tension can, after all, be related to each other. In the case of the extent of the atonement, the tension between universal atonement and particular election seems to be smoothed over by considerations of human response and cooperation; the hand of God extended to everyone is not, in return, grasped by an answering response from all. The theologian who attempts to smooth out the tension succeeds to the extent that the tension is adequately explained and then more or less set aside. At risk of great simplification, we could identify Thomas Aquinas as a successful theologian working in this mode.

To play up a biblical tension, on the other hand, would be to state both sides of it so strongly that the tension itself is raised to the level of a basic datum of theological work. In the case of the extent of the atonement, the gap between God's infinite power to save on the one

---

1. Calvin, "The Necessity of Reforming the Church," in *Selected Works of John Calvin: Tracts and Letters*, ed. Henry Beveridge and Jules Bonnet, 7 vols. (Grand Rapids: Baker, 1983), 1:192.

hand and the evident limitation of salvation's effectiveness on the other hand can be taken as a strong demonstration that humans are helpless to do anything for our own salvation. The gap is never filled; it stands open as a primary witness to the freedom of God and the gratuity of grace. The theologian engaged in playing up the tension succeeds to the extent that the tension is never put out of mind but remains an ever-present thought of the Christian and is constantly recommended as a source of awe or a summons to decision. Luther, Calvin, and Wesley, each in their own ways, excelled at making the most of this tension for the ends of proclamation and catechizing.

What I am suggesting is that there is something characteristically Roman Catholic about smoothing out this tension in the doctrine of grace by focusing on human response, infused virtues, and supernaturally enabled merit, and there is something characteristically Protestant about treating the tension as a place where the sheer gratuity of grace is encountered.

Levering may be primarily committed to the Thomist or Salesian mode of smoothing over the tension by explanation, but the smoothness he achieves remains in the territory of the doctrine of grace. When he lifts his eyes to the great background consideration, the character of God, Levering is eager to speak of a tension that remains unresolved. He notes two portraits of God's love in Scripture and that the tension between them is a permanent part of what theology has to work with:

> The biblical tension between two portraits of God—the eternal God efficaciously predestining and causing the unmerited salvation of some while allowing others to remain permanently in their sins, on the one hand, and the eternal God actively and superabundantly working for the salvation in Christ of all his human creatures, on the other—must be held together in tension rather than choosing either pole of the tension as a standard for measuring and limiting the other pole. (pp. 85–86)

Neither can be set aside because both are true, and the very tension between them is also something that must be accepted as part of the Christian message. Here at least is a welcome example of the way a Roman Catholic approach to theology can finally cast itself on the free mercy of God in a way that satisfies something of the deep Protestant impulse.

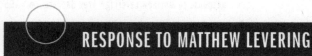

TOM GREGGS

I am grateful to Professor Levering in his chapter not only for such a lucid presentation of the classical Roman Catholic position, as well as helpful expositions of both Thomas and Augustine, but also for his own constructive engagement. I am also particularly grateful to him for two observations—one made at the start of his chapter and the other at the end.

Let me begin with the latter: Professor Levering points to the non-univocal nature of the biblical testimony around questions of sovereign election of God and the resistibility of grace (pp. 88–89). He wisely points to the reality that we "must hold two affirmations in tension without being yet able to see how they can be integrated" (p. 89). This is undoubtedly true, but one might also suggest that into this mix might come the universal expression of divine omnipotent love and the daring hope for the salvation of all (see my own chapter, p. 210–11). Indeed, this is perhaps hinted at as a possibility within the different readings Professor Levering offers when he writes, "From eternity God superabundantly loves without any constriction or narrowness each and every rational creature" (p. 89). By this, Professor Levering does not mean a "universalist" scope of salvation—even as a hope. And at least in part, this is because he follows Augustine. Indeed, the chapter states, "Augustine emphasizes that Scripture does not allow for an interpretation that would require universal salvation. Scripture is clear both that God predestines the elect by his powerful grace and that God allows some to turn away permanently from Christ" (p. 78). But even this discussion originates from the fact that there are certain passages that open the possibility of the universal salvation. If the *sensus plenior* of Scripture must include the universal offer of salvation and the sovereign electing (and rejecting) will of God, then one must surely say that the universal effectiveness of salvation is *possibly* present also. This aspect of the biblical testimony is perhaps a further tension.

The additional aspect at the start of the chapter for which I am grateful to Professor Levering is a related issue—his sense that the general instinct one should have should be in favour of a universal extent of the atonement and that the "*difficulty* . . . consists in how to handle the nonuniversal extent of predestination and how to understand Christ's knowledge of those who have permanently rejected him or will permanently reject him" (p. 1, emphasis added). Surely this is the right instinct to have. No Christian should ever desire to damn someone to hell or to place unwarranted limits on God's lovingkindness. As Karl Barth writes,

> It would be well, in view of the "danger" [of universalism] with which the expression is ever and again seen to be encompassed, to ask for a moment, whether on the whole the "danger" from those theologians who are forever sceptically critical, who are again and again suspiciously questioning because they are fundamentally legalistic, and who are therefore in essentials sullen and dismal, is not in the meantime always more threatening among us than that of an unsuitably cheerful indifferentism. . . . One thing is sure, that there is no theological justification for setting any limits on our side to the friendliness of God towards man which appeared in Jesus Christ—it is our theological duty to see and to understand that as even greater than we had done before.[1]

Of course, for Professor Levering, the meaning of this universal extent means, however, that Christ died for all and not only the elect, not that one might dare to hope salvation is universally and eschatologically effective for all humans.

These two ideas—Christ died for all and only for the elect—can be held together if we follow the lead of Karl Barth. Radically reinterpreting the tradition he inherited from Calvin (and through Calvin from Augustine), Barth claims that Christ is both the subject and object of election; in other words, the doctrine of election must be understood christologically. Election in Jesus Christ is less "decree" and more

---

1. Barth, "Humanity of God," *God, Grace and Gospel*, Scottish Journal of Theology Occasional Papers 8 (Edinburgh: Oliver and Boyd, 1959), 50.

movement: Christ is God in God's gracious movement towards and covenant with humanity.[2] Christ is God for humanity not only economically but ontologically in that Christ's election is not passive or confined to his human nature: his election is an active election in which Christ is simultaneously electing God.[3] In Christ's self-electing, one can see the self-determination of the electing God: "In so far as God not only is love, but loves, in the act of love which determines His whole being God elects."[4] In light of Professor Levering's account of Aquinas, it is interesting to note Barth's claim that Thomas overlooks this point.[5] Barth disagrees with those who claim Aquinas is not christocentric. But Barth argues that one has to go further in terms of one's chistrocentricity than Thomas does with predestination. For Barth, a continuity exists between the christological centre and the *telos* of God's temporal works; for Barth, it is necessary to bring together the work of God in Jesus Christ *and the eternal presupposition* of that work. Barth's concern (to his own mind in contrast to his predecessors) is to bring together the work of God and the eternal presupposition of that work.[6]

For Barth, it is *in Christ's election* that humanity is elected. That is, in Christ's singular election, one can consider the universal destiny of human nature:[7]

> The eternal divine decision as such has as its object and content the existence of this one created being the man Jesus of Nazareth, and the work of this man in His life and death, His humiliation and exaltation, His obedience and merit. It tells us further that in and with the existence of this man the eternal divine decision has as its object and content the execution of the divine covenant with man, *the salvation of all men*. . . . "In Him" means in His person, in His will, in His own divine choice, in the very basic decision of God which He fulfils over against every man. . . . His election is the original and *all-inclusive* election; the election

---

2. Barth, *Church Dogmatics*, ed. G. W. Bromiley and T. F. Torrance, trans. G. W. Bromiley et al. (New York: T&T Clark, 1957), II/2, 7.
3. Barth, *Church Dogmatics*, II/2, 107.
4. Barth, *Church Dogmatics*, II/2, 76.
5. Barth, *Church Dogmatics*, II/2, 107.
6. Barth, *Church Dogmatics*, II/2, 147–49.
7. Barth, *Church Dogmatics*, II/2, 118.

which is absolutely unique, but which in this uniqueness is *universally* meaningful and efficacious, because it is the election of Him who Himself elects.[8]

What of sin and judgement and rejection? It is here that Barth is at his most radical in terms of the scope of salvation: in the election of Jesus Christ, God elects the negative part of predestination—the death, rejection, and exclusion humanity deserves—yet God freely elects to suffer these things in Jesus Christ. This does not excuse human sinfulness, but in election God irreversibly takes its torment to Godself.[9] Christ wills in election to take to himself rejection in order that rejection is not the destiny of humanity: "He is *the* Rejected, as and because He is *the* Elect. In view of His election, there is no other rejected but Himself."[10] Barth writes in almost homiletic tone: "In Jesus Christ, thou, too, art not rejected—for He has borne thy rejection—but elected."[11] Barth's concern corresponds to Professor Levering's comment, "the God of election is not a two-faced God" (p. 83). Election for Barth is altogether good news. This vastly complex field of systematics would require more discussion than space allows, but for Barth, Christ dies for all and loves all, and this is an expression of God's self-electing will. Universal love and double predestination are held together in Christ.

So what might we do with those passages to which Professor Levering points which starkly present us with a limited atonement? Perhaps one way (in accordance with points made in my own chapter, pp. 214–16) might be to recognise the cosinfulness of the Christian and the non-Christian. Which of us is not spontaneously idolatrous? Which of us has never coveted? And which of us has not failed to have sufficient faith? Indeed, our very faithlessness is our sinfulness (see my own chapter, p. 216). We do well to remember that our anthropologies, even as people of faith, are not absolute.[12] As Karl Rahner reminds us, every one of us is an "inwardly plural being" about whom all kinds of different points

---

8. Barth, *Church Dogmatics*, II/2, 116–17, emphasis added.
9. Barth, *Church Dogmatics*, II/2, 166–67.
10. Barth, *Church Dogmatics*, II/2, 353.
11. Barth, *Church Dogmatics*, II/2, 322.
12. I explore this in my article, "Pessimistic Universalism: Rethinking the Wider Hope with Bonhoeffer and Barth," *Modern Theology*, 26, no. 4 (2010): 495–510, at 504–7.

might be made about her existence and its different aspects.[13] We are not absolute beings, and it is difficult to understand how the justice of God is fulfilled by making an absolute judgement to punish someone eternally in hell (cf. p. 88) for a life which is not absolute and which is temporal and not eternal.[14] Søren Kierkegaard points in this direction: "If others go to hell, then I will go too. But I do not believe that; on the contrary I believe that all will be saved, myself with them—something that arouses my deepest amazement."[15] Hell exists, but who is in it remains an open question, so rather than focus on those outside the church, we might be wise to be concerned with our cosinfulness with the world and its implications: we certainly do not want to be those judged by Jesus in Matthew 23:16, who are locked out of the kingdom. We are wise, I think, to follow Luther's reminder, even if this means a cheerful and daring *hope* for the salvation of all given the omnipotence of divine love:

> God receives none but those who are forsaken, restores health to none but those who are sick, gives sight to none but the blind, and life to none but the dead. He does not give saintliness to any but sinners, nor wisdom to any but fools. In short: He has mercy on none but the wretched and gives grace to none but those who are in disgrace. Therefore no arrogant saint, or just or wise man can be material for God, neither can he do the work of God, but he remains confined within his own work and makes of himself a fictitious, ostensible, false, and deceitful saint, that is, a hypocrite.[16]

Binary judgements are hard when we take seriously what it means for us (in our faithlessness as well as our faith) to fall on our knees and pray for God's unmerited mercy and grace.

---

13. Karl Rahner, SJ, "Purgatory," in *Theological Investigations*, vol. 19, *Faith and Ministry* (London: Darton, Longman & Todd, 1984), 184.

14. Cf. Paul Tillich, *Systematic Theology*, vol. 3, *Life in the Spirit: History and the Kingdom of God* (Welwyn: Nisbet, 1964), 434.

15. Kierkegaard, "Universalism in the History of Christianity," trans. Morwenna Ludlow, in *Universal Salvation? The Current Debate*, ed. Robin A. Parry and Christopher H. Partridge (Carlisle: Paternoster, 2003), p. 208.

16. Martin Luther, *Luther's Works*, vol. 14, *Selected Psalms III*, ed. Jaroslav Pelikan and Daniel E. Poellot, trans. Arnold Guebert (St. Louis: Concordia, 1958), 163.

Finally, I do wonder whether there might be aspects of the Roman Catholic perspective that offer this type of wider hope as well. There are the obvious explorations: von Balthasar's *Dare We Hope That All Men May be Saved*,[17] Rahner's discussion of anonymous Christians and Christianity,[18] and his redescription of purgatory[19] (though notably Rahner seems to advocate a broader account of the traditional scope of salvation rather than *necessarily* universalism). Indeed, it would be helpful to know how Professor Levering understands the traditional Catholic idea of purgatory or purgation to function in relation to these issues—whether it offers a hope beyond death—and what he makes of the faint and possible hope *extra ecclesiam muros* of salvation which Vatican II offers in *Lumen gentium* section 16 for those who have not received the gospel. Certainly, *Lumen gentium* offers no suggestion of a universalist position, but it holds open (even if in a more limited way than is often accounted) the possibility of revelation and salvation for those outwith the faith—those who have not decided for Christ and are yet not seemingly rejected in some binarized manner.

17. Hans Urs von Balthasar, *Dare We Hope That All Men May be Saved* (San Fransisco: Ignatius, 1993).

18. Karl Rahner, SJ, "Anonymous Christians," in *Theological Investigations*, vol. 6, *Concerning Vatican Council 2* (London: Darton, Longman & Todd, 1974).

19. Rahner, "Purgatory."

TRADITIONAL REFORMED VIEW

MICHAEL HORTON

Many Christians know Reformed theology only by the nickname "Calvinism," which is then reduced to the "five points," or TULIP: Total Depravity, Unconditional Election, Limited Atonement, Irresistible Grace, and the Perseverance of the Saints. Even many today who identify themselves as Reformed or Calvinist assume that these five points are the summary of the tradition's main teachings. However, this portrait, adopted by friend and foe alike, is simplistic to the point of being unhelpful. Before defending particular redemption (also called definite atonement), some corrections of these popular misunderstandings are in order.

Overcoming Stereotypes: Calvin and Calvinism in Context

More than anything else, Calvin and Calvinism are known for the doctrine of predestination. According to popular opinion, it is as if this doctrine were the central dogma of his system and a novelty in the history of the church. But both assumptions are false.

First, the doctrine of predestination was hardly a central dogma in Calvin's thinking.[1] In fact, he does not even mention election in his Geneva catechism. The doctrine is treated in the obvious places where it arises in his commentaries, but it holds no central position. In the *Institutes*

---

1. Richard Muller, *Christ and the Decree: Christology and Predestination in Reformed Theology from John Calvin to William Perkins* (Grand Rapids: Baker, 1988), 1–38. Cf. Francois Wendel, "Justification and Predestination in Calvin," *Readings in Calvin's Theology*, ed. Donald K. McKim (Grand Rapids: Baker, 1984), 160.

he discusses predestination principally in a section following prayer (3.21). Perhaps he is remembered for the doctrine more because of the polemical attacks he experienced, and responded to, from critics in Geneva and Basel. The article was well established before the Reformation, and then defended again by the first-generation Reformers. As such, there was little peculiar about a young Frenchman defending this doctrine in his commentaries, tracts, and his famous *Institutes*. The predestination that Calvin taught was catholic and evangelical, as it was faithful to the biblical text despite the scandal to human wisdom, speculation, and pride.

Second, the doctrine held by Calvin—namely, predestination to both salvation (election) and damnation (reprobation)—was insisted upon by many of the church fathers. Augustine took it for granted as the catholic teaching, in opposition especially to Pelagius. Reading Thomas Aquinas's articles on predestination in the *Summa theologiae* and his Romans commentary, one discerns nothing novel in Calvin's treatment. Aquinas wrote,

> From all eternity some are preordained and directed to heaven; they are called the predestined ones: "Having predestinated us unto the adoption of children according to the good pleasure of his will" [Eph. 1:5]. From all eternity, too, it has been settled that others will not be given grace, and these are called the reprobate or rejected ones: "I loved Jacob, and I hated Esau" [Mal. 1:2–3]. Divine choice is the reason for the distinction: ". . . according as he has chosen us in him before the foundation of the world." . . . God predestines because he loves. . . . The choice is not dictated by any goodness to be discovered in those who are chosen; there is no antecedent prompting of God's love [Rom. 9:11–13].[2]

Lodging the cause of election in the foreknowledge of human decision and action, says Aquinas, is the fountainhead of Pelagianism.[3]

But by the late Middle Ages, the popular theology of the era had been captured in the slogan, "God will not deny his grace to those who do what lies within them" (*facientibus quod in se est deus non denegat gratiam*). Thomas Bradwardine, the fourteenth-century archbishop of

---

2. Thomas Aquinas, *St. Thomas Aquinas: Theological Texts*, trans. Thomas Gilby (Durham, NC: Labyrinth, 1982; Oxford: Oxford University Press, 1955), 168.

3. Thomas Aquinas, *Summa theologiae* I, q. 23, a. 5.

Canterbury, recalled his discovery of God's electing grace from his own reading of Romans:

> Idle and a fool in God's wisdom, I was misled by an unorthodox error at a time when I was still pursuing philosophical studies. Sometimes I went to listen to the theologians discussing this matter [of grace and free will], and the school of Pelagius seemed to me nearest the truth. . . . In this philosophical faculty I seldom heard a reference to grace, except for some ambiguous remarks. What I heard day in and day out was that we are masters of our own free acts, that ours is the choice to act well or badly, to have virtues or sins, and much more along this line. . . . But every time I listened to the Epistle reading in church and heard how Paul magnified grace and belittled free will—as in the case in Romans 9, "It is obviously not a question of human will and effort, but of divine mercy," and its many parallels—grace displeased me, ungrateful as I was. . . . However, even before I transferred to the faculty of theology, the text mentioned came to me as a beam of grace and, captured by a vision of the truth, it seemed I saw from afar how the grace of God precedes all good works. . . . That is why I express my gratitude to Him who has given me this grace as a gift.[4]

Bradwardine wrote *The Cause of God against the Pelagians*, against "the new Pelagians who oppose our whole presentation of predestination and reprobation, attempting either to eliminate them completely or, at least, to show that they are dependent on our merits."[5]

"I received it all from Staupitz," Luther said of his mentor, Johann von Staupitz, the head of the Augustinian Order in Germany, whose most famous work was titled *Eternal Predestination and Its Execution in Time*.[6] "And thus the claim for man, namely, that he is master over his works from beginning to end, is destroyed," Staupitz wrote. "So, therefore, the origin of the works of Christian life is predestination,

---

4. Cited by Heiko Oberman, *Forerunners of the Reformation: The Shape of Late Medieval Thought Illustrated by Key Documents* (Philadelphia: Fortress, 1981), 135.

5. Oberman, *Forerunners of the Reformation*, 151.

6. Oberman, *Forerunners of the Reformation*, 175ff.

its means is justification, and its aim is glorification or thanksgiving—all these are the achievements not of nature but of grace." Staupitz even repeated the familiar formula that Christ's death is sufficient for the world but efficient for the elect only, along with a rigorous defense of the perseverance of the saints.[7]

No figure during the sixteenth century was as vehement in defending unconditional election and reprobation than Martin Luther in *The Bondage of the Will* (1525), written against Erasmus's *The Freedom of the Will*. Consistent with his Augustinian training, the early Luther wrote in his *Lectures on Romans* (1515–16), "The second argument [against predestination] is that 'God desires all men to be saved' (1 Tim. 2:4). . . . These verses must always be understood as pertaining to the elect only, as the apostle says in 2 Tim. 2:10 'everything for the sake of the elect.' For in an absolute sense Christ did not die for all, because he says: 'This is my blood which is poured out for you' and 'for many'—he does not say: for all—'for the forgiveness of sins' (Mark 14:24, Matt. 26:28)."[8] While not retracting this statement, his later ministry emphasized Christ's death for the world but in ways that Reformed theology also affirms. Embracing unconditional election, the orthodox Lutherans confess in the Formula of Concord (1577) that it is "a comforting article." "Accordingly we believe and maintain that if anybody teaches the doctrine of the gracious election of God to eternal life in such a way that disconsolate Christians can find no comfort in this doctrine but are driven to doubt and despair, or in such a way that the impenitent are strengthened in their self-will, he is not teaching the doctrine according to the Word and will of God."[9] At the same time, Lutherans reject particular redemption in the Book of Concord (Solid Declaration, art. 11).

According to the longest of the Church of England's Thirty-Nine Articles of Religion (1563/71), "The godly consideration of Predestination and our Election in Christ is full of sweet, pleasant, and unspeakable comfort to godly persons, and such as feel in themselves the working of the Spirit of Christ, mortifying the works of the flesh in their earthly

---

7. Oberman, *Forerunners of the Reformation*, 186.

8. Luther, *Lectures on Romans* (1515–1516), in *Luther's Works*, ed. J. Pelikan and H. Lehman (St. Louis: Concordia Publishing House, 1972), 25:375–76.

9. *The Book of Concord*, trans. and ed. Theodore G. Tappert (Philadelphia: Fortress, 1959), 497.

members, and drawing up their mind to high and heavenly things, as well because it doth establish and confirm their faith of eternal Salvation to be enjoyed through Christ, as because it doth fervently kindle their love towards God."[10] Since Cranmer, all of the archbishops of Canterbury were staunch Calvinists, until William Laud.[11] Delegates from the Church of England were sent to the Synod of Dort, where orthodox Calvinism was affirmed. Although Anabaptists inclined toward a more semi-Pelagian soteriology, Calvinistic Baptists in England adopted the Westminster Confession's articles on the doctrines of grace in the London Baptist Confession. (Interestingly, even the Ecumenical Patriarch Cyril Lucaris [1572–1638] embraced the conclusions of the Synod of Dort, although after his assassination by the Ottoman sultan, a council of Eastern bishops condemned Calvinism.)[12]

Thus the doctrine of unconditional election was held in common by all of the churches emerging from the magisterial Reformation, even as it had been affirmed by the best theologians of the pre-Reformation church. Only over the last century have these doctrines been summarized as "the five points of Calvinism" or by the TULIP acronym.[13] This is an unhelpful assumption for a couple of reasons.

First, this popular characterization loses the context in which these doctrines were formulated. The Dutch Reformed Church had a confession long before the Synod of Dort. Written by the martyr Guido de Brès in 1561, the Belgic Confession drew together the principal biblical doctrines under thirty-seven articles. Besides including the ecumenical creeds, the confession follows the outline of the Apostles' Creed, The Lord's Prayer, and the Ten Commandments. The church also had the Heidelberg Catechism (1563), which follows the same basic structure in teaching the Christian faith especially to children. The Belgic Confession includes what we think of as total depravity under the heading "Original Sin," condemning the Pelagian view that Adam was merely a poor example

---

10. W. H. Griffith Thomas, ed., *The Principles of Theology: An Introduction to the Thirty-Nine Articles*, with the text of the Articles (Grand Rapids: Baker, 1979), 236.

11. After Cranmer, to be specific, Edmund Grindal, John Whitgift, Richard Bancroft, and George Abbot preceded Laud, who then turned the tide toward Arminianism. The only exception is Cardinal Reginald Pole, who held the position during the restoration of Roman Catholicism under Queen Mary.

12. See George Hadjiantoniou, *Protestant Patriarch* (Richmond, VA: John Knox, 1961).

13. Kenneth J. Stewart, "The Points of Calvinism: Retrospect and Prospect," *Scottish Bulletin of Evangelical Theology* 26, no. 2 (2008): 189–93.

rather than the covenant head through whom we have received condemnation and corruption. The confession is no more controversial (in terms of the history of Christian interpretation) in its article on election:

> We believe that, all the posterity of Adam being thus fallen into perdition and ruin by the sin of our first parents, God then did manifest Himself such as He is; that is to say, merciful and just: merciful, since He delivers and preserves from this perdition all whom He in His eternal and unchangeable counsel of mere goodness has elected in Christ Jesus our Lord, without any respect to their works; just, in leaving others in the fall and perdition wherein they have involved themselves.[14]

The intent of the Belgic Confession is to summarize the catholic and evangelical faith while also affirming distinctly Reformed nuances of those doctrines. Nothing is said about the extent of the atonement in the confession or the catechism. In fact, election is referred to but is not given a separate question in the catechism, although there are several on the sacraments.

This is not to downplay the importance of predestination and its associated doctrines but to recognize the broader and richer context. As with Calvin, later Reformed pastors and teachers clarified and emphasized the doctrines of grace largely in the face of opposition. The Dutch theologian Jacob Arminius challenged the standard Reformed teaching, and by his death in 1609 the challenge had embroiled the whole church.[15] A national synod was called to settle the matter, but with "Arminianism" spreading, it became an international synod that included voting delegates from various continental Reformed churches as well as the Church of England and the Scottish Kirk. Thus the Synod of Dort (1618–19) represented the most ecumenical assembly of the post-Reformation era.

In short, the synod was called not to create a new confession

---

14. The Belgic Confession, art. 16, in *The Psalter Hymnal: Doctrinal Standards and Liturgy* (Grand Rapids: Board of Publications of the Christian Reformed Church, 1976), 77.

15. Arminius first aroused suspicions by teaching that Paul's argument in Romans 7 was nonautobiographical since it did not describe the life of a genuinely regenerated person. As he continued through his sermons on Romans, worries multiplied over his view of justification, election, effectual calling, and the perseverance of the saints.

summarizing the faith but to address specific errors. When treated as central dogmas, God's sovereignty and predestination become warped and in fact dangerously misunderstood. The terms "limited atonement" and "irresistible grace" do not appear even in the Canons of Dort and in fact distort Dort's teaching, which on the extent of the atonement repeats the traditional medieval refrain, "sufficient for the world, efficient for the elect only,"[16] and speaks of regenerating grace in noncoercive terms that "irresistible" hardly communicates.[17] The Synod of Dort was called because the Reformed churches believed that these distinctive doctrines were important. However, they are necessary but not sufficient elements in the total confession cherished by the Reformed churches.

With this historical prologue in place, the balance of this paper focuses on the Reformed understanding of Christ's saving work on the cross. With Dort in mind, my summary as well as argumentation situates the question concerning the atonement's *extent* in the wider context of its *nature*.

"Crucified from the Foundation of the World": The Triune Purpose in Redemption

According to classic Reformed theology, all of God's purposes are understood in terms of an eternal covenant between the persons of the Holy Trinity.[18] The Father chose a bride for his Son, the Son accepted this role as mediator of the elect, and the Holy Spirit pledged to bring the elect into a saving communion with Christ. In this perspective, the extent of Christ's redeeming work is inextricably related to this intra-Trinitarian purpose. I realize that there are alternative interpretations of each of the following passages. However, it may help to summarize

---

16. Canons of Dort, Second Head of Doctrine, art. 3, in *The Psalter Hymnal*, 99.

17. The Canons of the Synod of Dort typically use the more traditional language of "effectual calling" or "regeneration." Third and Fourth Heads, art. 16, in *The Psalter Hymnal*, 106: "So also this grace of regeneration *does not treat men as senseless stocks and blocks*, nor take away their will and its properties, or *do violence* thereto; but it *spiritually quickens, heals, corrects*, and at the same time *sweetly and powerfully bends it*, that where carnal rebellion and resistance formerly prevailed, a ready and sincere spiritual obedience begins to reign; *in which the true and spiritual restoration and freedom of our will consist*. Wherefore, unless the admirable Author of every good work so deal with us, man can have no hope of being able to rise from his fall by his own free will, by which, in a state of innocence, he plunged himself into ruin" (emphasis added).

18. See John V. Fesko, *The Covenant of Redemption: Origins, Development and Reception* (Göttingen: Vandenhoeck & Ruprecht, 2015); cf. Fesko, *The Trinity and the Covenant of Redemption* (Ross-shire, UK: Mentor, 2016).

briefly the exegetical basis for this intra-Trinitarian purpose especially as it relates to the extent of Christ's work.

Scripture teaches that the Father chose many, but not all, to eternal life and entrusted their salvation to the Son (John 6:38–39; 15:16; 17:9; Rom. 8:29; Eph. 1:4–5, 7, 15). The rest are "the objects of wrath—prepared for destruction" (Rom. 9:22 NIV). Prior to their decision—indeed their existence—God elected Jacob and rejected Esau, exhibiting God's prerogative to show mercy on whomever he chooses (Rom. 9:1–21). Scripture also teaches that the Spirit effectually calls the elect and unites them to Christ. Although they do indeed believe in Christ, it is because of God's sovereign grace rather than their own free will. The Spirit brings the elect to Christ, giving them faith (John 1:12–13; 6:44; 15:16; Rom. 8:30; 9:6–24; Eph. 2:8; 2 Thess. 2:13). Chosen in Christ "before the foundation of the world," the elect are redeemed by Christ and united to Christ by the Spirit (Eph. 1:3–14).[19] Luke reports that when a group of gentiles heard the gospel, "as many as were appointed to eternal life believed" (Acts 13:48).

Our entire salvation is credited not to the cooperation of sinners with God but to the cooperation of the persons of the Trinity. It would require a major revision in the doctrine of the Trinity to imagine that the Son's saving purpose was different from the Father's. No charge can be brought against "God's elect," since Christ has redeemed them and intercedes for them in heaven (Rom. 8:33–34). Therefore, Christ's death is referred to as "the blood of the eternal covenant" (Heb. 13:20). Peter wrote to believers as those who are chosen "for obedience to Jesus Christ and for sprinkling with his blood" (1 Peter 1:2), adding that we were purchased "with the precious blood of Christ, like that of a lamb without blemish or spot. He was foreknown before the foundation of the world but was made manifest in the last times for the sake of you who through him are believers in God, who raised him from the dead and gave him glory, so that your faith and hope are in God" (1 Peter 1:19–21).

John relates his vision of those who worship the beast, "everyone whose name has not been written before the foundation of the world in the book of life of the Lamb who was slain" (Rev. 13:8). In fact, a ribbon of passages in the Gospel of John testifies to the Father's gift of a people

---

19. Unless otherwise indicated, Scripture passages in this chapter come from the ESV.

before all time to the Son for the purpose of redemption. Jesus said that he came not to make salvation possible but to actually save "all that the Father gives me." He adds, "And this is the will of him who sent me, that I should lose nothing of all that he has given me, but raise it up on the last day. . . . This is why I told you that no one can come to me unless it is granted him by the Father" (John 6:37–39, 65). In John 10, Jesus said, "The good shepherd lays down his life for the sheep . . . I am the good shepherd. I know my own and my own know me, just as the Father knows me and I know the Father; and I lay down my life for the sheep" (John 10:11, 14–15), which includes gentiles as well as Jews (v. 16). With the cross looming, Jesus prays,

> Father, the hour has come; glorify your Son so that the Son may glorify you, since you have given him authority over all flesh, to give eternal life to all whom you have given him. . . . Yours they were, and you gave them to me, and they have kept your word. . . . I am praying for them. I am not praying for the world but for those whom you have given me, for they are yours. (John 17:1–2, 6, 9)

Once more Jesus includes all "who will believe in me through their word, that they may all be one" (v. 20–21). Throughout John's Gospel, then, there is an unmistakable thread that testifies to an eternal covenant of redemption between the persons of the Trinity, with the Father giving a people to his Son: "all that the Father has given to me."

In the Epistles as well, there is the correspondence between the will and work of the Father, the Son, and the Spirit in election, redemption, and calling that creates an unshakable ground of comfort. From the mass of fallen humanity, the Father has elected individuals "in Christ" (Rom. 8:30–34; Eph. 1:4–13).[20]

Jesus actually redeemed his elect (Rom. 8:32–35), his sheep (John 10:11, 15), his church (Acts 20:28; Eph. 5:25–27), and his people (Matt. 1:21). He gave "his life as a ransom for many" (Matt. 20:28; 26:28; cf. Isa. 53:12; Heb. 9:28). Sent to fulfill the Father's purpose, Jesus was confident that "nothing of all that he has given me" will be lost

---

20. See Stephen M. Baugh, "Galatians 3:20 and the Covenant of Redemption," *Westminster Theological Journal* 66, no. 1 (2004): 49–70.

but will be raised on the last day (John 6:38–39). The Savior entered Paradise as conqueror with the triumphant announcement, "I and the children God has given me" (Heb. 2:13). All of this shows "the heirs of the promise the unchangeable character of his purpose," which was "guaranteed . . . with an oath, so that by two unchangeable things, in which it is impossible for God to lie, we who have fled for refuge might have strong encouragement to hold fast to the hope set before us" (Heb. 6:17–18). "He has . . . *accomplished* redemption *for His people*" (Luke 1:68 NASB, emphasis added).

Thus particular redemption is not deduced from predestination as a necessary logical entailment. Rather, Reformed theology maintains that it is a truth taught explicitly in Scripture. That it coheres logically with myriad passages testifying to election and the Spirit's effectual calling of the elect is hardly a deficit. After all, since all the external works of the Godhead are undivided, it is to be expected that the Son's purpose in redemption would be the same as that of the electing Father and the regenerating, preserving, and glorifying Spirit. However, it is the weight of biblical passages testifying to that united purpose that persuades us of particular redemption.

What Did Jesus Do?

In the face of widespread challenges, it is not surprising that Reformed theologians (along with many evangelical Arminians) have emphasized the substitutionary aspect of the atonement. However, classic Reformed theology gives a wide berth to accommodate other crucial aspects, such as Christ's victory over the powers and recapitulation (the latter being particularly emphasized in the federal theology of the "two Adams"). Yet it is precisely on the basis of the legal satisfaction of divine justice—answering to God's curse in the original covenant—that Christ's victory over death, hell, and Satan is possible.

The extent of the atonement is bound up with its nature. This point becomes evident especially in the fact that Arminian theologians frequently express unease with the doctrine of substitution because it entails either Calvinism or universalism. Referring to the penal substitution theory as "the Calvinistic theory," H. Orton Wiley asserts, "It is in this attempt to impute our sin to Christ as His own that the weakness of this type of substitution appears."[21] He concludes, "Our final objection to the satisfaction theory is based upon the fact that it leads logically to antinomianism," for the following reasons:

> (1) It holds that Christ's active obedience is imputed to believers in such a manner that it is esteemed by God as done by them. They are, therefore, righteous by proxy. (2) This imputation in reality makes Christ's suffering superfluous; for if He has done for us all that the law requires, why should we be under the necessity of being delivered from penalty by His death? (3) If Christ's active obedience is to be substituted for that of believers, it shuts out the necessity of personal obedience to the law of God. . . . Man is therefore left in the position of being tempted to license of every kind, instead of being held strictly accountable for a life of righteousness.[22]

Wiley points out that Methodist theologian John Miley "is the outstanding representative of the governmental theory in modern times."[23] Wiley himself denies that Christ's death involved "a substitution in penalty as the merited punishment of sin."[24]

Of course, not all Arminians have rejected substitution (notably, John Wesley for example).[25] However, it was certainly the rule in Dutch Arminianism, and in the Anglo-American developments it became the norm for both the liberal Arminianism leading to Unitarianism and the revivalism of Jonathan Edwards Jr., Nathaniel Taylor, and Charles G. Finney. Drawing on the Dutch Arminian scholar Hugo Grotius (1583–1645), many Arminian theologians found the governmental theory more congenial than penal substitution, as Wiley observes.[26]

According to this view, God's nature does not demand absolute justice and the satisfaction of his righteous purposes. Rather, Christ's death makes it possible for God to offer salvation on easier terms than

---

21. H. Orton Wiley, *Christian Theology* (Kansas City, MO: Beacon Hill, 1952), 2:241, 245.
22. Wiley, *Christian Theology*, 2:249.
23. Wiley, *Christian Theology*, 2:255.
24. Wiley, *Christian Theology*, 2:257.
25. See Roger Olson on this point in *Arminian Theology: Myths and Realities* (Downers Grove, IL: IVP Academic, 2006), 224.
26. Wiley, *Christian Theology*, 2:241.

those required by the law. Christ's death is therefore not a real payment of a debt but merely the basis upon which God's just rule is exhibited. As Louis Berkhof concludes concerning this view, the basis of salvation is therefore not Christ's perfect fulfillment of the law and curse-bearing in the place of sinners, but the imperfect obedience of believers to a relaxed law.[27]

Going even further, the nineteenth-century American revivalist Charles G. Finney developed a scheme that was essentially Pelagian, beginning with a rejection of original sin.[28] Reflected throughout his *Systematic Theology* is a commitment to a combination of the moral influence and moral government theories. It is legally impossible for one person—even Jesus Christ—to fulfill the law and bear the sanctions of violating that law in the place of others, Finney insisted. "If he had obeyed the law as our substitute, then why should our own return to personal obedience be insisted upon as a sine qua non of our salvation?"[29] The atonement is simply "an incentive to virtue."[30] Rejecting the view that "the atonement was a literal payment of a debt," Finney can only concede, "It is true, that the atonement, of itself, does not secure the salvation of any one."[31] Going beyond most advocates of the subjective theories, Finney insisted that perfect obedience to God's law was "the sine qua non" of our justification.

More recently, Clark Pinnock reflected on his shift from Calvinism to Arminianism. "Obviously it caused me to reduce the precision in which I understood the substitution to take place," he related. "It caused me to look first at the theory of Anselm and later of Hugo Grotius, both of whom encourage us to view the atonement as an act of judicial demonstration rather than a strict or quantitative substitution as such." He concluded (perhaps prematurely), "It is my strong impression that Augustinian thinking is losing its hold on present-day Christians."[32]

---

27. Louis Berkhof, *Systematic Theology* (Grand Rapids: Eerdmans, 1996), 368.

28. Charles G. Finney, *Systematic Theology* (reprinted, Minneapolis: Bethany, 1976), 31, 179–180, 236. Arminian theologian Roger Olson points out that Finney's theology is much closer to Pelagianism than to Arminianism (*Arminian Theology* [Downers Grove, IL: IVP, 2005], 28, including footnote 20).

29. Finney, *Systematic Theology*, 206.

30. Finney, *Systematic Theology*, 209.

31. Finney, *Systematic Theology*, 209.

32. Clark Pinnock, "From Augustine to Arminius: A Pilgrimage in Theology" in *The Grace of God, The Will of Man: A Case for Arminianism*, ed. Clark H. Pinnock (Grand Rapids:

J. Kenneth Grider argues similarly that Christ could not have paid the penalty for sins, since he died for all and yet all are not saved. Of Wiley's defense of the governmental theory, Grider relates, "Importantly, he helped me to see that the Penal Theory of the Atonement fits Calvinism, and not Arminianism."[33] Again it is important to point out that evangelical Arminians have often been among the most stalwart defenders of Christ's substitutionary death for sinners. However, according to some of their leading theologians, this *should* lead them to the doctrine of particular redemption.

For Whom Did Jesus Do It?

From all that we have seen concerning the nature of Christ's work, it is apparent that Christ's death actually restores what was lost in Adam.[34] More than that, it brings those for whom Christ died into the everlasting Sabbath, the consummated glory of the new creation, a state that human beings have never entered. The powers of death and sin are vanquished. Christ's headship cancels Adam's. Our debts become Christ's and his righteousness becomes ours. Yet what conclusions can we draw from this concerning the extent of Christ's saving work?

One answer is that Christ's death objectively redeemed every person. The Scriptures unmistakably teach that God loves the world and that Christ died for the world (John 1:29; 3:16; 6:33, 51; Rom. 11:12, 15; 2 Cor. 5:19; 1 John 2:2). Therefore, advocates of this first view conclude that it was Christ's purpose to save each and every person who has ever or will ever live, and he bore their sins to that end. Officially condemned in the sixth century, Origen's theory of universal restoration (*apokatastasis*) held that all spirits (though not bodies), including Lucifer, would be reunited in heavenly bliss.[35] Refusing to bind God's freedom, Barth stopped short of a formal doctrine of universal salvation although his doctrine of election and reconciliation suggests it.[36]

Zondervan, 1989), 23, 26, 27.

33. J. Kenneth Grider, "The Nature of Wesleyan Theology," evangelicalarminians.org/the-nature-of-wesleyan-theology/.

34. The remainder of this essay is lightly revised from my chapter 4, "Mission Accomplished," in *For Calvinism* (Grand Rapids: Zondervan, 2011).

35. See *The Seven Ecumenical Councils*, in *Nicene and Post-Nicene Fathers*, vol. 14, ed. Henry R. Percival (Grand Rapids: Eerdmans, 1971).

36. Karl Barth, *Church Dogmatics*, trans. G. W. Bromiley, ed. G. W. Bromiley and T. F. Torrance (New York: T&T Clark, 1956–1975), II/2, 417–23; III/2, 136; IV/1, 91, 140, 410. For

Confessional Lutheranism also teaches a universal and objective atonement, but it also holds to a particular election of many, not all, to salvation in Christ. Only the elect will be finally saved, but some receive the saving benefits of Christ's work only for a time and then lose these benefits through mortal sin or unbelief. In this view, then, not all of those for whom Christ died will be saved, in spite of its universal intention.[37]

A second option is that Christ died to make salvation of every person possible. The intent of Christ's death, according to the Dutch Remonstrants (Arminians), was to make it possible for God to offer salvation by grace-enabled cooperation—namely, faith and evangelical obedience. It is generally recognized by Arminian theologians that if Christ actually accomplished the salvation of sinners at the cross (beyond making their salvation possible), then all for whom Christ died are actually saved. John Wiley therefore observes, "The penal substitutionary theory leads of necessity either to universalism on the one hand, or unconditional election on the other. Dr. Miley makes the charge that 'such an atonement, by its very nature, and by immediate result forever frees them from all guilt as a liability to the penalty of sin.'"[38] These Arminian theologians recognized that if Christ's death itself actually *accomplished* salvation for everyone for whom it was intended, then the only options are Calvinism and universalism.

There is another version of this second view. A mediating position between the orthodox Calvinism defined by the Synod of Dort in 1618–19 and Arminianism became known as "hypothetical universalism" (also "Amyraldianism," after its architect Moïse Amyraut). Christ bore the sins of every person without exception, but since God knew that no one would embrace Christ apart from the gift of faith, he elected some to receive the benefits of Christ's work. Many evangelical Protestants hold to either an Arminian or Amyraldian view, in either case agreeing with the position expressed by Lewis Sperry Chafer: "Christ's death does not

---

responsible evaluations, see especially G. C. Berkouwer, *The Triumph of Grace in the Theology of Karl Barth*, trans H. R. Boer (London: Paternoster, 1956), 215–34; Garry J. Williams, "Karl Barth and the Doctrine of the Atonement," in *Engaging with Barth: Contemporary Evangelical Critiques*, ed. David Gibson and Daniel Strange (Nottingham: Apollos, 2008), 232–72.

37. David Scaer, "Atonement in Lutheran Theology," *Bulletin of the Evangelical Theological Society* 10, no. 4 (Fall 1967): 175–87.

38. Wiley, *Christian Theology*, 2:246.

save either actually or potentially; rather it makes all men savable."[39] Similarly, Robert Lightner says that he rejects the Calvinist view "that the work of Christ on the cross was effective in and of itself."[40]

A third view is that Christ died for all of the sins of the elect, thereby redeeming them at the cross. According to this view, expressed by the Canons of Dort (ch. II, art. 3), Christ's death is "of infinite worth and value, abundantly sufficient to expiate the sins of the whole world," although Christ objectively and effectively bore the sins of the elect alone. Dort was repeating a common formula, "sufficient for the whole world but efficient for the elect alone." This formula is found in various medieval systems, including the writings of Aquinas, Gregory of Rimini, and Luther's mentor, Johann von Staupitz. As the formula indicates, this view does not limit the sufficiency or availability of Christ's saving work. Rather, it holds that the specific intention of Christ as he went to the cross was to save his elect.

As the seventeenth-century Puritan John Owen observed, every position that recognizes that some will finally be lost places a limit on the atonement at some point: either it is limited in its extent or in its effect. Owen summarizes the options: Christ died for (1) all of the sins of all people; (2) some of the sins of all people, or (3) all of the sins of some people.[41] If unbelief is a sin, and some people are finally condemned, then there is at least one sin for which Christ did not make adequate satisfaction.

Among the arguments in favor of particular redemption (the third view) are the following. *First, this view maintains that Christ's death actually saves.* Scripture nowhere teaches that Christ came into the world to make salvation possible, much less that it becomes actual because of faith in Christ. This would be to make the *instrument* of receiving salvation (viz., faith) the *basis* of redemption. The good news everywhere announced in the Scriptures is that God has reconciled us to himself through Christ's death, that this happened at the cross with the shedding of Christ's blood, and that it has secured an objective forgiveness of sins (Isa. 53:10–11; Matt. 26:28; John 1:29; 3:17; 4:42; 1 Tim. 1:15, etc.).

---

39. Lewis Sperry Chafer, "For Whom Did Christ Die?," *Bibliotheca Sacra* (October–December 1980): 325.

40. Robert Lightner, "For Whom Did Christ Die?," in *Walvoord: A Tribute*, ed. Donald K. Campbell (Chicago: Moody, 1982), 162.

41. John Owen, "The Death of Death in the Death of Christ," *Works of John Owen* (Edinburgh: Banner of Truth Trust, 1966), 10:233.

"For if while we were enemies we were reconciled to God by the death of his Son, much more, now that we are reconciled, shall we be saved by his life." (Rom. 5:10). All for whom Christ died have been redeemed, reconciled, and saved from the wrath of God. Through faith we receive this salvation that was accomplished at Golgotha. The "once and for all" accomplishment of Christ in his saving work at the cross leaves nothing for sinners to complete by their own actions, whether their decision or effort (Rom. 9:12–16). This is why the evangelistic appeals in the New Testament are unhesitatingly joyful and full of comfort. All who embrace this gift are assured that Christ's work *has already* secured their salvation, the benefits of which they now receive through the gracious work of the Spirit that was included in Christ's purchase of his people.

Second, this view displays the cooperation of the Trinity in the one work of redemption, united in purpose and accomplishment. As I have argued, the eternal covenant of redemption grounds the execution of this purpose in history. Particular redemption is not simply a logical deduction but is taught explicitly in Scripture as the outworking of God's electing plan.

Third, this view places the focus entirely on Christ rather than on the believer. It must be conceded that this is not always how this doctrine has been taught and applied in pastoral practice. How do I know if I am one for whom Christ died? The only answer given in Scripture is that we look to Christ, in whom we were chosen, and whose death is sufficient for every human being—indeed, for a thousand worlds. All that the sinner needs to know is that Christ's death is *sufficient* to save him or her and that by looking to Christ one is assured of being an elect and redeemed coheir with him.

During the magisterial Reformation, the doctrine of election was regarded as a corollary to justification, the nail in the coffin of synergism (i.e., justification and regeneration by human cooperation with grace). Pastorally, election was used to drive away despair and anxiety over one's salvation. John Bradford, an Edwardian divine and martyr under Mary's reign, wrote that this doctrine was a "most principal" tenet since it places our salvation entirely in God's hands. "This, I say, let us do, and not be too busybodies in searching the majesty and glory of God, or in nourishing doubting of salvation: whereto we all are ready enough."[42]

---

42. John Bradford, *The Writings of John Bradford* (Cambridge: Cambridge University Press, 1858), 2:316.

With Luther, Calvin cautioned against prying into the "hidden God." Rather, we must find our predestination in Christ. Even in the final edition of the *Institutes* (1559), Calvin declares concerning the doctrine of justification that we must "consider it in such a way as to keep well in mind that this is the principal article of the Christian religion" (3.11.1).[43] The discussion of election begins with the pastoral concern for assurance: "We shall never be clearly convinced as we ought to be, that our salvation flows from the fountain of God's free mercy, till we are acquainted with his eternal election" (3.21.1). But speculation on this topic is deadly. He writes,

> The discussion of predestination—a subject of itself rather intricate—is made very perplexed, and therefore dangerous, by human curiosity, which no barriers can restrain from wandering into forbidden labyrinths, and soaring beyond its sphere, as if determined to leave none of the Divine secrets unscrutinized or unexplored. . . . [The curious] will obtain no satisfaction to his curiosity, but will enter a labyrinth from which he will find no way to depart. For it is unreasonable that man should scrutinize with impunity those things which the Lord has determined to be hidden in himself. (3.21.1)

It follows, then, says Calvin, that if we want to know anything about predestination in general, or our own election in particular, we are to look no further than Christ and the Gospel: "as soon as the Lord closes his sacred mouth, he shall also desist from further inquiry" (3.21.5). We cannot obtain certainty of our election by attempting "to penetrate to the eternal decree of God," for "we shall be engulfed in the profound abyss." We must not seek to "soar above the clouds" but must be "satisfied with the testimony of God in his external word" (3.24.3–4).

When timid souls seek to discover their election beyond this external word—"Come unto Christ all ye sinners"—they will doubtless question their salvation, occupied with the question, "Whence can you obtain salvation but from the election of God? And what revelation have you

---

43. All parenthetical citations from the *Institutes* in this essay are from Calvin, *Institutes of the Christian Religion*, 2 vols., trans. John Allen (Philadelphia: Presbyterian Board of Christian Education, 1949).

received of election?" These questions can only torment the conscience, Calvin says. "No error can affect the mind, more pestilent than such as disturbs the conscience, and destroys its peace and tranquility towards God," than such speculations. The discussion of predestination is a dangerous ocean unless the believer is safely standing on Christ the rock (3.24.4).

> So how does one obtain assurance of election from the external word? In the first place, if we seek the fatherly liberality and propitious heart of God, our eyes must be directed to Christ, in whom alone the Father is well pleased. . . . Consider and investigate it as much as you please, you will not find its ultimate scope extend beyond this. . . . If we are chosen in Christ, we shall find no assurance of election in ourselves; nor even in God the Father, considered alone, abstractly from the Son. Christ, therefore, is the mirror, in which it behooves us to contemplate our election; and here we may do it with safety. (3.24.5)

Embracing Christ alone, one is assured of "every spiritual blessing in heavenly places in Christ," including election (Eph. 1:3–4). Further, says Calvin, to be "in Christ" is an ecclesiological matter: it is to be in the church, which is Christ's body. Thus the external word is joined to baptism, catechesis, the Eucharist, and the discipline and fellowship of the Savior's commonwealth. Although the reprobate are scattered among the elect in this community, there is no way of separating the sheep from the goats until the last judgment. Assurance of election therefore is linked to the proper use of the means of grace and incorporation into the visible Church (3.24.5–6). Thus certainty of election is obtained neither within oneself nor by oneself but in Christ and with his chosen people.

Grace really is grace: this is what Calvin and the Reformed tradition find most valuable in considering the doctrines of grace. While election may not be the center of Christianity, it is certainly the test of just how central the central things really are.

However, short of affirming universal salvation, the alternative views hold that in spite of Christ's objective work many for whom he died will be finally lost, bearing their own judgment. What then of Christ's promise above that he will not lose any of those whom the Father had given him? And why should I find assurance in the death of Christ if it did not actually save anyone? Though eccentric in the history of doctrine, Karl Barth's position illustrates this problem. Everyone is elect in Christ and redeemed by Christ: objectively saved and justified. However, he leaves open the possibility that some may be finally lost. However, if *one person* for whom Christ died is lost, even potentially or hypothetically, then his death did not actually save. The only way to maintain the objectivity of Christ's saving work on the cross as well as a universal atonement is to deny the possibility that any person will be finally condemned. However, if the notion of universal election is untenable exegetically, the concept of universal salvation is all the more so.

Calvinists proclaim Christ as the all-sufficient Savior for all people everywhere, and when people do believe, we assure them that there is not a single sin—past, present, or future—that "can separate them from the love of God in Christ Jesus" (Rom. 8:35). How do we know this? Is it because of what we have made of Christ or because of what he has made of us? On the contrary, Paul replies,

> And those whom he predestined he also called, and those whom he called he also justified, and those whom he justified he also glorified. What then shall we say to these things? If God is for us, who can be against us? He who did not spare his own Son but gave him up for us all, how will he not also with him graciously give us all things? Who shall bring any charge against God's elect? It is God who justifies. Who is to condemn? Christ Jesus is the one who died—more than that, who was raised—who is at the right hand of God, who indeed is interceding for us. Who shall separate us from the love of Christ? (Rom. 8:30–35)

We do not look for our election or redemption within ourselves, but outside of ourselves. Yet we can only do so because the objective judgment of God against us has been dealt with decisively, fully, and finally at the cross rather than in our subjective experience. If Christ's death did not actually bear away God's wrath for every person for whom he died, then, as Herman Bavinck concludes, "The center of gravity has been shifted from Christ and located in the Christian." Instead of Christ's objective work, "Faith is the true reconciliation with God."[44] In this view, then, faith not only receives this reconciliation but accomplishes it, and faith becomes a saving work—the basis of God's forgiving and renewing grace, not the instrument of receiving it.

Responding to Objections

1. *The New Testament teaches clearly that Christ died for the world.*

That Scripture explicitly teaches Christ's death for the world has never been in doubt among Calvinists; in fact, it has been celebrated as wonderful "glad tidings." We often take for granted that gentiles are made coheirs with Christ, spiritual children of Abraham along with believing Jews. However, this was a radical message for first-century Jews and gentiles. It lay at the heart of "the mystery of Christ" unfolded by Paul, the apostle to the gentiles (Eph. 2:11–3:13), and it is why some Jewish Christians opposed him. This mystery of Jews and gentiles united in Christ prompted the controversy that was finally resolved at the Jerusalem Council in Acts 15.

Yet all along, it had been God's purpose to save the world through Israel. This was anticipated as early as the announcement of the gospel in Genesis 3:15, was more clearly propounded in God's covenant with Abraham as "the father of many nations" (Gen. 15:5), is repeatedly promised in the prophets, and was to be proclaimed to the world by the risen Christ. Jesus did not come to restore the Mosaic covenant (a geopolitical theocracy) but to fulfill the Abrahamic covenant. He is the seed in whom all families of the earth are blessed (Gal. 3:11–18, 28).

However, throughout redemptive history, "salvation" always came through a remnant. The world was saved from the judgment of the flood through Noah and his family—eight people total (2 Peter 2:5). He saved Israel and Judah through a remnant. And he saved the whole world in the same way, not merely through a few, but through an innumerable company, having "ransomed people for God from every tribe and language and people and nation" as "a kingdom and priests to our God." (Rev. 5:9–10). "For God so loved the world, that he gave his only

44. Herman Bavinck, *Reformed Dogmatics*, ed. John Bolt; trans. John Vriend (Grand Rapids, Mich.: Baker Academic, 2006), 3:469.

Son, that whoever believes in him should not perish but have eternal life" (John 3:16). God's love for the world moved him to choose an innumerable company of enemies, to give his Son even "while we were enemies" (Rom. 5:10), and to unite these sinners to Christ by his Spirit as a massive choir celebrating his mercy and grace into all of eternity. In this way, the world is indeed saved.[45]

Calvinists proclaim as confidently as any Christian that Christ is "the Lamb of God, who takes away the sin of the world" (John 1:29). We declare not only generally to all but particularly to each person that Christ's death is sufficient to save him or her. In the words of the Canons of Dort, "The death of the Son of God is the only and most perfect sacrifice and satisfaction for sin, and is of infinite worth and value, abundantly sufficient to expiate the sins of the whole world."[46] No one can say, "I came to Christ, but there was no redemption for me." There is sufficient redemption in Christ's cross for every person in this world and in a thousand worlds besides. So there is no place in this view for thinking of the work of Christ as a limited reservoir of forgiveness with just enough for the elect. The question is never the sufficiency of Christ's work; the question is the purpose of the triune God.

2. *"It's a sin issue, not a Son issue."*

Some argue that Christ did accomplish objective forgiveness for every person so that unbelievers are condemned not for their *sins* but for their *unbelief.* However, John tells us that "whoever does not believe is *condemned already*, because he has not believed in the name of the only Son of God" (John 3:18, emphasis added). Born into the world guilty in Adam, we add to our debts each day. One does not become condemned the moment he or she hears and rejects the gospel. Paul says that God's wrath is being stored up for the ungodly because of their sins (Rom. 1:18) and lists examples of the sins for which God's wrath will be poured out on the last day (Col. 3:5–6). So clearly the basis of final judgment of unbelievers will be their works. Unbelief is simply one of the sins for which people will be condemned on the last day.

---

45. See B. B. Warfield, *The Plan of Salvation* (Grand Rapids: Eerdmans, 1942; repr., 1980), esp. 95.

46. Canons of Dort, Second Head of Doctrine, art. 3, in *The Psalter Hymnal*, 99.

3. *Isn't this "unfair"? How could God justly condemn people if Christ didn't die for them?*

If we accept the full force of the passages cited above, the Father did not choose to save everyone and the Spirit will not draw everyone effectually to the Savior. Therefore, this understandable objection is directed as much to election and the application of redemption as it is to its achievement. In Romans 9, the apostle Paul answers the fairness objection in relation to election simply by pointing to God's sovereign freedom to choose whom he will out of a mass of condemned humanity.

And that is the point. Christ did not die for neutral creatures but for sinners—enemies, hostile rebels. God's great love for humanity is manifest in the fact that even before Adam freely disobeyed God, enslaving himself and us to sin, the Father gave a people to the Son and gave his Son for his people. God was under no obligation to save any of his enemies, but even while we raged against him, he loved us and sent his Son for our salvation. Grace is not grace if it is compelled—even by an inner necessity of God's being. God could have justly condemned us all: that is the presupposition of grace and mercy.

Because the death of Christ is sufficient for everyone, no one is left out except those who refuse this gift. Of course, we would all have refused this gift apart from grace, but God is not held responsible for this sinful condition. On the day of judgment, human beings will have no one to thank for salvation but God and no one to blame for condemnation but themselves. To all who trust in Christ, we declare with Scripture that they are already now saved from God's wrath, death, and hell. Their salvation is not potential but actual. They are not savable but saved. It is not something that they are to complete or to make effective by their decision or effort, but they receive it as a gift.

Furthermore, the depths of God's love are revealed in the fact that he sent his Son to accomplish everything necessary for our salvation, not merely to make humanity "savable." He did not come halfway, as if to say, "I did my part, and now you need to do yours." Rather, he has carried his loving purposes all the way, accomplishing and applying redemption to those who were "dead in trespasses and sins" (Eph. 2:1).

ANDREW LOUTH

I did not expect to agree with the traditional Reformed view of the extent of the atonement, and I don't, but I did find in Michael Horton's essay a spirited attempt to put Calvinism in a better light (than accords with my usual prejudices, which I suspect are widely shared). Apart from Horton's detailed knowledge of the tradition from Calvin onwards, the rhetorical structure of his argument is engaging, at least at first sight. However, in his attempt to see Calvin as standing firmly within the Christian tradition rather than as some kind of freak, I felt there was much that proceeded by aposiopesis.

In common with most traditional Western theologians, Horton feels it perfectly acceptable to ignore the whole Greek dimension of the Christian tradition (save for Cyril Loukaris, whom he is pleased to claim for Calvinism; I fear my reaction, like that of most other Orthodox, would be that Horton is welcome to Cyril; he never convinced many of his fellow Orthodox). The Greek Christian tradition should not be unknown in the West; it is sad if it is indeed the case that Western patristic scholarship of the last century has made so little impact among Reformed theologians (I know that this is not universal, my own mentor in dogmatic theology, T. F. Torrance, was not in the least ignorant of the Greek Patristic tradition, though perhaps somewhat selective in his appreciation). Furthermore, as I argued above, it is a mistake to think that *gemina praedestinatio* was "taken for granted" by Augustine. It may have been the logic of his later thought, but it was a logic that betrayed itself, not one that he consciously developed. I am willing to accept that Aquinas may have taught it (given Levering's apparent endorsement), though it is not the only reading of the Angelic Doctor, but Horton's account of later medieval theology seems to me more a projection back of Luther's own perception, than an accurate account of current scholarship. I am not at all an expert in all this, but I have the impression that works of Heiko Oberman, such as *The Harvest of Medieval Theology* and *The Dawn of the Reformation* (not, I suppose, the latest scholarship), present a rather more nuanced picture of late medieval theology than Luther's view, as endorsed by Horton. Indeed, I rather had the impression that the tendency of Protestant theology in the past to work backwards from Luther—and, for instance, to project Luther's view of Paul and justification back on to the historical apostle—had largely been abandoned. I was, however, heartened by Horton's assertion that his survey of the way in which predestination became a contested issue even among the followers of Calvin had led him to situate "the question concerning the atonement's *extent* in the wider context of its *nature*." I then turned eagerly to the next section, with the fine title, "'Crucified before the Foundation of the World': The Triune Purpose of Redemption," with the suggestion that the nature of the atonement is only to be found in the context of the doctrine of the Trinity.

Nevertheless, I was puzzled to read that "according to classic Reformed theology, all of God's purposes [including, I presume, the atonement] are understood in terms of an eternal covenant between the persons of the Holy Trinity," for I have difficulty in grasping what could be meant by "an eternal covenant between the persons of the Holy Trinity." The notion of covenant is indeed central to the Scriptures of both the Old and New Testament, but it is a covenant (or series of covenants) between God and humankind; I can think of nowhere in the Scriptures where it is a question of a covenant between Father, Son, and Holy Spirit. Such a notion seems to me to be hopelessly anthropomorphic. So I found myself wondering how this notion might shed light on the *nature* of the atonement, in the context of which the *extent* of the atonement might become clearer. The answer seemed to be that all other aspects of the atonement—mention is made of Christ's victory over death in the cross and resurrection and the doctrine of recapitulation—are dependent on "the legal satisfaction of divine justice." In other words, the forensic aspect of the atonement is paramount, and this forensic aspect entails seeing Christ's death in substitutionary terms. This leads into a discussion of why "Arminian theologians frequently express unease with the doctrine of substitution," a discussion that picks up from the earlier discussion of the disputes over predestination among Calvin's heirs that are associated with the Synod of Dort. This circling back to pick up discussion of the Synod of Dort somewhat confused me (but I am easily confused over the details of Protestant theological history); I thought that the Synod of Dort took a strict Calvinist line against the Arminians or Remonstrants, but some of Horton's discussion seems to suggest that a weakening of the strict Calvinist line can already be discerned in the proceedings of the synod. Nevertheless, from what I could understand of Horton's essay, it seemed to me that what emerges from his discussion, particularly in the section entitled "What Did Jesus Do?," is the way in which the appalling spectacle of strict Calvinist predestinarianism led to a series of attempts to qualify aspects of this doctrine in ways that Horton argues turn the focus of the doctrine from Christ to the individual human soul, if not ultimately to a dissolution of Christian Trinitarian theology. It seems to me that such an outcome is a consequence of the quantitative approach to the atonement that is characteristic of Western theories of the atonement, which led to doctrine of "lowered mart," that is, that Christ's sacrifice on the cross lowered the price of redemption (the "mart" or the market price) for those who believe—which all might accept to be an unfortunate way of considering atonement.

A little later I picked up a reference to synergism, presented in wholly negative terms (justification as "a nail in the coffin of synergism"). Such a view is wholly at odds with the tradition of the Greek East, which is not without scriptural warrant. (It is not just in the use of συνεργέω or συνέργος in, e.g., Mark 16:20; 2 Corinthians 6:1; 1 Corinthians 3:9; and Colossians 4:11. It seems to be in the logic of passages such as Philippians 2:12–13 and Colossians 1:24–26, even though συνεργέω and its cognates do not appear.) This introduces a long exposition of the way the doctrine of election focuses the whole concern of salvation on God and "was used to drive away despair and anxiety over one's salvation" (p. 127), but the pages already devoted to the doubts of the "Arminians" seem to suggest that a strict doctrine of election could as easily lead to fear of eternal reprobation—*eternal* not just in the sense of everlasting but in the sense of being already decided before one's conception and birth.

I am sure it is a failing in myself, but I found it very difficult to find the details of the argument presented by Horton at all appealing, or even comprehensible.

RESPONSE TO MICHAEL HORTON

Although I disagree with the teaching of the Synod of Dort on limited atonement, I affirm Professor Horton's insistence upon the sovereignty and priority of God. It seems to me that if God did not have the power to convert our rebellious wills and thereby to enable us freely to accept him, no one would be saved. For human salvation, I count upon the grace of God to place us in communion with God. No doubt such conversion involves the action of our created will in synergy with God's activity, but God's activity has absolute priority and is the (noncompetitive) cause of our free positive response to God. I also concur with Professor Horton that, so far as we can tell from divine revelation (which is all that we have to go by), God does not save everyone.

Professor Horton argues that in accord with the biblical doctrine of predestination, we must hold that from eternity "the Father chose many, but not all, to eternal life" (p. 119). He affirms the triune God's eternal priority and sovereign power in accomplishing the purposes of his wisdom and will for his creatures. As he says, "The Spirit effectually calls the elect and unites them to Christ. Although they do indeed believe in Christ, it is because of God's sovereign grace rather than their own free will" (p. 119). In other words, we are sinners, and our wills are rebellious toward God, and how we get out of this situation is not by the goodness or power of our free will but by God's grace efficaciously healing and elevating our free will so that we freely choose God in Christ.

Put simply, God converts those who come to faith and charity, just as he converted Saul (Paul) but did not convert some of Paul's Pharisee friends. Paul emphasizes in his letter to the Romans that "at the present time there is a remnant, chosen by grace. But if it is by grace, it is no longer on the basis of works; otherwise grace would no longer be grace" (Rom. 11:5–6). Paul rebukes his Corinthian flock, whose members are tempted by pride, by asking them rhetorically, "What have you that you did not receive? If then you received it, why do you boast as if it were not a gift?" (1 Cor. 4:7). In Ephesians 1:3–5, Paul praises God the Father for having chosen "us in him [Christ] before the foundation of the world, that we should be holy and blameless before him. He destined us in love to be his sons through Jesus Christ, according to the purpose of his will."

For the community of Christ, it is glorious to look forward with confidence to eternal communion with the Lord who has called us to such an amazing relationship. Given the power of God's love, we can say with Paul that "we know that if the earthly tent we live in is destroyed, we have a building from God, a house not made with hands, eternal in the heavens" (2 Cor. 5:1). In Christ and through his Spirit, it is true that "we all, with unveiled face, beholding the glory of the Lord, are being changed into his likeness from one degree of glory to another" (2 Cor. 3:18). Given the sufferings endured by believers who follow the path of the cross, it is reassuring to know that "this slight momentary affliction is preparing for us an eternal weight of glory beyond all comparison" (2 Cor. 4:17).

But the question inevitably arises, what if we are not Jacob—as we hope—but rather Esau? Paul quotes Malachi 1:2–3: "As it is written, 'Jacob I loved, but Esau I hated'" (Rom. 9:13). What if Paul has "a house not made with hands" awaiting him in eternal life, whereas we, due to our sins (but not due to sins worse than those Paul committed as Saul), are headed to eternal misery? We may even be among those who can truly say to Christ, "Lord, Lord, did we not prophesy in your name, and cast out demons in your name, and do many mighty works in your name?" (Matt. 7:22). Why then does God not give us the grace of perseverance that God gave to Paul? Even if we know the evil that we have done freely and without repentance—and Paul spells it out for us when he states that "neither the immoral, nor idolaters, nor adulterers, nor homosexuals, nor thieves, nor the greedy, nor drunkards, nor revilers, nor robbers will inherit the kingdom of God" (1 Cor. 6:9–10)—we might still ask why we remained in our sins due to God's permission, whereas other sinners just as bad as us were by God's power "washed," "sanctified," and "justified" unto salvation (1 Cor. 6:11).

Paul identifies the obvious query: "You will say to me then, 'Why does he [God] still find fault? For who can resist his will?'" (Rom. 9:19). Paul answers in unsettling terms: "What if God, desiring to show his wrath and to make known his power, has endured with much patience the vessels of wrath made for destruction, in order to make known the riches of his glory for the vessels of mercy, which he has prepared beforehand for glory, even us whom he has called, not from the Jews only but also from the Gentiles?" (Rom. 9:22–24). What if, in the plan of God's wisdom and will from all eternity, there is no place for us in eternal life?

Due to the scriptural texts, the question of whether we are among the elect is present in some way among all Christians who are not universalists. One way to answer the question is to look for marks by which we can be assured that God wills to save us. Quoting Joel 2:32, Paul himself emphasizes that "every one who calls upon the name of the Lord will be saved" (Rom. 10:13). Likewise, citing Isaiah 28:16, Paul in the same context assures the members of his Roman flock that "if you confess with your lips that Jesus is Lord and believe in your heart that God raised him from the dead, you will be saved. For man believes with his heart and so is justified, and he confesses with his lips and so is saved. The scripture says, 'No one who believes in him will be put to shame'" (Rom. 10:9–11). The same Paul, however, also remarks that "if I have all faith, so as to remove mountains, but have not love, I am nothing" (1 Cor. 13:2). James warns in strong terms that we must "be doers of the word, and not hearers only" (James 1:22), and he concludes that "faith by itself, if it has no works, is dead. . . . Even the demons believe—and shudder" (James 2:17, 19). Furthermore, according to Paul, even if we are not "aware of anything against" ourselves, we are "not thereby acquitted" (1 Cor. 4:4). We cannot "pronounce judgment before the time, before the Lord comes" (1 Cor. 4:5).

After warning against speculating about whether one is among the elect, Professor Horton points out that "Calvinists proclaim Christ as the all-sufficient Savior for all people everywhere, and when people do believe, we assure them that there is not a single sin—past, present, or future—that can separate us from the love of God in Christ Jesus' (Rom. 8:35)" (p. 130). It follows that, as he goes on to observe, "no one can say, 'I came to Christ, but there was no redemption for me'" (p. 132). He suggests that if we believe in Christ, we will be saved.

The Catholic answer to the question of our status is that we do not receive sufficient clarity—other than through special revelation that very few people receive—to be able to know whether we are among the elect. It is always possible, even up to our final moment, that we will reject God in favor of a lesser good. This inevitably leads to anxiety, and so it is no wonder that Professor Horton and the Reformed tradition emphasize that no one who has faith can ever be separated by sin from eternal union with Christ.

Although Julian of Norwich (1342–1423) did not question her own faith and love for God, she did ponder how God could have permitted sin to mar his creation. Pondering sin in *Showings* (the short text), she describes herself as being "filled with compassion for all my fellow Christians," and she recognizes that "every kind of compassion which one has for one's fellow Christians in love is Christ in us."[1] In Christ's passion, she sees the immensity and perfection of God's love. She sees "his blessed will for all who will be saved. He comforts readily and sweetly with his words, and says: But all will be well, and every kind of thing will be well."[2] But she responds to this profound interior perception of God's superabundant love with a question, "Ah, good Lord, how could all things be well, because of the great harm which has come through sin to your creatures?"[3] God's response to her is that we must contemplate solely what he has revealed: "our savior and our salvation."[4] This must suffice because it is the revelation of his wondrous love for us. God warns her against seeking knowledge about "all which is additional to our salvation" since "this is our Lord's privy counsel, and it is fitting to God's royal dominion to keep his privy counsel in peace."[5] God then reiterates to her, in a Trinitarian fashion, "I will make all things well, I shall make all things well, I may make all things well and I can make all things well."[6] *Will* applies to the Father, *may* to the Son, and *can* to the Spirit. Yet Julian never says that all will be saved. Rather, she makes clear that God's goodness will be perfectly manifested: all will be well.

Saint Francis de Sales (1567–1622) endured a terrible spiritual crisis at the age of nineteen. He endured the agony of believing that he was not among the elect but rather was predestined to eternal alienation

---

1. Julian of Norwich, *Showings*, ed. and trans. Edmund Colledge, OSA, and James Walsh, SJ (New York: Paulist Press, 1978), 149.
2. Julian, *Showings*, 149.
3. Julian, *Showings*, 149.
4. Julian, *Showings*, 150.
5. Julian, *Showings*, 150.
6. Julian, *Showings*, 151.

from God. As a Catholic, he could not turn to the assurance that as long as you believe, you will be saved no matter what. Instead, he experienced God's superabundant love through an act of total abandonment to divine providence. He teaches his spiritual "daughter"—representative of all who come to him for spiritual direction—that she must constantly "praise His [God's] excellence, invoke His aid, cast yourself in spirit at the Foot of His Cross, adore His Goodness, offer your whole soul a thousand times a day to Him, fix your inward gaze upon Him, stretch out your hands to be led by Him, as a little child to its father."[7] He urges his spiritual daughter to make "an act of oblation by which you offer your affections and resolutions to God, in union with His Own Goodness and Mercy, and the Death and Merits of His Son."[8] This is the abandonment to divine providence, resting secure in the goodness, mercy, and love of God as revealed in the cross of Christ.

In the end, Francis de Sales found consolation not only by abandoning himself to divine providence and rejoicing in the superabundance of God's love in Christ but also by insisting that even if "the consent to grace depends much more on grace than on the will," nonetheless our free will cooperates with grace, and we can always "reject and deny consent" to God's grace.[9] This account of the resistibility of grace would not be something that Professor Horton could accept because it implies that the difference between those who are saved and those who are damned hinges upon the righteous or unrighteous exercise of free will under the influence of grace—even if de Sales tries to save matters by arguing that every "consent to grace depends much more on grace." When pressed on this point, he adds that only when the power of grace fills the heart can a human being have "either power or will to co-operate."[10] If grace gives us the will to cooperate, however, it seems that grace could overcome our resistance—and indeed if God does not have such power, then we fallen humans are in trouble.

A more satisfying answer, perhaps, may be found in the teachings of Brother Lawrence (1614–1691). In the course of his spiritual journey,

---

7. Francis de Sales, *Introduction to the Devout Life* (New York: Random House, 2002), 63.

8. De Sales, *Introduction to the Devout Life*, 55.

9. Francis de Sales, *Treatise on the Love of God*, trans. Henry Benedict Mackey, OSB (Rockford, IL: Tan Books, 1997), 96–97.

10. De Sales, *Treatise on the Love of God*, 180.

which began with ten years of spiritual darkness (though never the loss of faith), Brother Lawrence eventually came to focus on cultivating a "simple attentiveness and a loving gaze upon God which I can call the actual presence of God or to put it more clearly, an habitual, silent and secret conversation of the soul with God."[11] In this condition of faith and love for God, he finds that, sinner though he is, God in Christ shows him intense love and mercy. Indeed, he says, "The more weak and despicable I see myself to be, the more beloved I am of God."[12] In this condition, he abandons himself and his eternal destiny entirely to God, even to the point, as he puts it, that "I am so resigned that I would not lift a straw from the ground except in accordance with His order, or from any other motive than sheer love of Him."[13]

Similarly, consider the teaching of the spiritual manual *Abandonment to Divine Providence* by Jean-Pierre Caussade, SJ (1675–1751). Caussade argues, "In reality, holiness consists of one thing only: complete loyalty to God's will."[14] The key here, of course, is to realize that God's will is perfectly and infinitely good, superabundant love. God never restricts or withholds love for any of us. God loves each of us, no matter how sinful, with a superabundant and amazing love. The doctrine of limited atonement puts this into doubt by depicting an arbitrary God who superabundantly loves some sinners but who (however justly) abandons other sinners due to his will from all eternity to love Jacob and hate Esau.[15]

With Saint Gertrude the Great (1256–1302), we need to recognize that "the light of the godhead is so great and so incomprehensible that if each of the saints, from Adam up to the most recent, singly perceived a single insight so bright, profound and extensive that no creature could

---

11. Brother Lawrence of the Resurrection, *The Practice of the Presence of God*, trans. John J. Delaney (New York: Doubleday, 1977), 68.

12. Brother Lawrence, *The Practice of the Presence of God*, 69.

13. Brother Lawrence, *The Practice of the Presence of God*, 68.

14. Jean-Pierre de Caussade, SJ, *Abandonment to Divine Providence*, trans. John Beevers (New York: Doubleday, 1975), 24.

15. Matthias Grebe argues that limited atonement (with its corresponding doctrines of irresistible grace and absolute divine causality) "either calls into question the relationship between God's action and being in the atonement or it questions God's loving nature altogether. Either it attacks the notion that the atonement flows out of God's nature (essentially arguing that the atonement flows out of some arbitrary divine will); or, if it affirms that the atonement does flow out of God's nature (John Owen), then it attacks God's being, making God's love arbitrary because he would be seen to love some and not others." Grebe, *Election, Atonement, and the Holy Spirit: Through and Beyond Barth's Theological Interpretation of Scripture* (Eugene, OR: Pickwick, 2014), 210–11.

ever possibly grasp it . . . none the less the godhead would remain unspent forever, beyond all reach of understanding."[16] God's love is incomprehensibly glorious and so great that we cannot fathom it, other than to know that it is infinitely greater than the love we have for our dearest beloved. Even if we cannot see how the divine election of some and God's superabundant love for every rational creature go together, we must not let go of the fact that God powerfully loves each and every rational creature far, far more than we can ever imagine. This is, I hope, a point on which Professor Horton and I very much agree.

---

16. Gertrude the Great of Helfta, *The Herald of God's Loving-Kindness: Book Three*, trans. Alexandra Barratt (Kalamazoo, MI: Cistercian, 1999), 106.

FRED SANDERS

According to conventional wisdom, debate about the extent of the atonement is supposed to be a two-party system. The Calvinists are supposed to put the *L* in TULIP, arguing that limited atonement is part of a strict logical package, tightly bundled and adequately stated in five points. Remonstrants are supposed to remonstrate, denying the TULIP and especially that offensive *L* at its center. The well-trodden argument is supposed to be fairly straightforward from that point on. Thus far the conventional wisdom.

But conventional wisdom oversimplifies here, and the real situation has always been far more complex. For one thing, the *L* of limited atonement has historically been so manifestly the hardest letter in the acronym that it has spun off deviant forms of Calvinism left and right for centuries. Remonstrants, Arminians, and Wesleyans have always been able to gaze across the border into Reformed territory and wave sympathetically to the nearest four-pointers, Amyraldians, hypothetical universalists, and whatever Richard Baxter was. This waving causes understandable annoyance to the self-designated Truly Reformed.

Meanwhile on the Arminian side, the crowd is similarly diverse and internally conflicted. They are likely to agree with each other about the extent of the atonement (mainly agreeing that Calvinists are wrong) but disagree about everything else, and more deeply. Wesleyans as pure as John Wesley himself preach a self-consciously Protestant doctrine of grace and refuse to treat faith as a merely human possibility; Charles Finney, on the other hand, kept company with Pelagianism, gave long lectures on law and the simplicity of moral action, and couldn't understand why people won't just be good. Such major differences among those on the Arminian side of the divide have substantive implications when it comes to the extent of the atonement. When an Arminian like

Finney says, "Jesus died for all," he might mean that God has already done his part and now it's time for you to do yours; you can tell by the way he immediately describes the fact that God made salvation possible and calls on a human response to make it actual. When an Arminian like Wesley says, "Jesus died for all," he is only clearing the ground for further divine action; you can tell by the way he immediately begins filling in a vision of blood-bought prevenient grace and the regenerating work of the Holy Spirit.

On reflection it can seem like the central boundary line that defines the two-party system is drawn in the wrong place, at least in the sense that disagreement about the extent of the atonement turns out not to predict an overall theological profile very accurately. The present book is obviously an extended editorial attempt to approach the extent of the atonement in a way that flouts conventional wisdom and scrambles its expectations. Where readers look for the two standard views on the extent of the atonement, the editor instead solicits five. To make matters worse (or rather, hopefully, better), each of the five authors are committed to placing the extent of the atonement into the broadest possible perspective, contextualizing and resourcing the discussion with all manner of theological riches.

Michael Horton's chapter is no exception. Even though Horton might be expected to contribute the most predictable of the five views, he shares the conviction that this conversation has traditionally suffered from a diminished scope and context. So he joins the project of placing the extent of the atonement into a wider perspective. He immediately breaks out of the restrictions imposed by the popular reduction of Reformed theology to TULIP soteriology, calling the reduction "simplistic to the point of being unhelpful" (p. 112). In seeking a broader context for his Reformed contribution, he rightly takes his bearings from classic Trinitarian theology, arguing that "it would require a major revision in the doctrine of the Trinity to imagine that the Son's saving purpose was different from the Father's" (p. 119). And he makes his key move when he "situates the question concerning the atonement's extent in the wider context of its nature" (p. 118). That is exactly the right angle of approach for any theologian, and it is especially appropriate for the Reformed.

In all these ways and more, Horton shows again that here is a

Reformed theologian you can talk to: on the one hand he seeks common ground and classic doctrinal scope whenever possible, and on the other hand he can be counted on not to cheat or seek premature ecumenical compromise but to bring an actual Reformed confessional argument to the table. So the essay contains much we can agree upon, but when all is said and done, Wesleyans and Reformed theologians will finally have to disagree on some significant issues in soteriology.

The key disagreement surfaces most instructively in Horton's statement that "Arminian theologians frequently express unease with the doctrine of substitution because it entails either Calvinism or universalism" (p. 121). That stark choice between Calvinism and universalism indeed captures what makes Arminian theologians uneasy. But I do not think the stark choice attaches directly to the doctrine of substitution. Evangelical Arminians in the tradition of Wesley can wholeheartedly embrace the doctrine of substitution; it can quite readily serve as the fundamental meaning of atonement in a Wesleyan soteriology. It should be freely admitted that plenty of Arminian theologians have looked elsewhere for a key idea in their atonement theology and have especially tended to invest in a governmental model. Again, I will never attempt to undertake a theological defense of Finney or of anybody on that side of the Arminian assembly hall. But for evangelical Wesleyans, substitution is the basis of a doctrine of atonement that strangely warms their Arminian hearts.

The Calvinism-universalism disjunct, however, does kick in when the grace enacted in that substitutionary atonement is considered automatically effective. If grace is irresistible in that sense, then it certainly does follow that everybody for whom Christ died will be saved, so universal salvation would necessarily follow from universal atonement. The only alternative, if grace is automatically effective, is to reverse the equation and argue that since universal salvation is not the case, then Christ must not have died for everyone. But there are good reasons not to reverse that equation. The main reason is the New Testament's tendency to use comprehensive or universal language precisely in the context of the death of Christ, clustered strikingly around the cross of Christ. Edward Polhill refers to this scriptural evidence as "the general and large expressions in Scripture touching Christ and his death" and lists the following:

Christ died for all, (2 Cor 5:15), for every man (Heb 2:9); he gave himself for the world, (John 6:51), for the whole world (1 John 2:2); he is styled the Saviour of the world (1 John 4:14); and his salvation is called a common salvation (Jude 3), a salvation prepared before the face of all people (Luke 2:31), and flowing forth to the ends of the earth (Isa 49:6); the gospel of this salvation is to be preached to all nations, (Matt 28:19), and to every creature (Mark 16:19); there is a *charis soterios*, grace bringing salvation to all men (Tit 2:11); a door of hope open to them, because Christ gave himself a ransom for all (1 Tim 2:6).[1]

Not all of these citations carry equal weight, but taken together they justify Polhill's exclamation, "I know not what could be more emphatical to point out the universality of redemption."[2] At least it has seemed so to many Reformed theologians, and certainly to Wesleyans.

If universal atonement is taken to be the most straightforward conclusion to draw from the scriptural witness, it has seemed to Wesleyan theologians unwise to revise the starting point. So universal atonement it is. There must be another answer to the question why everybody is not saved. Several acceptable answers present themselves as possible. As Horton points out, following John Owen, "Every position that recognizes that some will finally be lost places a limit on the atonement at some point: either it is limited in its extent or in its effect" (p. 126). Edward Polhill, a few pages after rehearsing the biblical evidence and providing theological argumentation to support his view that Christ died for all, goes on to turn the corner and introduce his "limit on the atonement." He says that

albeit Christ died in some sort for all men, and, by virtue of his death, all men, if believers, should equally be saved; nevertheless Christ did not die equally for them all, but after a special manner for the elect, above and beyond all others.[3]

---

1. Edward Polhill, "The Divine Will Considered in its Eternal Decrees and Holy Execution of Them," in *The Works of Edward Polhill* (London: Thomas Ward and Co, 1844), 166.

2. Polhill, "Divine Will," 166.

3. Polhill, "Divine Will," 171.

Polhill describes this "special manner" in several ways, but his primary account is that "Christ purchased a salvability for all, but over and besides he purchased . . . for the elect . . . repentance."[4]

Some dangers lurk in that strange seventeenth-century word *salvability*, which we might now render *savability*. It can suggest that the death of Christ renders salvation merely possible, but something on the human side renders salvation actual. That possible-actual distinction is not what an author like Polhill is getting at. His version of Reformed hypothetical universalism is bound to be unsatisfying to a theologian like Horton, but it does not make the error of dividing human salvation between God the enabler and humanity the actualizer. Arminian theologians do sometimes make precisely that error. Arminian gospel appeals are littered with unfortunate examples of salvation presented as God reaching from heaven to earth and almost making contact with us but waiting on us to reach out our hand in response to his to complete the transaction. Gospel tracts do exist showing God voting for human salvation and Satan voting against it, with the human vote as the tiebreaker. That is not what Polhill meant by savable, but it is what some varieties of Arminianism have meant. I would call those varieties of Arminianism "the bad kind."

It is not acceptable to treat the death of Christ as something that only moves salvation into the maybe category, while shifting the actual completion of salvation to the side of the human response. Speaking for myself, I would say I'm Wesleyan but not crazy. Reformed theology at its best is a bright warning against treating the atonement as merely potential. The abiding theological lesson that Reformed soteriologies (whether their brief summaries count to four points or to five points) emphasize is that the effective power of salvation must be located on the divine side. In pondering this question of the extent of the atonement, we are not seeking an account of the so-called human side of salvation. We are seeking a recognition that a divine application of salvation is necessary. My own recommendation is that we should find that application in the way the work of the Spirit in our persons is coordinated with the work of the Son in our nature. In reaching that conclusion, the common Trinitarian and christological doctrines of core Christianity

---

4. Polhill, "Divine Will," 171.

have loomed large in my mind. But dialogue with Reformed soteriology has also been an important pressure on my thinking because of the abiding value of the Reformed witness to confessing that salvation is in the hands of God. Horton's presentation in this chapter is a solid and salutary statement of that witness.

TOM GREGGS

Professor Horton's account is one that helpfully and clearly sets out the concerns that the Reformed traditions have traditionally set forth in speaking about the extent of the atonement. His account of the context and proportionality with which one should consider the traditional doctrine of double predestination (pp. 112–121) is particularly helpful. Locating the doctrine in relation to Augustine (p. 113) and early Lutheran theology (p. 115) helpfully identifies the proportionate concerns of the doctrine. The issue for both is that God's salvation is *God's* salvation and that grace is fully and completely gracious. In an age in which Augustine (at the very least) has often been presented only from the perspective of theodicy in relation to double predestination, warped senses of what the doctrine was to accomplish have been articulated in such a way as to suggest that Augustine (a key proponent of original sin) was a miserly and condemnatory theologian set upon damning the majority in his account of the *massa damnata*. Of course, Augustine's salvific schema was far more generous than Pelagius's—only reliance upon divine grace and not upon human willing can bring salvation. The traditional account of double predestination seeks to see salvation within the context of who God is and what God graciously does in God's economy. A laudable theocentric concentration lies behind the doctrine of election: salvation is something God the Holy Trinity does in God's absolute, free, and unconditional grace. Professor Horton's essay highlights the "broader and richer context" in which the doctrine has its place in both historical and systematic topography of doctrinal loci. And along with him, I want to say that Christ's death actually saves (p. 126), the Trinity accomplishes redemption (p. 127), and the focus should be "on Christ rather than the believer" (p. 127).

However, I am always left in relation to this point wondering how the doctrines of creation and the last things relate to these doctrinal dynamics. While it is laudable not to separate the doctrine of salvation (and its scope) from the doctrine of God (and God's sovereignty and grace), there always remains for me the question of the doctrine of creation. If God creates electing the remnant and rejecting the majority, then this primary decree of God determines that God creates knowing that the vast majority of all people throughout all time will be predestined to eternal damnation in hell. Why should God create with the purpose of destining these people to an eternity of torment and suffering? Surely, it would be better not to create at all than to create with the purpose of damning the *massa* for the sake of the salvation of a remnant? I find difficult (while recognising that even the salvation of one is an unwarranted and unmerited act of grace) to square this account with all that I learn of the God who is the Father of the Lord Jesus Christ and who (with the Son) sends the Spirit. What do we make theologically, therefore, of God's creation and creating grace in light of this? Furthermore, if people raise questions about the justice of the universalist position (that it might include those we see as beyond redemption who have committed atrocities) and its challenge to the justice of God, the same must surely be applied to the account offered in traditional accounts of election (cf. p. 133): if the electing grace of God is utterly unmerited and beyond our knowing in the secret and eternal counsels of God, then in this position too we are challenged to know how best to understand human willing in time and space. In the universalist hope, at least God is saved from what seems like the unrighteousness of bringing about the eternal atrocity of hell's torment upon temporal beings who did not ask to be created for all eternity.

This is not to say that I challenge in any way the idea of unconditional election (p. 116) as an expression of divine sovereign grace. What I am concerned with is the insistence on the limited nature of that unconditional election. Or, rather, I would wish to agree with Barth that election is the self-election of God in Jesus Christ to be God who is eternally for us, and that the primary meaning of the "us" *in Christ* is as humans in Christ's humanity. We are elected in Christ's own humanity, in God the Son's eternal decision to be Jesus Christ.[1] We are elected in God's free grace in our humanity; in Christ's

1. Barth, *Church Dogmatics*, ed. G. W. Bromiley and T. F. Torrance, trans. G. W. Bromiley et al. (New York: T&T Clark, 1957), II/2, 117.

crucifixion and resurrection we are objectively participants as humans in the exaltation of humanity in Christ by the free grace of God.[2] Indeed, the emphasis placed by Professor Horton on salvation through Jesus Christ who is crucified "before the foundation of the world" is key. Recognizing the divine eternal life and the pretemporal, eternal self-willing of God to be God in Jesus Christ, we should reimagine the way in which we speak about the order of the decrees and economy of God: salvation in Christ takes place in God's eternity before the foundation of the world. Barth's presentation is particularly helpful here: in the crucifixion, in the Son's eternal obedience to the Father in foreknowledge and foreordination of all that He will suffer, Christ allows the righteousness of God to proceed against himself instead of them. Barth writes, "For this reason, He is the Lamb slain before the foundation of the world. For this reason, the *crucified* Jesus is the 'image of the invisible God.'"[3] Unlike the "hidden god" (p. 128), which is an inevitable problem for double predestination (the 'god' who would condemn as happily as save, who would reject as happily as elect), we must to the greatest degree explain (in Professor Horton's words) what it is to "find our predestination in Christ" (p. 128), not a hidden god behind the God of the gospel.

The principal question that I have of this account is why it must be limited (pp. 120–21). It is notable that Professor Horton recognises that his presentation of substitution logically involves either Calvinism or universalism (p. 121) and that there is a compelling logical case for universalism (pp. 129–30). While he refers to Karl Barth (surely the greatest theologian of the twentieth century) as "eccentric" in his account of election, Professor Horton does nevertheless recognise that there is a logical consistency in the position:

> Everyone is elect in Christ and redeemed by Christ: objectively saved and justified. . . . The only way to maintain the objectivity of Christ's saving work on the cross as well as a universal atonement is to deny the possibility that any person will be finally condemned. (p. 130)

---

2. Barth, *Church Dogmatics*, II/2, 118.
3. Barth, *Church Dogmatics*, II/2, 123.

He is correct to note that Barth wants to leave the (impossible) possibility of some being lost. But, evidently, Barth's account of election tends and leans in a universalist direction. Perhaps the difference here between the more traditional view and the one I am suggesting is not only material but formal: my own account wants to leave *open* the different accounts of salvation in Scripture rather than dogmatically claim only one of them and to allow them to stand and relate to one another (even in tension) by including the passages which are more universalist in direction. God is not a "thing" in the universe like anything else but is the sovereign and free Lord—the Subject of our thinking not the object of our thought. And Scripture allows different possibilities to stand.

It is indeed the assertion that Scripture does not allow the possibility of universal salvation that makes Professor Horton stop short of this position: "If the notion of universal election is untenable exegetically, the concept of universal salvation is all the more so" (p. 130). Yet Professor Horton does affirm, "The Scriptures unmistakably teach that God loves the world and that Christ died for the world (John 1:29; 3:16; 6:33, 51; Rom. 11:12, 15; 2 Cor. 5:19; 1 John 2:2)" (p. 124). Presumably, the issue at stake is what to do with the passages that involve rejection of humans. However, I have tried to make various cases for how these passages might be read in relation to the position of hopeful universalism I espouse. Not only is universalism expressed as a *daring hope*, but in the account I have offered, the rejection that Scripture speaks of is that which humans ought to suffer but which Christ, "who was crucified before the foundation of the world," takes eternally to himself in his objective substitution. Therefore, these passages can be understood kerygmatically or existentially as an expression of the wrath and condemnation sinful humans deserve and the possibility which lies before us in a life without God and as a checker against binding God to a principle of grace in a manner that reduces grace's graciousness (perhaps parallel to the way the doctrine of *aseity* functions dogmatically to remind us that God, who as Creator is not *a se*, is gracious in all God's acts). These passages are the *penultimate* words in the ultimate victory of Christ who is crucified and resurrected. We can debate how to read the *sensus plenior* of Scripture, but the *possibility* of universalism (however daring and however hopeful) is both hermeneutically and logically tenable; indeed, my own account wants to overcome, through the sovereignty of universal divine loving, some of the exegetical and hermeneutical problems which Professor Horton recognizes in the multivocity of Scripture (see my own chapter, pp. 202ff.). Indeed, even some of the passages that seem the most binary are not so straightforward in interpretation. Jacob, for example, does not come off well in relation to Esau! And there is no question, indeed, that even though God's covenant (*berit*) and its *responsibilities* rest with those who are elect, those who are rejected are nevertheless still in relationship with Yahweh in some way; God makes God's preparedness to bless Ishmael and to answer the prayers of Hagar (literally, "the stranger") intensely clear. I am not so firmly convinced that the account of election and rejection is so strongly binary throughout the narrative of the Bible.

Perhaps Professor Horton's sense of the "untenable" nature of the possibility of an interpretation of Scripture that tends in a universalist direction might well arise from his understanding of the condemnation of *apokatastasis* (p. 124). He is right to point out that *Origen's* theory is condemned, albeit historians of doctrine have shown it is really a gnosticised form of *Origenism*, which involves preexistent nonbodily souls and the salvation of the devil, that is condemned.[4] However, it is not *apokatastasis* per se, or the hope of universal salvation per se, which is condemned (see my own chapter, p. 201), since *Scripture* speaks of it. *Apokatastasis* is utilised in Acts when it speaks of Jesus who must "remain in heaven until the time of universal restoration [*apokatastasis*] that God announced long ago through his holy prophets" (Acts 3:21). That other chapters in this volume leave open the possibility of universal salvation from their own traditions (see Professor Louth's chapter, p. 34) indicates that there is no condemnation from the councils on the hope of universal salvation.

By way of one final point, the emphasis on God's saving activity and God's grace and Christ's sufficiency, all of which this chapter makes plain, is in part what has led me (an evangelical Methodist) to the perspective I hold as one who dares to hope in the possibility of universal salvation. So often the piety I grew up with was in effect semi-Pelagian in its common expression, and so much emphasis was placed on the human rather than God. However, coming from a Wesleyan background, it might perhaps be fairer to discuss the prevenience of

---

4. See Mark J. Edwards, *Origen against Plato* (Aldershot: Ashgate, 2002); and Elizabeth A. Clark, *The Origenist Controversy* (Princeton: Princeton University Press, 1992).

grace rather than "credit[ing] . . . the cooperation of sinners" (p. 119) in a manner that reflects more Professor Horton's discussion of "grace-enabled cooperation" (p. 125). However, I shall leave this to Professor Sanders to take up, should he choose, in his presentation of the traditional Arminian perspective.

WESLEYAN VIEW

FRED SANDERS

Overture: The Interpretive Task

"The grace of God has appeared, bringing salvation to all people," declares Paul in Titus 2:11, sounding a universal note that has sent many responsible translators scampering for some way to signal a compensating restriction. "For the grace of God that bringeth salvation hath appeared to all men," tried the King James Version, dislocating the *all* from *salvation* and reassigning it to *hath appeared*. But besides lacking grammatical warrant,[1] this foisted on Paul the implausible claim that grace has already been manifested to all people. The Revised Version revised, therefore, with surgical precision: "For the grace of God hath appeared, bringing salvation to all men." But unless the starkly universal word entails universalism (the actual salvation of all people contra the overwhelming scriptural witness), it cries out again for some sort of qualification. So the 1984 NIV once again let the *all* migrate toward the manifestation rather than the salvation ("The grace of God that brings salvation has appeared to all men"), but inevitably, more grammatical arguments prevailed by the time of the TNIV revision: "The grace of God has appeared that offers salvation to all people." To say that grace "offers salvation" is to conjure a new verb by way of explanation, offering much guidance to the reader. Too much guidance? Perhaps introducing the idea of an offer is not the best

---

1. I. Howard Marshall, with Philip H. Towner, *A Critical and Exegetical Commentary on the Pastoral Epistles* (London: T&T Clark, 1999), 268.

way to restrict the scope of that universal note.[2] But something must be done.

The metamorphoses of Titus 2:11 are merely illustrative of a wider phenomenon. We are not considering here how to manage a single stray verse, after all.[3] The universal note rings out over and over from the pages of Scripture, from multiple authors in various times and places. Nor are we simply asking how to hedge against possible misinterpretations, clearly marking what these texts are not teaching. Vital as that cautionary task is for theology, the more fundamental interpretive demand is for Christian teachers to apprehend what God is saying in Scripture when he draws our attention to the expansive scope of salvation. The question is: How can we do theological justice to the universal aspect of salvation that surfaces over and over in the biblical witness? If the universal note cannot entail universalism, what does it indicate?

Statement of the Theme

In this chapter I argue that the best way to do justice to the Bible's universal note is to consider the death of Christ to be the event that reconciles human nature to God. The Son of God takes up human nature by joining it to his own person and accomplishes the salvation of human nature in himself by taking that human nature (his and ours) through death and resurrection. The Holy Spirit applies the work of Christ to individual persons, bringing about each person's union with Christ. The atonement is thus the locus of the universal aspect of salvation, if by the word *atonement* we mean to pick out the paschal work of Christ—he died and rose for all. But if we intend the word *atonement* in a broader sense to include not only the accomplishing of salvation by the incarnate Son but also the application of that salvation to believers by the Holy Spirit, then we will have to say that atonement is the locus

---

2. "The event bringing salvation is universal in scope." Philip H. Towner, *The Letters to Timothy and Titus* (Grand Rapids: Eerdmans, 2006), 746. He goes on: "It is not immediately clear why this stress is added. . . . It underlines the vastness of the salvation produced by God's grace . . . and accords well with Paul's emphasis on the universality of access to God's grace throughout his letters."

3. After Marshall remarks on the grammar of Titus 2:11 that "the force is clearly that the salvation is intended for all people," he adds a parenthetical list of several passages with the same emphasis: Acts 17:30; 22:14f; cf. Luke 2:10, 14; 1 Tim. 2:4–6. Marshall with Towner, *Pastoral Epistles*, 268. I would list as the key verses 1 Tim. 2:3–6; 4:10; Titus 2:11; Heb. 2:9; 2 Peter 2:1; 3:9; 1 John 2:2; 4:14.

of both the universal and restrictive aspects of salvation. The death and resurrection of Christ for the salvation of humanity (universally) is applied by the Holy Spirit to those persons (restrictively) who hear the gospel and respond. This argument trades on three major doctrinal distinctions: the difference between nature and person, the difference between salvation accomplished and applied, and the difference between the Son and the Holy Spirit. This latter distinction must be understood primarily in their two distinctive missions in the economy of salvation, with special attention to the differentiation between the characteristic ways of working that each displays. But secondarily the distinction must be confessed to be grounded in their eternal being with the Father in the unity of the Trinity.

I have framed this chapter's argument in such a way that it takes up the challenge of articulating Scripture's witness to the fact that there is something universal and also something restrictive going on in salvation. I take this to be a deeply important question for Christian teaching, and I hope to commend the usefulness of certain conceptual tools (the person-nature distinction; the Son-Spirit distinction; the accomplished-applied distinction) from consensual Christian doctrine for framing a satisfactory answer. One of the ways a discipline like systematic theology can help in approaching a fundamental biblical question like this is to offer suggestions about which doctrinal heading it ought to be handled under. My recommendation is that the question about the universal aspect of salvation is best handled as a question about the extent of the atonement and that the question about the extent of the atonement is best handled under the heading of the accomplished-applied distinction. That is to say, it is a doctrinal task best undertaken by attending to the space between salvation accomplished by Christ and salvation applied by the Spirit. The accomplished-applied schematic is neither self-evident nor self-sufficient but depends for its power and its material content on the Son-Spirit distinction. Nevertheless, when it is grasped in its living connection with those underlying trinitarian realities, the accomplished-applied schematic can be quite illuminating. I believe it opens up the space for a Wesleyan or Arminian account of the extent of the atonement, and I conclude the chapter with an indication of what is Arminian about the argument.

Nature and Person

The distinction between nature and person will be basic to this argument, so we will establish it first. The notion that a human is constituted by these two elements is perhaps not something that is immediately apparent for the doctrine of theological anthropology. If we were constructing a theological anthropology from scratch, we might be led to make other distinctions: we might immediately attempt to explicate how humanity is in the image of God and identify elements of humanity's makeup from that master concept given by Scripture.[4] We might distinguish between body and soul, for instance, or among body, soul, and spirit.[5] Having established a dichotomous or trichotomous view of the human constitution, we might then go on to explore the theologically relevant states of humanity: the unfallen state of integrity, the fallen and corrupted state, the redeemed state, and the glorified state.[6] All of these are solid ways of proceeding in theological anthropology. But the person-nature schema is better if our goal is to examine divine action in soteriology. That is because there is a particular dogmatic history that commends using the categories of nature and person if our goal is ultimately to clarify a point in soteriology. The categories of nature and person are particularly apt because they are borrowed from the doctrines of the Trinity and Christology. They achieved prominence in Christian teaching because they were so helpful in comprehending something about God and Christ. They come to us, therefore, with a particular soteriological orientation that will be clarifying.

The distinction between person and nature became crucial for the doctrine of the Trinity because we needed nouns to help us confess what was one and what was three in God. When the one God brings about salvation in the act of the Father sending the Son and the Holy Spirit, it is helpful to be able to say that the one God is one being with one nature,

---

4. For an encyclopedic recent investigation, see John F. Kilner, *Dignity and Destiny: Humanity in the Image of God* (Grand Rapids: Eerdmans, 2015); for a more focused proposal, see Ryan Peterson, *The Imago Dei as Human Identity: A Theological Interpretation* (Winona Lake, IN: Eisenbrauns, 2016).

5. For the relevant considerations, see Marc Cortez, *Theological Anthropology: A Guide for the Perplexed* (New York: T&T Clark, 2010), 68–97.

6. For a classic Protestant statement of this schema, see Thomas Boston, *Human Nature in its Fourfold State: Of Primitive Integrity, Entire Depravity, Begun Recovery, and Consummate Happiness or Misery* (1720; repr., London: Banner of Truth, 1964).

while the sender and the two sent ones are persons. It is helpful to be able to specify that the Father and Son are united in having one nature but distinguished in being two persons. Notice that the terms as used in the doctrine of the Trinity are not especially thick or content-bearing terms. They are not richly descriptive terms that were ready at hand to apply to God, and they do not bring with them clarifying specifications that serve the theological purpose of naming the one and the three. It is enough if they are concise labels that are useful for picking out things we already knew from the actual revelation: the sender and the sent have something in common and something else that distinguishes them. If they serve this end (they do) and become standardized by usage (they have), then we have something that will keep us from renarrating the original story every time we want to refer to the Trinity. They keep us from stumbling our way through awkward sentences about the sender and the sent, or saying "what there is one of" versus "what there are three of" in God. When we read that the risen Jesus commanded his disciples to baptize in the name of the Father, the Son, and the Holy Spirit, the person-nature distinction enables us to say briefly that the category of "the name" picks out one God, while the Father-Son-Spirit series picks out three persons.

The same distinction must also apply to Christology, for obvious reasons. The first reason is that one person of the Trinity became incarnate. So when we say there are three persons in God, and one of them took on human nature, we are immediately making use of the person-nature distinction to clarify the relation between the doctrine of the Trinity and Christology. What there are three of in God (persons), there is one of in the incarnation: the second person in fact, one of the three persons of God. And what there is one of in God (nature), there are two of in the incarnation: the one divine nature and the created human nature. Because the terms stay the same, we can more readily point out what is different in Trinity and Christology. Gregory of Nazianzus says:

> The constituents of our Savior are different things (since invisible and visible, timeless and temporal, are not the same), but not different people. . . . I say "different things" meaning the reverse of what is the case in the Trinity. There we have "others" in order

not to confuse the subjects or hypostases, but not other things; the three are one and the same thing qua Godhead.[7]

Again, theological argumentation should be modest here. It is not the case that these terms bring extra content to the subject matter; instead, they are so helpful in labeling what we know from the subject matter itself that they actually enable us to do some rational reflection on these mysteries, with mathematical precision. In fact, we can even navigate certain issues of balance and emphasis using these categories. It has been pointed out that there is a conceptual reciprocity between the persons and natures in God and Christ. The clearer a theological project is about the distinction of the three persons in God, the more solid its confession of the unity of Christ, and the more a theological project emphasizes the oneness of God, the more sharply it will distinguish the two natures in Christ.[8]

Equipped with the person-nature distinction for Trinity and Christology, theology after Chalcedon was able to make some further clarifications that are illuminating for soteriology. As we approach the scope of the atonement, it will be helpful to draw out one further implication of the distinction, an implication having to do with the humanity of Christ. In the incarnation, one person of the Trinity took human nature into union with himself, thereby becoming one person with two natures. But the human nature which the Son of God assumed in the hypostatic union is precisely that: a nature, not a person. Every actual instance of human nature is a nature that is personalized, or joined to a person. This applies also to the human nature of Christ. But unlike every other human, the human nature of Christ is not personalized by a created person. That is, the person who personalizes the human nature of Christ is not a created human person. The person who is Christ is the eternal second person of the Trinity. Jesus Christ is a human person in a unique sense: he is the eternal second person of the Trinity, the Son,

---

7. Gregory Nazianzus, "Letter 101: The First Letter to Cledonius the Presbyter," in *On God and Christ: The Five Theological Orations the Two Letters to Cledonius* (Crestwood, NY: St. Vladimir's Seminary Press, 2002), 157.

8. Brian Daley, "The Persons in God and the Person of Christ in Patristic Theology: An Argument for Parallel Development," in *The Mystery of the Holy Trinity in the Fathers of the Church: Proceedings of the Fourth International Patristic Conference, Maynooth,* Irish Theological Quarterly Monograph (Dublin: Four Courts, 2007).

existing in a human nature. His personhood is from above. He has two natures: one is from above (the divine nature), and one is from below (the human nature). If we were to consider that human nature in itself, mentally abstracted from its personhood, the human nature of Jesus Christ would be simply human nature as such, not somebody with a human nature.[9] This is one way of grasping the fact that something universally human is happening in the incarnation. Insights like these would be hard to attain, if they could be glimpsed at all, without the person-nature distinction in place and informing our discussions of doctrine from the Trinity all the way down to anthropology and soteriology.

It will be crucial to distinguish nature and person in what follows because here again the error of universalism (the actual salvation of all persons) could creep in. As Kevin Vanhoozer has argued,

> The Incarnation unites the Son to human nature, to be sure, but it does not follow that it unites the Son to me (or me to the Son). To say the Son assumed humanity does not necessarily mean that he assumed my humanity, that is, the subsistent, hypostatic relation that is me. To be sure, Jesus' assuming humanity is a necessary condition for his being the mediator, the Messiah, and the second Adam.[10]

That is, you are not saved when the Son is united to human nature; you are saved when your person, "the subsistent, hypostatic relation that is [you]," is brought into union with Christ.

Son and Holy Spirit

The second distinction to recognize is between the Son and the Holy Spirit. At the level of the eternal Trinitarian being of God, it is of course

---

9. The classical term for this Christology is that it is anhypostatic and enhypostatic. It was especially developed around the time of the Second Council of Constantinople in 553. See my "Introduction to Christology: Chalcedonian Categories for the Gospel Narrative," in *Jesus in Trinitarian Perspective: An Introductory Christology*, ed. Fred Sanders and Klaus Issler (Nashville: B&H, 2007), 30–32.

10. Kevin Vanhoozer, "The Origin of Paul's Soteriology: Election, Incarnation, and Union with Christ in Ephesians 1:4 (with Special Reference to Evangelical Calvinism)," in *Reconsidering the Relationship between Biblical and Systematic Theology in the New Testament: Essays by Theologians and New Testament Scholars*, ed. Benjamin E. Reynolds, Brian Lugioyo, and Kevin J. Vanhoozer (Tübingen: Mohr Siebeck, 2014), 198.

a basic datum that the Son is not the Holy Spirit, that is, that they are distinct persons standing in relation to each other. That fundamental distinction is the presupposition and ground of everything else we will go on to say about Christology and pneumatology. Their distinction from each other is an aspect of their distinct relations to the Father. The Son stands in the relation of begottenness to the Father, and as the church fathers frequently pointed out, the Spirit cannot stand in the same relation. If the Holy Spirit were also begotten, he would be either another Son (if his begetting were parallel to the Son's begetting), or (if his begetting were somehow downstream from the Son's begetting) a Grandson. Instead, the Holy Spirit's relation to the Father is confessed not as a begetting but as a proceeding, a breathing, or a spirating. Like most of the elements of the doctrine of the Trinity, these things were only made known in the course of salvation history, as God revealed his eternal triunity in the act of the Father sending forth the Son and the Holy Spirit for our salvation. But they were antecedently true in God's immutable being as the living God who was always Father, Son, and Holy Spirit prior to making that triunity known.

We come to know and even to experience the Son and Spirit's distinctness as persons in their discrete missions. Though it might be too anthropomorphic to say that they have different personalities, it is nevertheless the case that the Son-Spirit distinction marks their respective missions in important ways. The most obvious differences can be visualized by comparing the visible mission of the Son to that of the Holy Spirit. The Son becomes incarnate by taking on flesh; the Holy Spirit is poured out on all flesh. The Son joins human nature to his own person by hypostatic union; the Holy Spirit indwells human persons by taking up residence within them. The Son takes up human nature and carries out a work in it that alters its status before God; the Holy Spirit applies that work to individual persons by interacting with them.

The distinction between the persons of the Son and the Holy Spirit that we can trace in their work is not, strictly speaking, a separation or a division between them. The missions of the Son and the Holy Spirit are not separate things, as if there were two ways of salvation, or even as if each mission constituted one half of salvation. God the Trinity has one work of human salvation, and it is the integrated, coordinated economy of salvation that is constituted by the sendings of the Son and the Holy Spirit. There are not two economies of salvation, one an economy of the Son and another of the Holy Spirit. The one divine economy maps onto the one divine being, making known the eternal unity of the Father, Son, and Holy Spirit in the economic history of the Father sending the Son and the Holy Spirit. In the eternal life of God in himself, the perfect unity of Father, Son, and Holy Spirit is a matter of the simplicity of their same divine nature and also a matter of the perichoretic mutual indwelling of each person in the others. In the missions of the Son and the Holy Spirit, there is an equally astonishing intimacy and mutuality, such that neither mission can be confessed without reference to the other. Indeed, each mission is constituted by the other mission, while still remaining itself and not being swallowed up by the other, lumped together as identical, or rendered redundant as a mere repetition of the other.

We can briefly consider each in turn. First, notice the constitutive role of the Holy Spirit in the mission of the Son. The incarnation itself, as the preparation of a physical body for the human nature of the Son, is a work of the whole undivided Trinity in which the Holy Spirit takes the most prominent role. Jesus Christ is "conceived by the Holy Spirit," as the Apostles' Creed confesses. The very title "Christ" signifies one who is marked out and anointed by the Holy Spirit; Jesus received the Spirit without measure and promised to bestow that Spirit on his followers. The miracles he did were worked through the power of the Holy Spirit. He offered himself to the Father through the eternal Spirit (Heb. 9:14) and was raised from the dead by the Holy Spirit (Rom. 8:11). There is even a pneumatological goal to the life and work of Jesus Christ, and his cleansing of the temple of human nature can be seen as preparatory to the indwelling by the Holy Spirit. Yet for all this, the mission of the Son is still his own: the Spirit is not incarnate, nor is the Spirit the personal agent of the actions of the incarnation. Second, notice the constitutive role of the Son of God in the mission of the Holy Spirit. In the Old Testament, the Spirit spoke of the Son through the prophets, and the New Testament speaks of the Spirit of the Son and the Spirit of Christ. The Holy Spirit's distinctive ministry is not to bear witness to himself but to bear witness to Christ. There is no second gospel of the Holy Spirit and no separate act of faith in the Spirit added to a prior faith in Christ. The work of the Spirit constantly points away from itself to the work of Christ, and after the ascension of Christ, the Holy Spirit's personal presence is the vehicle of the ascended Jesus's personal presence. There is even a christological goal to the work of the Spirit as he applies to each believer the work accomplished by Jesus Christ. Yet for all this, the mission of the Spirit is still his own.

In this case, we distinguish in order to unite: it is valuable to distinguish the work of the Son and the Holy Spirit precisely so that we can confess their ordered unity with more force and precision. To this end, it is worth noting how Scripture leads us to develop a relatively independent vocabulary for each person and his work.[11] The Son becomes incarnate, substitutes for us, dies for us, is a propitiation and a mediator; we confess him, believe in him, imitate him, are conformed to his image. Almost none of these terms would be proper to say of the Holy Spirit, who is not incarnate, propitiatory, or our pattern for imitation. Scriptural usage gives us plenty of ways of affirming the full equality and true personhood of the Holy Spirit without ever encouraging us to apply to him language more fitting of the incarnate Son. The Holy Spirit, for example, guides us, empowers us, indwells us, and renews us. It would be a blunder to say that the Holy Spirit is the mediator between God and man, that we should be conformed to the image of the Spirit, or that the Holy Spirit substitutes himself for us representatively in our place. To speak this way is to treat the Holy Spirit as another Son and the Spirit's mission as a hazy duplication of the Son's. We should be equally careful not to transfer pneumatological language to Christ, turning Christ into another version of the Holy Spirit. This sometimes happens when we describe Christ as indwelling us directly without indicating that the whole reason Christ dwells in believers is because the Holy Spirit makes him present. Again, keeping their distinctions in mind helps us underline their unity: Christ, whose mission is to take on human nature and reconcile it to God by propitiation, is present to us spiritually because of the Holy Spirit's mission to apply the work of Christ to us, indwell believers, and bring us personally into contact with God in Christ.

---

11. The language of "relatively independent" vocabularies for Christology and pneumatology is from A. A. Van Ruler, "Structural Differences between the Christological and Pneumatological Perspectives," in *Calvinist Trinitarianism and Theocentric Politics: Essays toward a Public Theology* (Lewiston: Mellen, 1989), 27–46.

Accomplished and Applied

The work of the Son and the Holy Spirit are thus two sides of one reality: God is with us. In the work of the Son, God is with us as the one who takes human nature to himself permanently. In the work of the Holy Spirit, God is with us as the one who dwells among us as in a temple. Mutually presupposing each other, the missions of the Son and the Holy Spirit together simply are the one economy of salvation. God saves by sending the Son and the Holy Spirit.

The final distinction to rehearse in order to understand the scope of the atonement is the distinction between redemption accomplished and applied. To distinguish salvation into these two aspects is to recognize an objective and historical aspect of salvation and a subjective and contemporary aspect. It is especially helpful to do this when considering that Christian salvation is a matter of union with Christ. God the Father brings about salvation by sending forth his Son, who takes hold of human nature and reconciles it to God. Christ lives out a perfect human life of obedience and submission to God, subjects human nature in his own person to the righteous wrath of God, and is raised from the dead to live a renewed human life in indissoluble union with God. Christian salvation is not a separate affair in which God carries out some further activities in our life that somehow parallel or rhyme with what he did in the life of Christ. Instead, salvation is a matter of being included in Christ such that what happened in him is also made to apply to us. The stronger a theologian's commitment is to understanding salvation as union with Christ, the more important the accomplished-applied dynamic will be. John Calvin, for example, spends book 2 of the *Institutes* cataloging the work of Jesus Christ for our salvation, and he concludes, "We see that our whole salvation and all its parts are comprehended in Christ."[12] And as he turns the corner to book 3, he poses this question:

> How do we receive those benefits which the Father bestowed on his only-begotten Son—not for Christ's own private use, but that he might enrich poor and needy men? First, we must understand

---

12. Calvin, *Institutes of the Christian Religion*, ed. John T. McNeill, trans. Ford Lewis Battles (Louisville: Westminster John Knox, 2011), 2.16.19.

that as long as Christ remains outside of us, and we are separated from him, all that he has suffered and done for the salvation of the human race remains useless and of no value for us.[13]

The immediate answer that Calvin gives for how the blessings of salvation are to be brought home to us and made effective is that we must have faith. But by itself, this answer might suggest that something in our own response (having faith) is what causes us to be in Christ. So Calvin immediately probes for the reality behind the rise of faith within us: "Reason itself teaches us to climb higher and to examine into the secret energy of the Spirit, by which we come to enjoy Christ and all his benefits." As he puts it later, "The Holy Spirit is the bond by which Christ effectually unites us to himself."[14] This is an element of Calvin's teaching where his deeply traditional doctrinal profile is most evident, and the lines of continuity with the patristic tradition are in effect.

What is crucial for making the accomplished-applied dynamic function in our theology of salvation is that it is seen in the context of the unity of the Son and the Holy Spirit. If in the previous section we emphasized the distinctness of the Son and the Holy Spirit in their work, here we must emphasize their underlying unity. Without that unity, when we "climb higher" to examine the work of the Spirit in uniting us to Christ, we risk climbing up to some foreign element or alien power. But the whole point is that the Spirit is not such a power; in his person he is eternally together with the Father and the Son as the one God, and in his work he is applying to believers what the Son has already worked out in his appropriated human nature. The Puritan theologian John Flavel wrote two books making this point at great length, one volume on redemption accomplished in Christ, and the other on redemption applied in the Holy Spirit. He took great pains to show both the sufficiency of salvation as wrought in Christ, and the necessity of its application by the Spirit. He sets both the Son and the Spirit in the context of the Father's gracious election:

---

13. *Institutes* 3.1.1.
14. *Institutes* 3.1.1.

It is confessedly true, that God's good pleasure appointing us from eternity to salvation is, in its kind, a most full and sufficient impulsive cause of our salvation, and every way able (for so much as it is concerned) to produce its effect. And Christ's humiliation and sufferings are a most complete and sufficient meritorious cause of our salvation, to which nothing can be added to make it more apt, and able to procure our salvation, than it already is; yet neither the one nor the other can actually save any soul, without the Spirit's application of Christ to it. The Father has elected, and the Son has redeemed; but until the Spirit (who is the last cause) has wrought his part also, we cannot be saved. For he comes in the Father's and in the Son's name and authority, to complete the work of our salvation, by bringing all the fruits of election and redemption home to our souls in this work of effectual vocation.[15]

We might say that salvation is complete in each of its aspects, both as salvation accomplished and as salvation applied. What Flavel wants us to avoid at all costs is thinking of the work of the Spirit as some alien work that brings about some other salvation than the very same salvation worked out in the incarnate Son. In that sense, the work of the Son, taken all by itself if that were possible, would not be salvation. But the point is that it cannot be taken all by itself. The idea of a salvation worked out in Christ and not completed by the Holy Spirit is a figment of the imagination, a mere abstraction drawn from reality by a mental act of subtracting. To call the Son's accomplishment of salvation incomplete without the Spirit is to presuppose that it can be separated from the Spirit.

Salvation, in other words, is accomplished by the Son and applied by the Spirit. The power of the accomplished-applied distinction is in fact dependent on the underlying Son-Spirit distinction, and our guideline for understanding its effect on us is the person-nature distinction.

---

15. John Flavel, *The Method of Grace: In the Holy Spirit's Applying to the Souls of Men the Eternal Redemption Contrived by the Father and Accomplished by the Son* (New York: American Tract Society, 1845), 19. It was originally published in the late 1600s. The 1845 edition, the most widely available, includes some silent modifications that render it less useful for historical accuracy. In particular, readers will want to beware of the way the American Tract Society has suppressed several notes of Flavel's Reformed theology, not least by omitting several paragraphs in which he defends limited atonement!

Atonement and the Work of the Trinity

If we use *atonement* in the broadest sense theologically, it indicates the full scope of salvation, encompassing both salvation accomplished and salvation applied. If, on the other hand, we use it more restrictively to refer to the sacrificial death of Christ (not neglecting the incarnational presuppositions and triumphant implications that illuminate that death's saving power), then atonement obviously belongs entirely on the accomplished side of the ledger. There is good biblical warrant and traditional precedent for either usage, yet in what follows I will be restricting the sense of the word atonement to refer to the work of Christ accomplished once for all on the cross, or "the atonement of the death of Christ."[16] The reason for this is to underline the distinction between what happened to human nature in the death of Christ then and there, and what happens to human persons in the proclamation of the gospel here and now.

Salvation accomplished	Salvation applied
By the Son	By the Holy Spirit
In human nature	To human persons
Universally	Particularly
Objectively for all	Subjectively to each

The set of distinctions we have established can be tabulated thus: With these distinctions in place and correlated with each other in this way, we can state more fully our recommendation for doing justice to the Bible's universal note. The scope of the atoning death of Christ is universal because it is the work of the incarnate Son accomplishing salvation in and for human nature, objectively, once and for all. This atonement is applied to particular human persons by the Holy Spirit when each one hears and responds to the word of the gospel. Understanding the extent of the atonement as universal has the interpretive advantage of aligning well with the biblical passages that sound the universal note, enabling

---

16. The title of H. D. McDonald's book, *The Atonement of the Death of Christ* (Grand Rapids: Baker, 1985).

readers to rejoice in what Scripture is affirming in those places.[17] It enables us to read 1 John 2:2 ("He is the atoning sacrifice for our sins, and not only for ours but also for the sins of the whole world") without wincing at the introduction of the universal note in such close proximity to the propitiation. We can read 1 Timothy 2:6 (Christ Jesus "gave himself as a ransom for all people") with the same expansive scope, following the line of thought out to the way the ransom was given for humanity as such. We can even read Titus 2:11 ("the grace of God has appeared, bringing salvation to all people," NET) without worrying overmuch about the lack of restriction offered by the context. There are, of course, honorable ways to handle passages like these while denying the universal extent of the atonement. Calvinist exegesis, for example, may not be free to glide elegantly along the stream of Scripture's phraseology here, but it is not reduced to special pleading or obfuscation.[18]

Another interpretive option would be to account for the universal note by referring it entirely to the incarnation. That is, we might deny that the atonement has universal extent for human nature as such but retain the universal scope of God's saving intentions as something that is witnessed in the incarnation. The Son of God took to himself human nature: this is a statement about human nature as such, and cannot be limited to being just an episode in the history of the Son of God that leaves humanity as such untouched. There is by common consent a universal note in Christmas preaching, in the announcement of peace on earth and joy to the world.[19] It might be possible to refer the universal note in the Bible's announcement of the gospel to the incarnation as such, while locating the restrictive note in the atonement. This would

---

17. For a similar reading of these passages, including an arrangement of them by category, and extensive exegetical engagement, see the Puritan John Goodwin's work *Apolutrosis Apolutroseos, or, Redemption Redeemed* (London: Lodowick Lloyd, 1651); republished as *Redemption Redeemed: A Puritan Defense of Unlimited Atonement*, ed. John Wagner (Eugene, OR: Wipf and Stock, 2001).

18. Among the many examples of honest exegetical reasoning about such passages by scholars with explicit commitment to limited atonement, I recommend Thomas Schreiner, "'Problematic Texts' for Definite Atonement in the Pastoral and General Epistles," in *From Heaven He Came and Sought Her: Definite Atonement in Historical, Biblical, Theological, and Pastoral Perspective*, ed. David Gibson and Jonathan Gibson (Wheaton, IL: Crossway, 2013), 376–97. The exegetical case on either side is much broader than the Pastoral and General Epistles of the New Testament, but Schreiner is right to focus on the hard edges of these explicit statements.

19. Indeed, in Isaac Watts's handling, "Joy to the World" is a messianic interpretation of Psalm 98 that intends the proclamation of good news to all creation under heaven, not just human nature.

be to acknowledge a deep tension between Christmas and Easter, but perhaps that is a burden that must be borne. There would still be a range of options within that proclamation: the more universal way of putting it would be that the Son of God assumed the nature of every human but died only for those who are finally redeemed as actual persons; the more restrictive way of putting it would be to distinguish even within the incarnation between a universal base of operations and a restrictive intent. It seems preferable to acknowledge that the Son took on human nature as such in order to atone for it as such.

Interpreting the atonement as intended for, and effective for, human nature as such does entail locating the necessary restrictive element in the Holy Spirit's work of application. This move has the advantage of accounting for why a universal atonement is not universally applied. Though there is some explanatory power in acknowledging the distinction between the work of the Son and the work of the Spirit, there is also mystery here that will remain resistant to being dispelled. The factor that splits the human race between those who are finally personally reconciled to God and those who finally are not is an issue that resists final systematic solution, however clear Scripture may be about the facts. A theological account of why some persons abide in permanent rejection of reconciliation with God is necessary, but it must avoid two errors. On one side is the error of an overly tidy parallelism that locates some persons in a hell toward which they were always directed. Most versions of Reformed theology avoid this error, confessing that "the chief end of man is to glorify God and enjoy him forever," which makes it impossible to think of the damned as having achieved the purpose for which they were made. On the other side is the error that locates the answer so completely in human response that the principle of sorting ends up equally tidy: good people choose God and bad people do not. Most Wesleyan theology avoids this error, which cannot be reconciled with the utter dependence on God's prevenient initiative in salvation that is the hallmark of evangelical Arminianism. But whatever we say about the abiding mystery of those who are finally lost, recognizing the distinction between the work of the Son and the Holy Spirit helps us recognize that the damned are those who are personally at cross-purposes with their true nature. It is unnatural to go to hell, and it is against God's enacted will for the destiny of human nature.

But Is It Wesleyan?

The argument of this chapter recommends the doctrine of universal atonement on the grounds that it is the best way to do justice to Scripture's recurrent universal note in speaking of salvation. It uses consensual dogmatic tools from the doctrines of the Trinity and Christology in order to establish a field within which the atonement can be confessed as universal but with a particular application. Because the goal of this chapter is to enter into critical dialogue with other Christian traditions, it is worth asking to what extent the argument presented here is identifiably, characteristically, or distinctively Wesleyan. Most of the conceptual tools, drawn from the doctrines of the Trinity and Christology, are the common property of all churches, which makes the argument more or less ecumenical. I do in fact view the Wesleyan account of the atonement as standing within the main consensus of the church's traditional teaching. If, for the sake of clarifying contrast, we needed an opponent to bring out the distinctive profile of the Wesleyan teaching, we would have to turn not to Roman Catholicism or Eastern Orthodoxy but to the Reformed tradition. There is world enough and time for conflict between Wesleyans and Calvinists on the issue of limited atonement; my point here is simply that outside of that polemical context the Wesleyan view will not present a strikingly unique profile. And even if we draw out the contrast with Reformed theology at greater length, there would be no small irony in the fact that this chapter's case has often been constructed with resources from classic Reformed authors.[20]

Of course, the classic Reformed case for limited atonement depends a great deal on the overarching systematic coherence that binds together a number of commitments—at least five, by a conventional way of counting the distinctive points of Calvinism. Limited atonement is part of a package. Without the rest of the distinctively Reformed system of soteriology in place, not many thinkers have ventured to treat the extent of the atonement as limited to the elect. This is because the logic of limited atonement generally only becomes compelling if a particular notion

---

20. Or that modern Reformed authors have found elements of my own argument useful. For a use of my Trinitarian soteriology to serve the doctrine of limited atonement, see Jonathan Gibson, "The Glorious, Indivisible, Trinitarian Work of God in Christ," in Gibson and Gibson, *From Heaven He Came and Sought Her*, 331–74.

of election is already operative. That Reformed soteriological view of election is, in traditional Wesleyan judgment, based on a misreading of the argument of Romans 9, one which extends its salvation-historical argument transcendentally into the sphere of a pretemporal distinction between individuals as regards their final salvation. In traditional Wesleyan theology, the thrust of Paul's argument in Romans 9 is not to establish such a realm but to work out the implications of Israel's corporate election, of a divine election to service, and of the way election has been revealed as recentered in Christ.[21] The present chapter has been focused on explaining how a Wesleyan view of the extent of the atonement can make the most sense of the language and argument of the universal passages of the New Testament. To many Reformed critics, the Wesleyan view seems to sidestep the more restrictive passages, but it is a different notion of election that enables it to do so without shirking exegetical responsibility.

But aside from contrasting with Reformed theology, there are two ways of demonstrating that the argument of this chapter has good Wesleyan credentials. One is to show that it makes conceptual space for the appeal to free will that has been characteristic of Wesleyan theology and practice, or at least opens up christological and Trinitarian space for that appeal; the other is to show that it has historically been held by some prominent Wesleyans.

A thick account of the distinction between the work of the Son and the work of the Holy Spirit in the application of redemption does in fact open up the possibility of a theological recognition of free human response to the gospel. A theology that developed this distinction inadequately would risk picturing Christ as testifying effectively to his own work rather than recognizing the testimony of the Holy Spirit to the work of Christ. When a person recognizes Christ as savior, that person stands in the midst of the Son-Spirit distinction in a particular way. Before him stands Christ, and within him stands the Holy Spirit testifying to Christ and awakening a genuine personal response to the truth of Christ.

---

21. The most detailed account of this reading, especially commendable for its attention to intertextual concerns, are Brian J. Abasciano's *Paul's Use of the Old Testament in Romans 9.1–9* (New York: T&T Clark, 2005), and *Paul's Use of the Old Testament in Romans 9.10–18* (New York: T&T Clark, 2011).

Christ does not simply show himself to us as the light and then open our eyes to himself as our vision. The person of the Son does not both speak the word of promise and open our ears to hear it, or vouch for himself in two voices. Instead, as the Son manifests himself to us, the Holy Spirit within us prepares us to receive the message, enlivens our receptive power to receive what is being given, awakens our response, and causes the miracle of faith. As Thomas Smail has argued, "The Freedom of a Christian to confess Christ is in the last resort dependent on the reality of the distinction between Jesus and the Spirit. . . . Jesus does not dictate or manipulate our response to him, he receives it. He presents his evidence and awaits our verdict just as he did with Peter."[22] We must confess Jesus as Lord, but (1 Cor. 12:3) nobody can do this except by the Holy Spirit. Smail pursues the thought to the edge of the question of grace and freewill:

> In saying this we have not, of course, explained the mystery of the relationship between God's grace and our freedom; we have elucidated it by seeing it in a trinitarian context and so suggesting that the mysterious relationship between grace and freedom is closely connected with the even more mysterious relationship between the Spirit and the Son.[23]

I am not aware of any Wesleyan accounts of conversion that more elaborately exploit the Son-Spirit distinction as Smail has suggested. Certainly more would have to be done with the category of prevenient grace to round out these suggestive remarks. But my point is that the christological and Trinitarian resources I am commending are extremely hospitable to Wesleyan concerns.

As for whether historical Wesleyans have held a view like the one described in this chapter, the answer is yes, though I hope that I have made more explicit the Trinitarian and christological background of the view. The position sketched here has much in common with the affirmation of the universal extent of the atonement in the work of Methodist theologian Thomas Oden, whose three-volume *Systematic*

---

22. Thomas A. Smail, *The Giving Gift: The Holy Spirit in Person* (London: Hodder & Stoughton, 1988), 69.

23. Smail, *The Giving Gift*, 69.

Theology is an attempt to trace the classic consensus of Christian doctrine without introducing any novelty, or making his own confessional stance especially prominent. "The atonement," he writes, "is addressed to all humanity, intended for all, sufficient for all, yet it is effectively received by those who respond to it in faith."[24] He expands on this somewhat:

> As to sufficiency, the cross is *for all, for the world.* As to efficacy, the cross becomes effective *for some, for the faithful.* From this derives the distinction of universal sufficiency and conditional efficacy: *as to sufficiency it is universal; as to efficacy it is limited to those who accept God's offer of salvation through Christ.*[25]

Oden repeats this relation several times, varying the terminology and drawing on different sources,[26] but always to the same effect: to draw the contrast between universal, unlimited atonement, and restricted application of it to believers.

Looking further back in Wesleyan history, another theologian whose discussion of the extent of the atonement maps closely onto the argument presented here is William Burt Pope, who likewise wrote a three-volume systematic theology with the special intention of drawing out the great lines of continuity with the united Christian tradition.

> The Price was paid down for all men for the entire race, or for the entire nature of man in all its representatives from the first transgressor to the last. Redemption as such is UNIVERSAL; or it is general, as distinguished from the Special Redemption of the individual.[27]

---

24. Thomas C. Oden, *Systematic Theology*, vol. 2, *The Word of Life* (San Francisco: Harper and Row, 1989), 388. Oddly, Oden's parenthetical reference here is to Wollebius, Olevianus, and Heppe. It is for the reader to decide whether this is because Oden's harmonistic temperament got the best of his judgment or because he accurately perceived shared commitments and reflected them in one part of his summary sentence.

25. Oden, *Word of Life*, 388, italics in original.

26. Christopher Bounds has pointed out that Oden does not cite the early church fathers very much in this subsection but that he could have. Bounds, "The Scope of the Atonement in the Early Church Fathers," *Wesleyan Theological Journal* 47, no. 3 (Fall 2012): 7–26.

27. William Burt Pope, *A Compendium of Christian Theology* (NY: Phillips and Hunt, 1881), 2:294.

Pope makes the same contrast between a universal (he sometimes says "racial") atonement and its selective application to believing individuals: "While Universal Redemption is a great reality, it is such only as the basis of a particular application."[28]

And reaching back all the way to a Wesley (either one will do), we can call on the hymns of Charles Wesley to show that the doctrine of an unlimited atonement was not a side issue, a solution to some hard texts, a point for polemics against Calvinists, or a truth to be held privately. John and Charles Wesley held it to be the teaching of Scripture, the manifestation of God's heart, the motive for universal gospel preaching, and a truth close to the heart of the revivals, to be sung in worship:

> Father, whose everlasting love
> Thy only Son for sinners gave,
> Whose grace to all did freely move,
> And sent Him down the world to save;
>
> Help us Thy mercy to extol,
> Immense, unfathomed, unconfined;
> To praise the Lamb who died for all,
> The general Savior of mankind.
>
> Thy undistinguishing regard
> Was cast on Adam's fallen race;
> For all Thou hast in Christ prepared
> Sufficient, sovereign, saving grace.
>
> The world He suffered to redeem;
> For all He hath the atonement made;
> For those that will not come to Him
> The ransom of His life was paid.

---

28. Pope, *Compendium*, 2:296. On this same page, Pope outlines the biblical case for the doctrine of unlimited atonement, but he concludes with the words, "It is however the glory of this argument that it needs not the support of individual texts." There may conceivably be much wisdom in such a claim, but it would be an ineffective way to open a conversation on the subject.

ANDREW LOUTH

From the beginning of this essay, I felt that I was in a curious way almost at home. Right from the beginning, the approach seemed not only congenial but almost familiar: the insistence, in the initial discussion of Titus 2:11, on the grace of God bringing salvation to all people rather than reading into the phrase a tortuous syntax to evade its universalist declaration and, a couple of pages later, a remark associating atonement with the paschal work of Christ, not just with his death. The headings listing the themes to be discussed felt very familiar: "Nature and Person," the economies of "Son and Spirit," "Atonement and the work of the Trinity." These are very much Orthodox themes. It is widely held among Orthodox that the theme of person in relation to (if not in opposition to) nature is a theme developed by the Greek fathers (in contrast to the Latin fathers) and is central to the distinctiveness of Orthodox theology (one need only mention the names of the Greek theologians John Zizioulas, Metropolitan of Pergamon, and Christos Yannaras).[1] The parallel treatment of the economies of the Son and the Spirit is a striking feature of what is perhaps the best-known work of Orthodox theology in the West, Vladimir Lossky's *The Mystical Theology of the Eastern Church*.[2] An insistence on the Trinitarian nature of theology is another emphasis one is likely to find among Orthodox theologians. It is not that there is no disagreement among Orthodox theologians about these matters (Lossky's apparent separation of the economies of the Son and the Spirit was sharply criticized by Georges

---

1. For Zizioulas, see the first chapter, "Personhood and Being," of *Being and Communion* (London: Darton, Longman, and Todd, 1985), 27–65; for Yannaras, see his *Person and Eros*, trans. Norman Russell (Brookline, MA: Holy Cross Orthodox Press, 2007).

2. See chapters 7 and 8 ("The economy of the Son" and "The economy of the Holy Spirit") in Vladimir Lossky, *The Mystical Theology of the Eastern Church* (London: James Clarke, 1957), 135–73.

Florovsky, for example),[3] but they are characteristically Orthodox. There is nothing of this, however, in Sanders's account of a Wesleyan view. His resources are entirely Western, not least his account of the nature/person distinction, which should give pause to those Orthodox who regard the notion of personhood as something disclosed solely to the Orthodox through the Greek fathers. And, so far as historical sources are concerned, it is indeed to the Greek fathers that Sanders goes in his development of the person/nature distinction.

The person/nature (ὑπόστασις-πρόσωπον/φύσις) distinction was devised by Greek theologians of the fourth century, especially the so-called Cappadocian fathers, in order to affirm the threeness of the persons in the one nature or being of God. It is not much developed, at least not until the sixth century. Once devised, it is used without too much reflection about what the distinction entails. As Sanders says, "Notice that the terms as used in the doctrine of the Trinity are not especially thick or content-bearing terms. They are not richly descriptive terms that were ready at hand to apply to God" (p. 160). Soon the same distinction was applied to Christology, notably by the Council of Chalcedon (451), a transference made all the easier by the relatively undefined nature of the terms.

I was a little surprised that Sanders illustrated his argument by quoting Gregory of Nazianzus (Gregory the Theologian), for, notoriously, Gregory does not use the person/hypostasis distinction. In the passage cited, he makes the distinction by gender, using the masculine for the three and the neuter for the one (ἄλλος-ἄλλο), or in the case of Christ, ἄλλο-ἄλλο for his natures, human and divine, and ἄλλος for the one person he is. The use of the term ὑπόστασις in Gregory is probably not technical, as Lionel Wickham's translation as "subjects or hypostases" is intended to intimate. Nevertheless, Gregory the Theologian's distinction here came to be represented (and was already by his friend Basil and Basil's brother Gregory of Nyssa) by the person-nature distinction. I am not sure that Sanders's rendering of this distinction is not somewhat wooden: the distinction is not a division (though, inspired by last-century existentialism, both Zizioulas and Yannaras are inclined to err in this way too).

---

3. See Georges Florovsky, review of *The Mystical Theology of the Eastern Church*, by Vladimir Lossky, *Journal of Religion* 38, no. 3 (July 1958): 207–8.

Sanders's second distinction is between Son and Spirit, a distinction that is grounded in their different relationships to the Father within the eternal divine being (this way of putting it is very much that of the Orthodox, who use it to criticize the notion of the *filioque*, the term inserted into the Western version of the Niceno-Constantinopolitan Creed to assert the "double procession" of the Spirit from Father and Son; Sanders is happy both with and without the *filioque*). This leads Lossky to a sense of the two *economies* of the Son and the Spirit, complementary but distinct, a term Sanders also uses, accompanying it with mission. Sanders goes on to draw out the complementary nature of the economy of the Son and the economy of the Holy Spirit: not two economies but two indivisible, though distinguishable, aspects of the one divine economy. He is very careful to avoid any "Joachimism," a kind of second gospel of the Spirit, advocated by the twelfth-century monk Joachim of Fiore.

At the end of the section, after an account of the way in which Son and Spirit are complementary in the divine economy, I made a note: *epiklesis*, which is the central part of the Eucharistic prayer, or anaphora. In the Orthodox understanding of the Divine Liturgy, Christ becomes present in response to the *epiklesis*, uttered by the bishop or priest on behalf of all gathered together, calling upon (ἐπικαλέω) God to "send down the Holy Spirit upon us and upon these gifts here present." This is not something isolated: throughout the history of salvation, continuing into the Divine Liturgy, the Holy Spirit brings about the presence of Christ, overshadowing the Virgin Mary at the annunciation so that Christ becomes present in her womb, coming upon the apostles gathered together with Mary in the upper room and turning a group of frightened disciples into the body of Christ, making Christ to dwell in the hearts of the believers, and effecting the presence of Christ in the Eucharist.

Sanders then sets up a parallelism between the Son and the Spirit, drawing on the distinction between nature and person, so that the Son is *present* in human *nature*, *universally*, and *objective* to all while the Spirit is *present* to human *persons*, *particularly*, and *subjective* to each. Sanders adds another distinction between accomplished and applied. The atonement is *accomplished* by the Son in assuming human nature, an accomplishment universal and objective, and what has been accomplished is *applied* by the Spirit, particularly and subjectively to each. I am not sure that *applied* is the right word; it is too impersonal. Sanders seems to suggest that what we are talking about here is personal apprehension or appropriation through the Spirit. Perhaps the Protestant fear of synergy is at work here, a synergy that becomes so intimate that the term *deification* seems the only word appropriate to describe the transformation (transfiguration) involved:

> *Changed from glory into glory*
> *Till in heaven we take our place.*[4]

A little later on, Sanders made a striking—and to my ears puzzling—point. He notes "a universal note in Christmas preaching, in the announcement of peace on earth and joy to the world," and suggests that one might accept this "while locating the restrictive note in the atonement [presumably in the cross or, better, in the Paschal mystery]"—which "would be to acknowledge a deep tension between Christmas and Easter" (p. 170–71). I find this strange, though I recognize here the way the Western celebration of Christmas seems to exalt the feast even above Easter. Certainly in the popular imagination of the West, Christmas is *the* Christian feast while Easter is made much less of (the liturgical texts celebrating Christmas and Easter in the historical rites of West and East are, however, equal in making Easter the "Feast of Feasts"). There is tension here, but I am surprised that Sanders is willing to accept it as a "deep tension," that is perhaps "a burden that must be borne." What could be more universalist than the conviction that Christ descended into hell and released the souls of those who had died before his coming? (In Byzantine folklore—or perhaps more accurately "monk-lore"—there is a tradition that Plato was one of the first to acknowledge Christ as he descended into hell.)[5] The opposite side of that is the way in which in the Byzantine celebration of Christmas the cross is never forgotten. One of the songs (*troparia*) for the days immediately before the Feast of the Nativity (called the "Forefeast") says,

---

4. Charles Wesley, "Love Divine, All Loves Excelling," in *Hymns for Those That Seek and Those That Have Redemption in the Blood of Jesus Christ* (Bristol: William Strahan, 1747), hymn 9.

5. See Anastasios of Sinai, *Quaestiones et Responsiones* 61, *Corpus Christianorum Series Graeca* (*CCSG*) 59, ed. Marcel Richard and Joseph Munitiz (Turnhout: Brepols, 2006), 111–12.

Get ready, Bethlehem, Eden has been opened to all. Rejoice, Ephratha, because the tree of life has blossomed from the Virgin in the cave. For her womb has been shown to be the spiritual paradise, in which is the divine plant; eating of which we shall live—and not have died like Adam. Christ is born, raising up the image that once fell.

In celebrating Christ's nativity, we are led back to Adam, in whom the image fell, and forward to the cross, the tree of life, bearing the fruit of immortality.[6]

Sanders ends considering whether the understanding of the atonement that he has put forward is Wesleyan. The fundamental points he makes are worth pondering. First, "a thick account of the distinction between the work of the Son and the work of the Holy Spirit . . . open[s] up the possibility of a theological recognition of free human response to the gospel," for "when a person recognizes Christ as saviour, that person stands in the midst of the Son-Spirit distinction in a particular way. Before him stands Christ, and within him stands the Holy Spirit testifying to Christ and awakening a genuine personal response to the truth of Christ" (p. 173). A little later on, he quotes from a modern Wesleyan theologian, Thomas Smail:

In saying this we have not, of course, explained the mystery of the relationship between God's grace and our freedom; we have elucidated it by seeing it in a trinitarian context and so suggesting that the mysterious relationship between grace and freedom is closely connected with the even more mysterious relationship between the Spirit and the Son.[7]

Seeing, in this way, the real question as the mystery of divine grace and human freedom rather than the mystery of God's electing will, creating

---

6. This breadth of perception was not unknown to the medieval West. In the National Gallery in London, there is a painting, not much noticed, called *The Dream of the Virgin* by Simone dei Crocifissi (*fl.*1355–99). In it, the pregnant Virgin is lying asleep on a bed; from her womb is growing the tree of life, the cross, on which Christ is hanging. Below the bed, Adam and Eve are grasping the roots of this tree. It seems to me almost a pictorial transcription of the *troparion* for the Forefeast of Christmas.

7. Thomas A. Smail, The Giving Gift: The Holy Spirit in Person (London: Hodder & Stoughton, 1988), 69.

some for life and some for death, we are focusing on what is tangible to us as human beings, not getting lost in an eternal, divine labyrinth, conjured up by human thought. Furthermore, setting this in the context of the economy of the Son and the Spirit turns a philosophical puzzle into a theological mystery, or so it seems to me.

RESPONSE TO FRED SANDERS

MATTHEW LEVERING

In emphasizing the Trinitarian character of atonement, Professor Sanders has opened a crucial aspect of the theology of Christ's Pasch. I can hardly do more than agree, but let me first place Professor Sanders's perspective in the context of similar efforts by Reformed theologians. Influenced by Karl Barth, recent studies of atonement by Adam Johnson and Matthias Grebe have illuminated the importance of thinking about Christ's Pasch in a Trinitarian manner.[1] Johnson points out that for Barth, "the unity of God is the precondition of the work of the incarnate Son reconciling us to God," while the Trinity of God "is the condition for God's ability to take up into his own life the sinful human condition through the incarnation of the Son so as to save us by doing away with our sin and guilt in faithfulness to himself and sharing with us the fellowship proper to his triune being."[2] Johnson also finds in Barth the tools for speaking rightly about "the unified and differentiated work of the Father, Son and Holy Spirit in the work of Christ, without lapsing into tritheism."[3]

Grebe, in his study of Barth, argues that the Holy Spirit is operative in Christ as he undergoes death and resurrection. The Spirit joins believers to Christ's death and resurrection, thereby applying the universal effects of Christ's saving to particular believers.[4] Were the Spirit not acting in Jesus, then Jesus, too, would have been unable to overcome the unruliness of sinful flesh. Grebe describes the atonement itself as that "whereby humanity was incorporated into Christ through the Spirit."[5]

---

1. Matthias Grebe, *Election, Atonement, and the Holy Spirit: Through and Beyond Barth's Theological Interpretation of Scripture* (Eugene, OR: Pickwick, 2014); Adam Johnson, *God's Being in Reconciliation: The Theological Basis of the Unity and Diversity of the Atonement in the Theology of Karl Barth* (London: Bloomsbury, 2012); Adam Johnson, *Atonement: A Guide for the Perplexed* (London: Bloomsbury, 2015).

2. Johnson, *God's Being in Reconciliation*, 84.

3. Johnson, *God's Being in Reconciliation*, 84.

4. Grebe, *Election, Atonement, and the Holy Spirit*, 222.

5. Grebe, *Election, Atonement, and the Holy Spirit*, 225.

On this view, there is no atonement outside the effects of the atonement upon particular people. Moreover, for Grebe, the atonement includes not only the cross and resurrection, but also the incarnation and life of Christ. Christ's saving work is a unity, and it includes all the mysteries of his life, death, and resurrection. Like Professor Sanders, Grebe posits that when people remain in Christ, they do so "through the power of the Spirit" rather than by the power of their will cooperating with the Spirit.[6]

Earlier Christians too can be called upon to contribute to the conversation that Professor Sanders develops in his essay (as Professor Sanders well knows). Naming some examples will be helpful in opening up the theme. Saint Athanasius, while circumspect regarding the Holy Spirit in *On the Incarnation* (though freely extolling the Spirit in later writings), draws the Father firmly into his discussion of Christ's saving work without thereby suggesting that the Father suffered. For Athanasius in *On the Incarnation*, the sin of Adam and Eve consists in turning away from "the Word and Reason of the Father" and choosing to act irrationally and against the true human good.[7] As a result, lawlessness spread through the human race, and the human race was headed for oblivion. God the Father perceives this situation and acts to fix it. Having lovingly created the human race, the Father was not going to let the human race destroy itself. Thus the Father, having created humankind in his rational Image (his Word), sent this very same Image to renew the human race. The purpose of Christ's saving work is to bring the human race back to knowledge of the Father. As Athanasius puts it, by becoming incarnate the Word "teaches those who would not learn by other means to know Himself, the Word of God, and through Him the Father."[8]

Furthermore, even in the midst of his passion, the Word rested "in the Father alone" and "was in constant union with the Father."[9] The Word never ceased to be divine in becoming incarnate and acting as man. Therefore, the Word was able perfectly to accomplish his mission of revealing the Father. Athanasius states that when the Son paid our debt (the penalty of death) on the cross, and when the Son rose from the

---

6. Grebe, *Election, Atonement, and the Holy Spirit*, 232.

7. Athanasius, *On the Incarnation*, trans. and ed. a Religious of C.S.M.V. (Crestwood, NY: St. Vladimir's Orthodox Press, 1993), §11, p. 38.

8. Athanasius, *On the Incarnation*, §14, p. 43.

9. Athanasius, *On the Incarnation*, §17, p. 45.

dead, these actions both flowed from "the good pleasure" and "loving wisdom" of the Father.[10]

Athanasius, in later writings, draws the Spirit into this picture. In his *Second Discourse Against the Arians*, Athanasius explains that human beings gain from the incarnate Word the power "to become sons of God . . . by receiving the Spirit of the natural and true Son."[11] This Trinitarian formulation makes clear that the adoptive sonship described by Paul in Romans 8 comes to us through a Trinitarian work of salvation. Athanasius goes on to say that the Spirit's uniting us to the Son (and thus to the Father) is what deifies us, "for man had not been deified if joined to a creature, or unless the Son were very God; nor had man been brought into the Father's presence, unless He had been His natural and true Word who had put on the body."[12] Athanasius describes this economy of salvation in some detail, focusing on the Word and the Father, since the Father wills for us to become sons in the Son through Christ's saving work. But he does not leave out the Spirit since the Son pours forth the Spirit to unite us to God. As Athanasius says in his *Third Discourse Against the Arians*, "The Son is in the Father, as His own Word and Radiance; but we, apart from the Spirit, are strange and distant from God, and by the participation of the Spirit we are knit into the Godhead; so that our being in the Father is not ours, but is the Spirit's which is in us and abides in us."[13]

Moving to the medieval period, I note that the twelfth-century theologian Hildegard of Bingen remarks that the Word, who from all eternity was indivisible from the Father, became incarnate in time "by the Holy Spirit's sweet freshness," without thereby ceasing to abide inseparably with the Father.[14] In the fullness of time, without being separated from the Father, the Word became incarnate, endured his Passion, and delivered his elect from hell and slavery to death. For Hildegard, even the fact that Christ remained three days in the tomb

---

10. Athanasius, *On the Incarnation*, §20, p. 49.

11. Athanasius, *Second Discourse Against the Arians*, in *Athanasius: Select Works and Letters*, ed. Archibald Robertson, trans. John Henry Newman, in *A Select Library of the Nicene and Post-Nicene Fathers*, 2nd series (*NPNF*[2]), ed. Philip Schaff and Henry Wace (Peabody, MA: Hendrickson, 1995), 4:348–93, at 380.

12. Athanasius, *Second Discourse Against the Arians*, in *NPNF*[2] 4:386.

13. Athanasius, *Third Discourse Against the Arians*, in *NPNF*[2] 4:393–432, at 407.

14. Hildegard of Bingen, *Scivias*, trans. Columba Hart and Jane Bishop (New York: Paulist, 1990), 151.

was for the purpose of confirming the threeness of the one God. She describes the Resurrection as a Trinitarian event in which "the noble body of the Son of God . . . was touched by the glory of the Father, received the Spirit and rose again."[15] The same is true for the ascension of the Son to the Father, who reign together with the Holy Spirit in perfect joy. The victory over sin includes Christ's passion, resurrection, and ascension—and the entire Trinity is involved.

In addition to supporting Professor Sanders's essay by means of the above examples, let me support his essay by adding a bit more about what it means to say that the atonement is a Trinitarian event. According to classic Trinitarian doctrine, the Son is not different in any way from the Father other than in the fact that the Son is begotten and the Father is unbegotten. Therefore, when we speak of the Son becoming incarnate (or dying on the cross), this is because of a change on the side of the creature—even though the Son is the personal agent of all the acts of Jesus Christ. Even the hypostatic union does not change the Son because the Son is already infinitely, fully Son in his being begotten by the Father. If the Son were to change, then the hypostatic union would no longer be the joining of the human nature to the divine nature in the person of the Son because a changed Son could not be the only Son of the Father.[16]

Further helpful clarification comes from Gilles Emery. Emery has noted that for the pro-Nicene Fathers, the distinct persons are constituted by "paternity and innascibility (Father), filiation (Son), and procession (Holy Spirit)" but not by any division or separation of the divine nature.[17] Thus Trinitarian faith involves absolutely no fall into a worship of three gods, as it would if each of the persons possessed his own distinct intelligence and freedom—in which case one person's will would reach a finite limit precisely where the other persons' wills begin. At the same time, when the persons act as one ad extra, they do not thereby lose their constitutive properties. Emery points out that the Son, in acting as one with the Father and the Spirit, acts in his property of

---

15. Hildegard of Bingen, *Scivias*, 156.

16. Thomas Weinandy discusses this at length. See Thomas G. Weinandy, OFM Cap., *Does God Change?* (Petersham, MA: St. Bede's, 1985); Weinandy, *Does God Suffer?* (Notre Dame, IN: University of Notre Dame Press, 2000).

17. Gilles Emery, OP, *The Trinity: An Introduction to Catholic Doctrine on the Triune God*, trans. Matthew Levering (Washington, DC: Catholic University of America Press, 2011), 111.

being begotten by the Father. But it remains the case that the *missions* of the Son and the Spirit do not describe changes in the Son and the Spirit; rather, they describe changes in creatures who are temporally related in various salvific ways to the Son and Spirit by the divine power of the Father, Son, and Holy Spirit (a power in which the persons act in their personal properties).

If I understand him correctly, Professor Sanders stands with Emery and Weinandy and with the classical Trinitarian tradition. Any other approach would result in additional real distinctions in the Godhead that would negate the unity of God and would add to the number of distinct Persons. Professor Sanders states, "The distinction between the persons of the Son and the Holy Spirit that we can trace in their work is not, strictly speaking, a separation or a division between them. The missions of the Son and the Holy Spirit are not separate things, as if there were two ways of salvation, or even as if each mission constituted one half of salvation" (p. 173). This is a crucial insight. Sanders here preserves us from anthropomorphizing the Son and Spirit by turning them into two gods whose divine unity is similar to the unity of two humans who share in human nature. The divine Persons do not enter into the world as finite entities, pushing different volitional agendas. As Professor Sanders says, "In the eternal life of God in himself, the perfect unity of Father, Son, and Holy Spirit is a matter of the simplicity of their same divine nature and also a matter of the perichoretic mutual indwelling of each person in the others. In the missions of the Son and the Holy Spirit, there is an equally astonishing intimacy and mutuality" (p. 164). Note that these missions are not the Son and Holy Spirit descending to earth from heaven, but rather involve relations by which human nature is caught up into the Trinitarian life—preeminently, of course, the hypostatic union and Christ's actions as the Spirit-filled Son incarnate. Sanders rightly points out "the constitutive role of the Holy Spirit in the mission of the Son," insofar as the humanity of the Son is unthinkable without the graced transformation of that humanity by the indwelling Spirit (p. 164).

Notably, Professor Sanders states that "interpreting the atonement as intended for, and effective for, human nature as such does entail locating the necessary restrictive element in the Holy Spirit's work of application [i.e., the application to particular persons of the effects of Christ's universal work of redemption]" (p. 171). Assuming that all persons are not saved, some account of why Christ's saving work is not efficaciously transformative of everyone is needed. The problem here, however, is that the Son's mission ends up seeming more generous—more loving because it is all-encompassing—than the Spirit's mission. To my mind, this problem may be resolvable by taking account of the Son's invisible mission in the souls of believers, that is to say, the Son's indwelling of believers (John 14:23). Thomas Aquinas puts it this way: "If we consider mission as regards the effect of grace, in this sense the two missions are united in the root which is grace, but are distinguished in the effects of grace, which consist in the illumination of the intellect and the kindling of the affection."[18] This point—that the interior indwelling of the Son is associated with the illumination of the intellect (faith)—might restore the balance between the Son and Spirit, so that the Spirit does not seem less generous than the Son. Likewise, the Spirit's action in the Son's universal atonement for "human nature as such" should be underlined: the Spirit fills Christ's holy humanity and enables him to endure in charity his self-sacrificial cross.

Professor Sanders asks whether his account is Wesleyan in the traditional sense of being opposed to the traditional Reformed doctrine of limited atonement. I am not sure. Matthias Grebe quotes a passage from a traditional Reformed book titled *The Five Points of Calvinism, Defined, Defended, and Documented*, a passage distinguishing between the "outward general call" to salvation extended universally by Christ on the cross and a "special inward call" extended to particular persons by the Holy Spirit. Only the latter is efficacious. The Reformed authors write, "The *Holy Spirit*, in order to bring God's elect to salvation, extends to them *a special inward call* in addition to the outward call contained in the gospel message. Through this special call the Holy Spirit performs a work of grace within the sinner which inevitably brings him to faith in Christ."[19] This seems to be exactly the division between accomplishment and application that Professor Sanders is proposing. But it seems that Wesleyans (including Sanders?) generally posit an Arminian understanding of grace as fundamentally resistible by human free will. I suggest that this point may need further elucidation.

---

18. Aquinas, *Summa theologiae* I, q. 43, a. 5, ad. 3.
19. Cited in Grebe, *Election, Atonement, and the Holy Spirit*, 209n53.

RESPONSE TO FRED SANDERS

MICHAEL HORTON

Fred Sanders proposes a way of distinguishing and thereby defending simultaneously the universality of Christ's work and the particularity of its application by the Holy Spirit. "This argument trades on three major doctrinal distinctions: the difference between nature and person, the difference between salvation accomplished and applied, and the difference between the Son and the Holy Spirit" (p. 158).

The first distinction underscores the fact that the Son assumed a universal human nature, not a person. The upshot for our topic is that "salvation" occurs in conversion, when we are united to Christ by faith, not at the cross. "That is, you are not saved when the Son is united to human nature; you are saved when your person, 'the subsistent, hypostatic relation that is [you],' is brought into union with Christ" (p. 162). "It seems preferable to acknowledge that the Son took on human nature as such in order to atone for it as such. . . . This move has the advantage of accounting for why a universal atonement is not universally applied" (p. 171). I think that this is the strongest part of his argument. However, human nature did not sin; human beings did. Therefore, wouldn't it be the case that Christ atoned for *human transgressors* rather than for *human nature as such*?

I agree that we must distinguish between the missions of the Son and the Spirit (pp. 162–65), but I wonder if the unity of the Godhead in every work (*opera Trinitatis ad extra indivisa sunt*) is given its due. How can the will and work of the Son differ in purpose and scope from that of the Father and the Son? And do not the passages concerning the Son's definite purpose to save the elect (his chosen, his sheep, the church, many, his people, etc.) demonstrate this unity?

Like fellow Wesleyans whom he cites, Sanders appears to see this distinction between salvation accomplished and applied as synonymous with the sufficient-efficient formula (Christ's death as "sufficient for all, efficient for the elect"). This rule was common in the medieval schools and is repeated in the Canons of Dort. However, I do not think that Wesleyans are using the formula in the same way as traditionally conceived. For example, the quotation from Tom Oden correlates sufficiency (for all) and efficiency (for the faithful) but then changes the definition of terms to "universal sufficiency and conditional efficacy" (p. 175). From a Reformed perspective, Christ's work is indeed universally sufficient but efficient for the elect only, not conditionally (if they believe) but truly *efficiently* (because the Spirit applies the fruit of Christ's accomplished redemption, which includes the gift of faith). There are not two "redemptions," Christ's in the past and the Holy Spirit's in the present, as the quote from William Burton Pope implies, but one redemption accomplished and applied.[1] Thus Christ did not make salvation possible but saved his people from their sins. Otherwise, as Herman Bavinck judges, "The center of gravity has been shifted from Christ and located in the Christian." Instead of Christ's objective work, "Faith is the true reconciliation with God."[2]

We recognize that our Arminian brothers affirm prevenient grace, not the moral ability of sinners to convert themselves. Nevertheless, we are once again closer to Aquinas than to Arminius: what we require is not merely sufficient grace to make it possible for us to be regenerated if we believe but efficient grace to regenerate us so that we do in fact believe. The line that Sanders quotes from the Charles Wesley hymn, "For all Thou hast in Christ prepared / Sufficient, sovereign, saving grace" (p. 176), reflects this confusion between "sufficient" and "sovereign, saving grace." If the latter is universal, then are not all saved?

Far from suppressing or canceling human agency, Reformed churches confess that the Spirit's gracious work effectively liberates people from bondage to sin and death. Evangelical Arminians like Fred Sanders extol the Spirit's liberating work in terms that all of us love to sing (verse 4 of Charles Wesley's "And Can It Be?" comes to mind). Nevertheless, in Sanders's presentation we meet the traditional Arminian *ordo*: first response, then new birth (pp. 166–68).

---

1. See John Murray's excellent treatment, *Redemption Accomplished and Applied* (Grand Rapids: Eerdmans, 2015).

2. Herman Bavinck, *Reformed Dogmatics*, ed. John Bolt; trans. John Vriend (Grand Rapids: Baker Academic, 2006), 3:469.

His statement that the Spirit "prepares us to receive the message, enlivens our receptive power to receive what is being given, awakens our response, and causes the miracle of faith" (p. 174) gets better with each clause. However, I wonder how the clauses "awakens our response" and "causes the miracle of faith" fit with the notion that the Holy Spirit applies the atonement "when each one hears and responds to the word of the gospel" (p. 169).

So I suppose what I'm asking Fred is this: Why isn't the older meaning of sufficient-efficient better? It acknowledges that there is no restriction on Christ's work to save a million human races; "Come to me, all who labor and are heavy laden, and I will give you rest" (Matt. 11:28). Yet this rest was accomplished specifically for all who would believe, the elect, in Christ's death and resurrection. It was there that the debt was paid, the devil was conquered, death itself died, and Christ became the source of eschatological life for his new humanity.

TOM GREGGS

I am grateful to Professor Sanders for such a compelling and elegantly argued account of the Wesleyan understanding of salvation. It is the position *from which* I think most easily and the foundation from which my own theology is built. The presentation in this chapter of the universal scope of salvation accomplished in Christ finds strong scriptural grounds and is exegeted with care and logical precision, but I wonder three things: whether it overly complexifies the biblical passages cited, whether it sufficiently accounts for the eternal and sovereign omnipotence and majesty of God, and whether it places too much causation on the human person. Beyond this, in a less materially significant way, as a Methodist, I wonder if the presentation fully captures the theology of the Wesleys.

Professor Sanders's powerful and biblical opening to his chapter is arresting in pointing us to the statement in Titus 2:11: "The grace of God has appeared, bringing salvation to all people" (p. 156). Indeed, he points us towards the extent to which translators will go in order to avoid this universal claim (p. 156). Later in his chapter, he also cites a run of verses that point to the universal atoning work of Christ. He cites 1 John 2:2 ("He is the atoning sacrifice for our sins, and not only for ours but also for the sins of the whole world") and states that his interpretation enables one to read the passage "without wincing at the introduction of the universal note in such close proximity to the propitiation" (p. 170). He also cites 1 Timothy 2:6 (Christ Jesus "gave himself as a ransom for all people") and Titus 2:11 once more and states how his interpretation can prevent us from "worrying overmuch about the lack of restriction" (p. 170). I cannot but agree with him that it is difficult to interpret such passages from a Calvinist perspective. However, it seems that his worry is born from avoiding universalism in its plainer sense. He asserts, "The actual salvation of all people [is] contra the overwhelming scriptural witness" (p. 156). For him (though the position is not expanded), "the universal note cannot entail universalism" (p. 157). But is it not, surely, the most literal and straightforward reading of these texts to say (as the Reformed will) that when Scripture speaks of the salvation God brings in Christ, it *is genuinely speaking of salvation*? Jesus does not give Himself as a *possibility* for the ransom of all people or the *potential* of being an atoning sacrifice for our sins and those of the whole world or to bring the *opportunity* for salvation for all people. Rather, he *has* given himself for all; that he *is* the atoning sacrifice of the sins for all the world; that he has appeared to bring *salvation* to all people. These universal claims are ones which both Reformed and traditional Arminian theologians are anxious about (as the language of *worrying* and *wincing* makes clear). As I have discussed elsewhere (in response to Professor Levering), would it not be better to worry more in the opposite direction—in our preparedness to put limits on the sovereign friendliness of God to us in Jesus Christ? Indeed, to explain these passages, Professor Sanders must make a series of differentiations that are not innate to the text but imposed upon them schematically. In my own account, I wish on these issues (to a degree) to employ Ockham's razor: why not take the simplest and straight forward readings of these texts *and then* try to understand issues to do with rejection and judgement and hell? Might we not place the lens of the universal nature of salvation in front of texts about judgement, decision, and so forth rather than *vice versa*, or is just asserting or presuming this impossible?

Of course, the claim could be that these demarcations are innate to the *sensus plenior* of Scripture. After all, theology involves inevitable abstractions. But the question is whether those theological abstractions are either borne out by Scripture or meaningful in relation to the scriptural texts cited. The principal issue among these which I wish to consider is the demarcation of nature and person. Much depends on this, since it leads Professor Sanders to be able to read seemingly universalist texts in terms of a universal possibility for individuals. He quotes Vanhoozer: "To say the Son assumed humanity does not necessarily mean that he assumed my humanity, that is, the subsistent, hypostatic relation that is me" (p. 162). I heartily commend Professor Sanders's instinct that discussing soteriology and the scope of salvation is a doctrine that is dependent on the foundational dogmatic *res* of Trinitarian theology and Christology. However, I am unsure that the demarcation between nature and person in the manner offered is as helpful as it might first appear. Two comments are worth making.

First, the question of what it means for Christ to have a human nature perhaps needs to be explored further. I wish to affirm fully that Christ is the hypostatic union of God and humanity in the one person Jesus Christ. But I am not sure that language of "nature" and "person" as employed here can be used so straightforwardly or univocally. There is a question of what takes precedence (logically) in our thought in holding person and nature together. My own reading of Chalcedon is to say that *the one person of Jesus Christ* is its starting point, which it goes on to expand, whereas I sense the reading offered by Professor Sanders prioritizes language of nature first (pp. 161–62). Space sadly does not allow a detailed exposition of what I mean by this, but the point I wish to make is that I am not sure it is straightforward to say that we have a clear sense of what "human nature" is *outside of who Christ is*. Most pertinently for this discussion, I think we are wiser to say that we share in Christ's humanity rather than to presume we know what a human nature is and to say only that he shares in ours. If Jesus Christ is the one "who is slain before the foundation of the world," Christ's enhypostatic humanity (p. 162) is something the Son possesses from eternity; creation is through him, and humans are made in the image of God because we share in the humanity he has enhypostatically in the perfect simultaneity of his divine eternity. Put more plainly, there is no human without Jesus Christ: he is the prototype, as the Last Adam, the one in whose image the first Adam was created. Or else, we might say (recognizing the importance of the doctrine of God to doctrines of creation, reconciliation, and redemption): not only does God reconcile and redeem because God creates; God also creates because God reconciles and redeems. Our humanity is found in his *personhood* as the one who is true God and true human (in a way we as yet are not), and in his humanity in which we share, he mediates us to the Father and substitutes for us in God's grace. Furthermore, we might say that part of being human, of human nature, *is personhood*. Can we have a notion of being human which does not involve being a person? There is at least space to ask whether it is possible to have a univocal use of language of personhood any more than Chalcedon allows this with *hypostasis*. Christologically, Jesus is *one person* and *one hypostatsis* in two natures, but one of those natures (true God) is also termed in Trinitarian language a *person* and a *hypostasis*, and this does not mean the same thing as speaking of a human being as a person. We become human in Christ, subsisting in Christ's own humanity.

Beyond these abstract issues, second, there is the issue of whether the distinction between nature and person can be meaningfully employed in the biblical texts that Professor Sanders points us towards. Titus 2:11 does not state that God "has appeared, bringing salvation" to human nature but to "all people." What sense can be made of this passage if "people" does not involve "person"? Does "all people" (with the inevitable personhood this involves) fall neatly into the distinction offered? Similarly, does "the whole world" (1 John 2:2) really function in the same way as "human nature" but not "persons"? Or can we understand Jesus giving himself as a ransom "to all people" (1 Tim. 2:6) in depersonalised terms of nature? And what if, given the logic of the position espoused, no one chooses or seeks the applicative: If that is the case, in what possible sense has *God* ransomed all people?

A further aspect I laud in Professor Sander's account is the full expression of Trinitarian dynamics. Indeed, if (as I have argued) I were to remove the nature-person row, I would whole heartedly endorse his helpful table (p. 169). Where I differ, however, is in the extent to which application becomes causation. I am unsure what salvation *without effect* might mean ultimately and, therefore, whether application language helps. The question for me is where the *efficient* causation of that application rests: Is it the grace of God, or is it human willed faith? If it is the former, then we are led back to the questions of arbitrariness, which might be mounted against Calvinism (why does God's prevenient grace operate through the dynamics of God's Spirit for some and not others?). If it is the latter, then we open the possibility of *human* activity being the cause of grace (the argument of semi-Pelagianism often mounted against the Arminian position). If it is only in the application that we receive the benefits of grace eternally (and that salvation becomes effective in us), does this not simply pay lip service to the claim that Christ's death is for all people? My own hope (and for a universalist, I do not think it can be more than that—a daring hope) is that Christ's work is objective and *de iure*, accomplished once and for all (in the most straight forward meaning of this word) for human beings (even in their passivity to this reality), and the Holy Spirit enables the believer to participate subjectively and *de facto* in time *already* (actively in their active participation in this reality) in the salvation God determines from eternity to eternity for creation. The economic dynamics of the Spirit and the Son make meaningful both the objective universal language about the salvation the Son brings and the urgent call to repentance and formation into the likeness of Christ (through sharing actively in the same Spirit who rested fully upon him), which the Spirit brings about in creation here and now. Without the Spirit, the creature continues to live in time (even if we might hope not eternally) in the existential condition of the possibility of hell, of condemnation, of death. With the Spirit's grace, the creature is freed in time to live in the present in the objective reality of God's salvation. My concern in describing the economy in these ways is to uphold not only the meaningfulness of the life of faith, but also (and perhaps primarily) the omnipotent sovereignty of the divine will—a will which is shown to us in Jesus Christ and in the love that is the basis for the incarnation. In the end, I think we need to focus more upon God and all God has done in salvation rather than presuppose some form of human action is more powerful than the sovereignty of divine love. And in this we might *dare to hope* that all people are saved by the eternal God, who is—altogether and at once in God's eternity—Creator, Reconciler, and Redeemer.

Indeed, it may well be that the Wesleys themselves came to some potential version of this. In the hymn with which Professor Sanders ends, Charles Wesley speaks not of "sufficient . . . saving grace" but also of "sufficient, *sovereign*, saving grace" (p. 176). Later in life, John Wesley in his *Explanatory Notes on the New Testament* included a number of comments which tended in a universalist direction on passages in Scripture.[1] Perhaps most notable of them all were his comments on the eschatological imagery of Revelation 5:13 in which he is at pains to make plain that "every creature" means just that—*every* creature. He too confronts the reality with which I am concerned that we read passages with a degree of seeking the plain sense—which perhaps for us a *deuxieme naïvité*.

I wish there were more space to engage with Professor Sanders excellent essay, not least since it describes the ecclesial, theological, and spiritual context in which I am most at home and (as this response might make plain) with which I continue to wrestle before God.

---

1. See, e.g., Wesley's comments on Eph. 1:10; 1 Cor. 15:28; and 2 Cor. 5:18–19.

CHRISTIAN UNIVERSALIST VIEW

TOM GREGGS

Christian universalism is the view that the extent of the atonement is such that it is not only universally offered to all human beings but also universally effective for all human beings. Christian universalism comes in a variety of forms, but these distinctive forms are united in advocating that the sovereign loving will of God is ultimately irresistible and that salvation is ultimately extended to all humanity. In this way, universalism combines the Arminian position that God *wills* the salvation of all people with the Calvinist position that God's sovereign will cannot be resisted: universalism is the belief in the omnipotence of divine love as fulfilled in the atonement. Christian universalism demarcates itself not only from other accounts of the extent of the atonement but also from other accounts of eschatology. In advocating the irresistible sovereignty of divine love, Christian universalism rejects traditional separationist accounts of the eschaton in which the saved and the damned are divided for all eternity, with the former group destined to go to be with God and the latter destined to everlasting torment, the absence of God, or annihilation. Unlike pluralistic universalism, Christian universalism is an account of the atonement that takes seriously the uniqueness of the atoning work of Christ's life, death, and resurrection and seeks to build upon scriptural accounts of this economy in order to understand its unique effectiveness as universally applicable to humanity: Christian universal salvation argues that in Scripture the atonement is an atoning for humanity and that Christ's objective work of salvation is effective for all human beings (not simply a select few by either election or exercise of free will) by God who is the God of salvation. In other words, Christian universalism seeks to ask the question of how *fitting* an account of universalism might be to describe the work of salvation in Jesus Christ as attested in Scripture.

Particularist "Christian" Universalism

Christian universalism is a minority stream within the Christian tradition. Separationism remains the dominant, majority version of traditional, mainstream Christianity's view of eschatology and of the extent of the atonement. The essential requirement of separationism, as an alternative to universalism, is not that the majority or even a good portion of humanity may not be saved but simply "that *some* men [and women] . . . will finally not be saved":[1] that is, that there are some humans who will not receive the benefits of Christ's atoning sacrifice. For separationists, the extent of the effects of the atonement on either side of the separation is a secondary issue (as is the means by which they may be saved) to the reality that the effects of the atonement are not universal but (to differing degrees and for differing reasons) limited in scope. For the Christian universalist, in contrast, the extent of the atonement is not a question of the breadth of the atonement such that it might include more or fewer humans, by virtue of either divine election or a judgement by God on the basis of the knowledge available for a human to exercise her free will. Universalism, instead, appeals to the irresistibility of the loving and atoning work of the Son of God. The issue in relation to the atonement is not whether it involves more or fewer people; the point is that atonement is universal and its benefits are received ultimately by all. According to Christian universalism, the reception of salvation is not conditional upon either a profession of faith or the eternal decision of God to elect or reject the individual: God has elected all in God's love, and it is for these all that God atones in the person of Jesus Christ, the God-human. This *all* is the decisive feature of Christian accounts of universal salvation in contrast to other accounts of the extent of the atonement.

---

1. Nigel M. de S. Cameron, "Universalism and the Logic of Revelation," in *The Best in Theology*, vol. 3, ed. J. I. Packer (Carol Stream, IL: Christianity Today, 1989), 154, emphasis added; cf. p. 166. It is noteworthy that in 1995 the Church of England's Doctrine Commission seemed to reject the idea of hell, the Commission nevertheless replaced hell with the equally separationist view of "total non-being."

But universalism is not found in only one form. In its pluralistic form, universalism has emerged in response to the contextual issue of living in a complexly multireligious and secular society and the problems this raises for separationist accounts of the extent of the atonement. The argument of pluralistic universalism has been in essence that Christians should give up entirely on the significance and sufficiency of the atonement. In this form, universalism within modern theology has emerged from an acceptance of modernist, universalistic relativism in which the singularity and power of the atonement is removed or else comes merely to account for a general way "God" is in the world. Such pluralistic forms of universalism arise from questioning both the absoluteness of Christian claims and the unique significance of the person of Jesus Christ and the event of his life, death, and resurrection. These accounts of universalism arise for many Christians out of the sense that, in the words of Rousseau, religion is simply "*une affaire de geographie*" and out of a critical historicist approach to the events of the Scripture. Indeed, pluralistic accounts of universalism arise (ironically) out of a nervousness about the universal claims of Christianity. Adapting the insights of Ernst Troeltsch in *The Absoluteness of Christianity* in a more radical direction, pluralistic universalists, such as John Hick, seek to reconcile the sceptical historicist approach to the claims of Christianity with the sense that religions provide evidence of an ultimate reality at a noumenal, but not phenomenal, level: in this sense, Jesus Christ's atonement is not a particular event but a mythical and generalist event that gives insight into what Hick (in his rejection of theistic absoluteness) calls "The Real."[2] Albeit still working within a soteriological schema that is no doubt alien to other faiths, Hick's belief in the relativity of the historical phenomenon of Christianity and its claims leads him to a position that stresses divine love and universal salvation—the noumenal reality that is identified as the core of the phenomenal exoteric symbols within given religions.

It is easy to see how those debating the extent of the atonement could be dismissive of this approach to universalism. Pluralistic approaches undermine the very uniqueness and efficacy of the atonement as an

---

2. See John Hick, *An Interpretation of Religion: Human Responses to the Transcendent* (London: Macmillan, 1989), 10–11; cf. John Hick, *Problems of Religious Pluralism* (London: Macmillan, 1985), 39–44.

event. While they seem in one way to universalize the atonement, in reality they remove the atonement and its effects, or reduce the atonement merely to the level of the symbolic. In recognizing this issue, separationists identify an important problem: all too easily the uniqueness of Jesus Christ can find itself being replaced by some notion of generalized religiosity or spirituality in universalism. Pluralistic universalism can leave one wondering why one is a Christian rather than a Sikh, Hindu, Muslim, or a member of any other faith tradition; or else pluralistic approaches often work on the basis of a lowest common denominator between faiths, ignoring the exclusivist elements faiths contain. The danger exists that a lack of particularity, which a doctrine of universal salvation could bring about, could lead to the unhelpful descriptive inadequacy of sameness between peoples who understand themselves to be particular or even unique, and—moreover—that the person and work of Jesus Christ becomes a meaningless and ineffective narrative that at best merely symbolizes the work of God (or "the Real") in salvation (or "liberation").

Christian universalism should properly be demarcated from relativist and nonabsolutist accounts of religions in which some version of pluralism is the way a universal hope of salvation (however meaningful those terms might be) is expressed. *Christian* universalism, by contrast, seeks to offer a *particularist* account of the work of salvation in the life, death, and resurrection of Jesus Christ and to claim that *this particularity and the uniqueness of the incarnation and atonement has universal effects*.[3] Christian universalism seeks to arise out of a deeply particularist theological account of the unique atoning sacrifice of Jesus Christ, one that takes Scripture seriously, and to create room for Christian particularity by advocating that a limited atonement is not the only way to make sense of human ethical decision and faith commitment,[4] as well as the seriousness of the decision of faith, the Christian church, and the call to holy living.[5]

---

3. De S. Cameron, "Universalism," sees the term *particularist* as the antonym of *Universalist*. See also here Veli-Matti Kärkkäinen, "Evangelical Theology and the Religions," in *The Cambridge Companion to Evangelical Theology*, ed. Timothy Larsen (Cambridge: Cambridge University Press, 2007), 201–4.

4. David Fergusson, "Will the Love of God Finally Triumph?," in *Nothing Greater, Nothing Better: Theological Essays on the Love of God*, ed. Kevin J. Vanhoozer (Grand Rapids: Eerdmans, 1997), 241.

5. On this, see Trevor Hart, "Universalism: Two Distinct Types," in *Universalism and the Doctrine of Hell: Papers Presented at the Fourth Edinburgh Conference in Christian Dogmatics*,

One response to this kind of particularist universalist account may be to say that it is impossible to have Christian universalism—that universalism is itself unchristian, that universalism is a position which has been condemned as heterodox. Such an account is based on the supposed position of the fifth ecumenical council—the Second Council of Constantinople (553 CE), which anathematized Origen. *Apokatastasis* (the universal restoration of souls to God) is mentioned in this council in relation to the fifteen anathemas held against Origen (or, more likely in reality, Origenism),[6] and it is cited on three occasions (anathemas 1, 14, and 15). However, in each occasion, the anathema is cited in reference to another area of Origenist theology:[7] in 1 and 15, it is the idea of *apokatastasis* held in conjunction with some belief in the pre-existence of souls that is anathematized, and in 14, it is the doctrine held in conjunction with immateriality that is condemned. The local council of Emperor Justinian (543) may have condemned *apokatastasis*, but even this—without the status of an ecumenical council—did not condemn Christian universalism outright but only the particular form of it Origen reputedly offers.[8] Christian universalism in and of itself is never outrightly condemned; in fact, it would be difficult to do so since the word *apokatastasis* is used in Scripture in Acts, when it speaks of Jesus who must "remain in heaven until the time of universal restoration [*apokatastasis*] that God announced long ago through his holy prophets" (Acts 3:21).[9] Rather than a question of heterodoxy, the questions around Christian universalism are questions of fittingness: How fitting is an account of universalism to describe the work of salvation in Jesus Christ as attested in Scripture? The key issues concern, therefore, the extent to which an account is consistent with the revelation of the divine life; the manner in which it accords with the account of the atoning life, death,

---

1991, ed. Nigel M. de S. Cameron (Grand Rapids: Baker, 1993), 22–29, who lists various charges that can be cited against universalism. These are that universalism trivializes of sin, emasculates the doctrine of atonement, denies the reality of hell and judgment, denigrates justification by faith, impugns the righteousness of God, undermines Christian mortality, and lacks foundation in the Bible.

6. On this see Elizabeth A. Clark, *The Origenist Controversy: The Cultural Construction of an Early Christian Debate* (Princeton, NJ: Princeton University Press, 1992); and Henri Crouzel, *Origen* (Edinburgh: T&T Clark, 1989), 171–72.

7. I use the term Origenist deliberately in contrast to Origen's.

8. See Gregory MacDonald, *"All Shall Be Well": Explorations in Universal Salvation and Christian Theology, from Origen to Moltmann* (Eugene: Cascade, 2011), 4–11.

9. Unless otherwise indicated, Scripture quotations in this chapter come from the NRSV.

and resurrection of Jesus Christ; the degree to which universalism is biblical and has followers within the Christian tradition; the sense in which the seriousness of the choice of faith is meaningful; the degree to which sin and its seriousness can be appropriately accounted for; and the sense in which the Christian life and discipleship are not undermined by a belief in universal salvation. It is to these themes that this chapter now turns.

The Positive Contribution of Christian Universalism: The Omnipotence of Divine Love in Jesus Christ

Universalism in its Christian form proceeds in the belief that love is the very nature of God (1 John 4:8) and that, since God is love and God is immutable, all of God's actions in relation to God's creation must be consistent with God's nature as love. Furthermore, since God is omnipotent, God is thus omnipotent in God's loving of God's creatures. The love of God is, therefore, ultimately irresistible for the creature. The material form that this love of God takes is God's perfect expression of love in the atoning work of Christ on the cross. As the writer of 1 John states,

> God's love was revealed among us in this way: God sent his only Son into the world so that we might live through him. In this is love, not that we loved God but that he loved us and sent his Son to be the atoning sacrifice for our sins. (1 John 4:9–10)

God's love is cruciform. That God reveals God's love in this manner says something about the form of atoning love God is and performs in relation to creation. This love is antecedent (and incomparable) to any response to that love. God's is a prevenient love that does not depend on a response since nothing can alter the divine nature of love and the divine loving consistent with that nature. God's acts towards creation are to be understood as consistent with God's nature (and *vice versa*). If God is described as love then God's ways with the world are ways of love. For a Christian universalist, to describe God's loving as limited only to those within the church, those who choose to follow Christ, or those who are elect makes God seem either impotent—since God's loving is not sufficiently effective to overcome human sin unaided by

faith—or capricious—for deciding that some should have eternal torment and others salvation. Indeed, the capriciousness of the eternal and
omniscient God creating a world knowing that most of the world will
exist for all eternity in torment or will be annihilated ultimately is a
deeply problematic feature of separationism: Why should God create
anything if God eternally knows that the majority of creation (either by
its exercise of free will or by God's electing will) will be rejected from
salvation and damned? What does it say about God's nature that God
should elect to damn the majority of the world (or even a part of it) in
God's sovereign foreknowledge? How would God be so thoughtless in
God's foreknowledge to create a world that never asked for its creation
knowing that the vast majority of people will wrongfully exercise free
will and be denied salvation?[10]

In contrast to this capricious or arbitrary presentation of God, the
Christian universalist associates the love that is described as God's being
with the acts of God's grace. These acts are directed towards the whole
of creation, and in them God is not less than sovereign. As Trevor Hart
describes it,

> The central Christian conviction that love is the very nature of
> God, and that the most fundamental relation of this God to all
> his creatures must therefore be one of love if he is to be true to
> himself; the concomitant conviction is that this same God must
> ultimately have the final good of all his creatures in view, that
> "he desireth not the death of (any) sinner, but rather that he
> may turn from his wickedness and live"; the gospel stress on the
> utter unconditionality of salvation wrought in Christ, and the
> rejection of any notion that some might be more deserving than
> others of redemption; the clear affirmations in Scripture con-
> cerning the universality of the scope of Christ's saving passion
> and resurrection and the completeness of the salvation effected

---

10. Jürgen Moltmann, *In the End—the Beginning: The Life of Hope* (London: SCM, 2004),
considers how unchristian certain separationist views are (140ff.). While separationists argue
universal salvation might lead to a weakening of the doctrine of God's freedom, universalists
are surely justified in advocating that separationism may bring into question God's love,
omnipotence, justice, and holiness (if God is understood to will and allow the destruction
of a significant proportion of the humanity God created). Cf. Friedrich Schleiermacher,
The Christian Faith (Edinburgh: T&T Clark, 1968), §§117–120, 163.

by the same (i.e. some sense God *has* saved all in Christ); and lastly the insistence that God, as Lord of all, must prevail, that the universal saving will springing inevitably from his nature must be fulfilled in his creatures.[11]

Although there is a minority view of universalism that rests in some degree on the individual—given eternity and purgation—eventually making the correct decision and willing salvation for themselves,[12] the majority of forms of Christian universalism rest on the foundational beliefs that God is love, God's ways are loving because God is love, and in God's loving God is omnipotent.

This irresistibility of the immutability of divine loving will no doubt present some with the problem of the lack of free will: divine love is so irresistible that human freedom may seem to be evacuated. However, Christian universalism questions the idea that freedom exists in rejecting God. True freedom is to be found in the freedom we have as creatures to be for (not against) God.[13] Freedom in Christianity is not the same as eighteenth-century concepts of liberty, but the freedom of the creature to be for God in Jesus Christ. To be in sin is not to exercise free choice. According to Scripture, to be in sin is to be in bondage. Outside God's atoning work, we are not free but are instead slaves.[14] True freedom rests in willing with the divine willing. It is simply false to state that the only condition that makes the possibility of human love of God real (rather than coerced) is the possibility that we might reject God;[15] freedom is found in and with loving the immutably divine love, not in the (perversely coercive) willed avoidance of hell, eternal torment,

---

11. Hart, "Universalism," 15–16.

12. Origen could potentially be read this way. For more on Origen, see my *Barth, Origen, and Universal Salvation: Restoring Particularity* (Oxford: Oxford University Press, 2009); *"Apokatastasis:* Particularist Universalism in Origen," in MacDonald, *"All Shall be Well"*, 29–46; "The Many Names of Christ in Wisdom: Reading Scripture with Origen for a Diverse World," *Journal of Scriptural Reasoning* 7 (2008), http://jsr.shanti.virginia.edu/back-issues/vol-7-no-1-january-2008-spreading-rumours-of-wisdom/the-many-names-of-christ-in-wisdom/; and "Exclusivist or Universalist? Origen 'the Wise Steward of the Word' (CommRom V.1.7) and the Issue of Genre," *International Journal of Systematic Theology* 9 (2007): 315–27.

13. As Augustine puts it, true freedom is the *non posse peccare* (the inability to sin), not the *posse non peccare* (the possibility of sinning). See, for example, Augustine, *City of God*, 21.15.

14. See Rom. 6:17–20, for example.

15. Cf. Fergusson, "Will the Love of God Finally Triumph?," 199–200; and Grace Jantzen, "Do We Need Immortality?," *Modern Theology* 1 (1984): 40.

or annihilation. To quote 1 John 4:19, "we love because he first loved us," and not because we are free to reject that first loving of humanity by God. There is a difference between the atonement's objective (or *de iure*) effects and its subjective (or *de facto*) effects. Salvation is universally effected in Christ, objectively and *de iure*, in that God first loved humanity, and it is subjectively and *de facto* effected in the lives of those who love in response to and in accordance with that objective loving. The objective loving of God in Jesus Christ is the basis for the free response subjectively and *de facto* in the life of the believer as the objective reality is realized in the life of faith by the Holy Spirit.[16] The condition for the creature's free love of God is not the creature's capacity in sin and bondage to reject that love; the condition for the creature's free love of God is God's free love of the creature.

Another way to discuss these issues relating to freedom and will might be to differentiate between the view from above (that which is ultimate) and the view from below (that which is penultimate). As creatures we can make all kinds of penultimate decisions, but we are ultimately creatures belonging to the Creator, and in living out and fulfilling our purpose, we find true freedom from sin and for God. When the view from below recognizes the reality from above, there is an effect on created, temporal, human existence: from below, in the slavery of sin, such possibilities of hell and disobedience are real; only in knowing the omnipotent divine loving of creation is the creature truly free. It is worth considering the verses which follow Scripture's emphatic claim that God is love:

> Love has been perfected among us in this: that we may have boldness on the day of judgement, because as he is, so are we in this world. There is no fear in love, but perfect love casts out fear; for fear has to do with punishment, and whoever fears has not reached perfection in love. (1 John 4:17–18)

The reality of the divine loving has to be perfected within the creature, who is enabled thereby to have boldness at the eschaton. Knowledge of

---

16. For a further discussion of these themes, see my *Barth, Origen, and Universal Salvation*, esp. ch 7; and Adam Neder, *Participation in Christ: An Entry into Karl Barth's Church Dogmatics* (Louisville: Westminster John Knox, 2009), esp. 17–28, 40–59.

this loving casts out fear, especially the fear of punishment. For those who in the reality of life in time and space do not see, know, or recognize the universal atoning work of God in salvation, there is a reality of fear and punishment (from below). But for those *in whom* love is perfected, there is a reality of salvation (from below) as they know the reality of God's atoning sacrifice in Christ and its universal effects (from above).

Karl Barth offers an interesting account of the reality of the possibility of rejection by God (from below), and he does so within a schema that universalizes the scope of salvation. He argues that even those who seem to have the form of the "rejected" have the purpose of manifesting the grace of the gospel.[17] For Barth, it is an impossible possibility that we as creatures might reject our election in Christ; nevertheless, there is nothing which can change God's decree *for* humanity. Here, it is worth quoting Barth at length:

If we truly hear, then in face of this election and its meaning it is not possible for us not to be able to hear or obey that Yes, not to will to be amongst those who are affirmed by God. This is not a possibility but an impossibility. It is a turning of the sense of that election into nonsense. It is a descent into the abyss of the divine non-willing and the divine non-electing. Even in such a descent the creature cannot escape God. Even in this abyss it is still in the hands of God, the object of His decision. Yet that does not mean that it has been flung, or even allowed to fall, into the abyss by God Himself. God is and God remains the One who has decided for the creature and not against it. It is by love itself that the creature is confounded. Even there, in the midst of hell, when it thinks of God and His election it can think only of the love and grace of God. The resolve and power of our opposition cannot put any limit to the power and resolve of God. Even in our opposition there comes upon us that which God has foreordained for us. But that means that what comes upon us cannot alter in the slightest the nature and character of the foreordination which is God's decree. In that decree as such we find only the decree of His love. In the proclaiming

17. Karl Barth, *Church Dogmatics* II/2 (London: T&T Clark, 1957), 457.

and teaching of His election we can hear only the proclaiming of the Gospel.[18]

Barth speaks of the creature "in the midst of hell" and "in this abyss," but nevertheless he also speaks of the creature's resolve and power (to reject its election) as being one which "cannot put any limit to the power and resolve of God." From below, we must always recognize in the divine freedom the possibility of God's rejection (of the limiting of God's atoning work in God's freedom). However, while God has the freedom to reject the creature and condemn it, in grace, God always offers a divine "Nevertheless" towards the creature. There is nothing, for Barth, that could ever undermine the love of God, but the possibility of rejection from this side of the eschaton remains an existential reality. J. A. T. Robinson speaks of the need in this way to preach hell, even for the universalist;[19] and Trevor Hart has described this as a "kerygmatic hell."[20] Despite the possibility of this reality of hell and rejection, there is an ultimate irresistibility to divine love; but hell and rejection remain an existential reality for those who have not received the benefits of Christ penultimately. This existential reality for most of humanity is indeed the reason for the Christian universalism to evangelize. Without the knowledge of God's saving and loving acts in Jesus Christ, the human being stands under the fear of death and hell before their own view of a capricious "god" or else their sense of an unending abyss of nothingness. The imperative to proclaim and witness to the good news in Jesus Christ is not altered by the ultimate reality of universal salvation in Christ: not knowing this ultimate reality, humanity exists in fear and without the hope and assurance of God's salvation in its penultimate condition from below. Evangelism continues to be needed so that people can live free from the fear of death and hell, and free for God. While Christ brings universal salvation for all, God continues in the person of God's Holy Spirit to relate the ultimate objective reality of salvation to the penultimate conditions of human subjectivity, bringing the assurance that God is the Father of the Lord Jesus Christ, the God of our salvation.

---

18. Barth, *Church Dogmatics* II/2, 27.
19. J. A. T. Robinson, *In the End, God . . . : A Study of the Christian Doctrine of the Last Things* (London: Clarke, 1950), 119.
20. Hart, "Universalism," 21.

The world does not yet know this ultimate reality and lives in the condition of the unreality of the curse of sin and its associated expectation, death. Thus the good news of salvation (and not the bad news of condemnation) continues to need to be proclaimed to the world for a Christian universalist.[21]

Indeed, it is possible here to hit upon an interesting note on how Christian universalism contributes to the debate on the extent of salvation in relation to classical Calvinist (or Augustinian) or Arminian perspectives. As Thomas Talbott puts it,

> For even as many Augustinians are utterly convinced that God's salvific will cannot be defeated forever and many Arminians are utterly convinced that God at least will will the salvation of all human sinners, so I am equally convinced that *both* claims are true. . . . If you simply take the Augustinian idea of God's sovereignty in the matter of salvation . . . and put it together with the Arminian idea that God at least wills or desires the salvation of all, then you get universalism, plain and simple.[22]

If thought about from a predominantly theological perspective as relating to the doctrine of God, the real tension between the Arminian position and the Calvinist/Augustinian position regards not the exercise of the human will (a concern from the perspective of systematic theology primarily for the theological locus of theological anthropology) but the extent of the divine willing. Before the question of the irresistibility of the divine will in relation to the human willing arises, in terms of the issue of the extent of the atonement, comes the question of the scope of the divine willing of salvation—some (Augustine and Calvin) or all (Arminius). Christian universalism seeks to offer an account of the divine life which is neither an expression of what may seem to be divine arbitrariness (electing some but not others), nor an expression of what may seem to be divine impotence (the human creature's freedom over against the sovereign freedom of the divine life). Christian universalism

---

21. See my *Barth, Origen, and Universal Salvation*, chs. 5–7.
22. Thomas Talbott, "A Case for Christian Universalism," in *Universal Salvation? The Current Debate*, eds. Robin A. Parry and Christopher H. Partridge (Grand Rapids: Eerdmans, 2003), 7.

is a neat theological response to the problems of both the Calvinist/ Augustinian approach and the Arminian approach by combining the Calvinist account of divine sovereignty with the Arminian account of the divine willing. Christian universalism rests on the same premises as both the Calvinist and the Arminian accounts, and potentially offers a more consistent account of the person and work of God in relation to the extent of the divine work of atonement. To quote Talbott again,

> If it is not heretical for Arminians to believe that God, being unlimited in love, at least wills (or sincerely desires) the salvation of all (proposition [1]), how could it be heretical for universalists to believe this as well? And if it is not heretical for the Augustinians to believe that God, being almighty, will in the end accomplish all of his redemptive purposes (proposition [2]), why should it be heretical for universalists to believe this as well? And finally, if it is not heretical to accept proposition (1), as the Arminians do, and not heretical to accept proposition (2), as the Augustinians do, why should it be heretical to accept both (1) and (2)?[23]

As Talbott recognizes, there could, of course, be a reason why it might be acceptable to believe that holding both propositions together might be heretical: if the Bible were to be accepted as having ultimate authority in matters of faith (as a particularist account of universal salvation might suggest), and if the Bible were to teach that the coalescence of these two propositions were heretical, then it would be necessary to accept that this were so. It is to the biblical issues relating to universalism to which this chapter now turns.

Is Love the Whole of the Story? Sin, Judgment, and the Life of Faith

The response of both the Calvinist and the Arminian parties will, however, no doubt be to claim that the shadow side of the account of the extent of the atonement continues to exist within Scripture: rejection and condemnation are present in Scripture as well as election and salvation.[24]

---

23. Talbott, "A Case for Christian Universalism," 11.

24. Some of the material presented here is a condensed account of a section of chapter 5 from my *Theology against Religion: Constructive Dialogues with Bonhoeffer and Barth* (London: T&T Clark, 2011), 117–23.

Separationists of all varieties claim that it would be a fulsome denial of Scripture and its authority to suggest anything other than an ultimate division between the saved and the damned, anything other than a limited atonement in some form.[25] It is impossible to deny the kerygmatic urgency of the choice of faith in the salvific work of Christ in the New Testament. The Gospels reverberate with this message—the wide or narrow gate, the sheep or the goats, hell, condemnation, and destruction. But even the most determined separationist may need to acknowledge that the New Testament also contains messages that (in a plain-sense reading) suggest a universal salvation for all humanity, indeed all creation. There are numerous passages (especially in Paul) that point towards universal salvation, enough indeed for universalism to be a quiet but continual strain throughout the history of Christian theology.[26] Consider, for example:

> Therefore just as one man's trespass led to condemnation for all, so one man's act of righteousness leads to justification and life for all. For just as by the one man's disobedience the many were made sinners, so by the one man's obedience the many will be made righteous. (Rom. 5:18–19)[27]

It is difficult not to read this passage as suggesting that all will be saved by Christ's righteousness and obedience. Even in context, it is difficult to see where one might gain the idea of the "all" or the "many" here meaning only both Jews and gentiles; the plain-sense meaning seems to be "all human beings."[28] Similarly, the visions of cosmic reconciliation in Paul are also suggestive of universal salvation. For example:

---

25. See, for example, I. Howard Marshall, "Does the New Testament Teach Universal Salvation?," in *Christ in Our Place: The Humanity of God in Christ for the Reconciliation of the World. Essays Presented to James Torrance*, eds. Trevor Hart and Daniel Thimell (Exeter: Paternoster, 1989); or I. Howard Marshall, "The New Testament Does *Not* Teach Universal Salvation," in Parry and Partridge, *Universal Salvation*, 55–76; see the responses to the presentation of Romans 5 in Richard Bell, "Rom. 5:18–19 and Universal Salvation," *New Testament Studies* 48 (2002): 427–29.

26. For an overview of the history of the idea of universal salvation in Christianity, see MacDonald, *"All Shall Be Well"*.

27. See, for further exegesis, Bell, "Rom. 5:18–19 and Universal Salvation."

28. Cf. N. T. Wright, "Towards a Biblical View of Universalism," *Themelios* 4, no. 2 (1979): 54–58.

And through him God was pleased to reconcile to himself all things, whether on earth or in heaven, by making peace through the blood of his cross. (Col. 1:20)

Or

He has made known to us the mystery of his will . . . as a plan for the fullness of time, to gather up all things in him, things in heaven and things on earth. (Eph. 1:9–10)

Or

That is, in Christ God was reconciling the world to himself, not counting their trespasses against them, and entrusting the message of reconciliation to us. (2 Cor. 5:19)

Indeed, the words of Thomas Johnson are wise: "The case for universalism is stronger than is usually realized. God's saving love for the world is a prominent biblical theme from Genesis through Revelation."[29] Texts pointing to a final division between categories of people and those suggesting ultimate universal hope exist side by side in the New Testament. The question is how one understands them in relation to each other. One approach may be to deny the meaning or significance of one side or another; another approach may say that there is no consistent message within the New Testament regarding this and that, even within the same author or book, images of universalism and separation stand side by side without logical inferences being able to be drawn.[30] But another approach might be to read one set of themes through the other. For an Arminian, for example, the universal passages could be held out to be the desire of God, while the separationist accounts could be held

29. Thomas Johnson, "A Wideness in God's Mercy: Universalism in the Bible," in Parry and Partridge, *Universal Salvation*, 97. By far and away the best account of the biblical material in relation to an account of universal salvation is Gregory MacDonald, *The Evangelical Universalist* (London: SPCK, 2008), esp. chs. 2–6; this book offers an excellent overview of the passages of Scripture which are universalist in tone and an account of how to interpret those texts which are separationist.

30. This is the perspective of M. Eugene Boring with regard to Paul. See Eugene Boring, "The Language of Universal Salvation in Paul," *Journal of Biblical Literature* 105 (1986): 269–92.

.out to be the reality of human decisions:[31] the universalist passages are sublated to the separationist passages in order to discover their meanings. But in advocating a universal scope to the extent of the atonement, a universalist might suggest reading the separationist passages in light of the universalist ones, as warnings of the reality of life without God, of the threat of hell and death (without Christ's atoning sacrifice) rather than its prediction—images and parables of the consequences of rejecting God.[32]

Let us consider, in relation to the approach I am outlining, the Bible's discussion of hell in this way. While it is surely true to say that much contemporary imagery of hell owes more to Milton and Dante than it does to the teaching of Jesus Christ, there is in the New Testament, and particularly in Jesus's eschatological discourses, a clear discussion of the existence of hell. The primary word for hell used in the New Testament is *Gehenna*. This word appears thirteen times in the New Testament, and over half of these occurrences appear in the Gospel of Matthew.[33] When reading these references to *Gehenna*, it is important for the contemporary reader to remember the term's context. For the Gospel's original listeners, there was a significance to *Gehenna* that is possible to miss as a contemporary reader—a reference to an existing location used to symbolize the possibility of the absence of God. On the south side of Jerusalem existed the Valley of Hinnom, which in Hebrew is "*Ge Hinnom*" from which *Gehenna* is derived. The Valley of Hinnom was seen as a place of unrighteousness associated with the idolatry of Manasseh and the human sacrifices of Molech. For the Jewish listeners to Jesus and the early Jewish gospel communities (hence the focus of the material in Matthew), the teachings about *Gehenna* would have had meaning in relation to an existent, physical location.[34] For them, the discourse would have been seen as one based on imagery concerning the Valley of Hinnom—an image of unrighteousness and judgement rather than a physical place called *Gehenna* after death. To interpret the imagery of hell in the New Testament in this manner, as an image

31. See Marshall, "The New Testament Does *Not* Teach Universal Salvation."

32. See Richard Bauckham, "Universalism: A Historical Survey," *Themelios* 4 (1978): 52–54.

33. The other word used for *hell* in the New Testament is *Hades*, which occurs ten times.

34. In this way, I disagree with the (albeit excellent and informative) presentation of MacDonald, *Evangelical Universalist*, 144–45.

indicative of unimaginable distance from God (an existential state) based upon the worst physical location that the audience might be able to imagine, allows this image to stand alongside the more universalistic passages about salvation discussed in the preceding.[35] The twofold claims of Scripture, the universal and separationist, can be preserved by prioritizing the universalistic passages in Scripture and seeing the passages on hell as contextual imagery related to an existential distance from God for those facing death in the present without the assurance of salvation through faith in Christ. From below, in the context of the penultimate (see the preceding discussion), hell and judgement are indeed realities ("kerygmatic"[36] realities), but the sovereign and gracious love of God will ultimately reign in all creation at the eschaton.

It is also worth noting that in many of the passages on judgement, in the most harrowing and most binary of these stories, it is not always clear which side of the divide "Christians" find themselves. The separations that separationists presume do not neatly fit the division of faith and unbelief. This issue in relation to the text adds a tremendous level of complexity into any binary, separationist approach.[37] In Jesus's parabolic use of the imagery of the sheep and the goats (Matt. 25:31–46), the sheep think they are goats, and the goats think that they are sheep: on each side of the eschatological divide some expect to be in the other camp in terms of their present lives. The religious self-categorization of one body of people confident of their salvation through their faith or churchmanship in comparison to another has nothing to do with the eschatological determination of the people in this parable. Quite the reverse—the "believers" seem to be those who are sent to damnation.[38] The separation is not as neat as one might hope it would be, and those who believe they will receive salvation do not. Faith, assurance of

---

35. In the words of Boring regarding separationist and universalist passages in the New Testament: "As propositions, they can only contradict each other. As pictures, they can both be held up, either alternatively or, occasionally, together, as pointers to the God whose grace and judgment both resist capture in a system, or in a single picture" (Boring, "The Language of Universal Salvation in Paul," 292).

36. Hart, "Universalism," 21; cf. Robinson, *In the End, God . . .*, 118–19.

37. For a more detailed account of this, see my "Beyond the Binary: Forming Evangelical Eschatology," in *New Perspectives for Evangelical Theology: Engaging with God, Scripture and the World* (London: Routledge, 2010).

38. Cf. Christopher Rowland, "The Lamb and the Beast, the Sheep and the Goats: 'The Mystery of Salvation' in Revelation," in *A Vision for the Church: Studies in Early Christian Ecclesiology in Honour of J. P. M. Sweet*, ed. Markus Bockmuehl and Michael B. Thompson

salvation, and reception of the sacraments play no role here; those who believe themselves never to have met Christ find themselves categorized as righteous.[39]

But does this mean, then, that sin and judgement are of no significance in a universalist account of the scope of salvation? Not necessarily. Accounts of universal salvation may in fact take sin as seriously as separationist accounts.[40] Indeed, universalism may well account in a more convincing way for the continued sin that exists in Christians. Dietrich Bonhoeffer addresses this theme in his *Sanctorum Communio*. In discussing the existence of the community of saints within the community of sinners, Bonhoeffer asks Christians to recognize their roles in bringing sin into the world and their coresponsibility for sin in the world. Instead of a binarized, separationist picture, Bonhoeffer accounts for the severely limited quality of Christian faithfulness and the way in which Christian faithlessness binds the Christian to the non-Christian in shared sinfulness. For Bonhoeffer, "The culpability of the individual and the universality of sin should be understood together; that is, the individual culpable act and the culpability of the human race must be connected."[41] In Bonhoeffer's account, every human being is found wanting in any and every sin committed. This is because no human being is different in principle from Adam, the first sinner, but rather each human being is in effect also Adam.[42] This shared cosinfulness does not determine that sinners are not responsible for individual acts of sin; rather, living individuals are responsible with Adam (and all other humans) for the sin in the world. The Christian who sins is coresponsible for the sin of the non-Christian—and for the sin of Adam.[43] Rather than a straightforward separationist logic, Bonhoeffer states that the church stands under the judgement of sin, and this judgement is only

---

(Edinburgh: T&T Clark, 1997), 181–92. Rowland not only considers this passage but also separationist discourses in Revelation.

39. One can see here some biblical basis for Rahner's anonymous Christianity; see Karl Rahner, *Theological Investigations*, vol. 6, *Concerning Vatican Council II* (London: Darton, Longman and Todd, 1974), 390–98.

40. For a more detailed account of the argument that follows, see my "Pessimistic Universalism: Rethinking the Wider Hope with Bonhoeffer and Barth," *Modern Theology* 26 (2010): 495–510.

41. Dietrich Bonhoeffer, *Sanctorum Communio: A Theological Study of the Sociology of the Church* (Minneapolis: Fortress, 1998), 110–11.

42. Bonhoeffer, *Sanctorum Communio*, 115.

43. Bonhoeffer, *Sanctorum Communio*, 116.

replaced eschatologically.[44] Salvation and sanctification do not place the members of the church in a different position. For Bonhoeffer, it is not so simple as to see Christians freed from sin and non-Christians bound by sin: both the separation and unity of Christian and non-Christian in relation to sin must be accounted for. He writes:

> We must not speak of a dual outcome . . . without at the same time emphasizing the inner necessity of the idea of apocatastasis. . . . On the one hand, the concept of the church, as Christ's presence in the world which calls for a decision, necessarily demands the dual outcome. The recognition that the gift of God's boundless love has been received without any merit would, on the other hand, make it seem just as impossible to exclude others from this gift and this love.[45]

This argument is, according to Bonhoeffer, the strongest argument for a universal scope for salvation: being responsible for bringing sin into the world, the Christian stands alongside the non-Christian in continual need of God's gracious and unmerited salvation.

To accept such an unwillingness to categorize humans into binary, separationist categories brings with it a fundamental shift in attitude towards those who do not share in faith. They are not to be seen as the rejected but as those who are likewise tainted by sinfulness, beloved of God, and in need of God's gracious and unmerited salvation.

But what, we might say, of the role of faith in this? Since grace is unmerited, it is received not by works or righteousness but according to faith. But is it really so straightforward to separate sin and unbelief? Karl Barth reminds us that sin is in and of itself unbelief. He writes:

> Man's [and woman's] sin *is* unbelief in the God who was "in Christ reconciling the world to himself," who in Him elected and loved man from all eternity, who in Him created him, whose word to man from and to all eternity was and will be Jesus Christ.[46]

---

44. Bonhoeffer, *Sanctorum Communio*, 124.
45. Bonhoeffer, *Sanctorum Communio*, 286–87.
46. Barth, *Church Dogmatics* IV/1, 415, emphasis added.

Faith is not the simple assent to a *credo* which might wipe sins magically away; unbelief [*Unglaube*] *is* faithlessness—it is sin. There can be no crude distinction between faith and works in this way. Christians cannot simply understand their continued sin as being cancelled out by their faith; rather, their continued sin is indicative of their continued faithlessness and unbelief. The Christian's continual sin joins them to the unbeliever as a fellow unbeliever—another faithless rejecter of the gospel message (a goat who believes it is a sheep). In response to the question of a universal scope to salvation impugning the righteousness of God by offering a broader hope which does not take sin seriously, there can be no easy recourse to the *sola fide* that separates faithlessness from sinfulness. Indeed, taking seriously the realities of faith in Jesus Christ and the implications of faithless behaviour may make universalism all the more possible for an account of the scope of salvation. Again to quote Barth:

> The power of the revelation of the salvation accomplished for each and all on Golgotha consists in the fact that they are brought, and brought into, the peace which was there concluded in their name, so that they can consider and respect and to that extent have it even in the midst of strife. When this power is at work, man can no more imagine that on the frontier of his life he is confronted by an enemy whom he can meet only in a pitiful submission to his merciless rule or with a defiant shout of freedom. When this power is at work the One with whom he has to do, as a brother of Jesus Christ, is God as his Father. Nor need he see in his fellows only those who constantly disturb the peace, so that his only course is either to avoid them, or resist them, or at very best tolerate them. On the contrary, he now finds that these men are unmistakeable and undeniable, if sometimes very doubtful and difficult, brothers of Jesus Christ and therefore his own brothers.[47]

A universalist account of the scope of salvation may well take the existence of sin with great seriousness, but it also believes that sin is not as sovereign a power as the sovereign love of God.

---

47. Barth, *Church Dogmatics* IV/2, 314.

Conclusion

Christian universalism is the hope that, because of the sovereign loving of God, the extent of the atonement will be universal not only in its potentiality but in its actuality—not only as a work of God offered to all but as an eschatological reality for all. The best forms of Christian universalism seek to take Scripture and the traditions of the church seriously and seek to give expression to the unique saving work of Christ who they understand to be irresistibly and lovingly *Pantokrator*. Indeed, the best forms of Christian universalism seek not to bind God to a principle that all people should be saved but to say that it seems consistent with God's loving sovereign grace as revealed in the life, death, and resurrection of Jesus Christ that in the end all may be saved. To affirm that the extent of the atonement is universally effective is for the universalist (or the one who hopes for universal salvation) an attempt at affirming what it means to say Jesus Christ is victor, and at his name "every knee should bend, in heaven and on earth and under the earth, and every tongue should confess that Jesus Christ is Lord, to the glory of God the Father" (Phil. 2:10–11).

RESPONSE TO TOM GREGGS

ANDREW LOUTH

I am not sure what I expected to find as I approached this essay, for it seems to me that advocacy of universalism is on an ascending gradient. For two millennia, if any opinion has been ruled out of court, it is universalism. The prevalence of the sense of God as judge seems to rule out the possibility that all will be acquitted in the end, and nowhere is the sense of God as judge more ubiquitous than in the Psalms, the influence of which on Christian sensibility cannot be underestimated; this is the Christian way of praying, if we are to judge by practice rather than simply by precept.

Furthermore, any attempt to promote universalism has to take into account the fear of Origenism in the early centuries—a fear so great that it is now difficult to know fully what accounted for it. That fear has led to the loss of the Greek original of most of Origen's works, and what does survive is marred by selectivity dictated by concerns of generations much later than Origen or by a stated desire (by Rufinus, to whom we owe the bulk of the Latin Origen) to modify or correct anything dubious on the grounds that the text is likely corrupt. The traditional story—supported by the condemnations of Origen, or at least Origenism, in the sixth century (instigated by Emperor Justinian)—is that central to Origen's condemnation was his notion of ἀποκατάστασις παντῶν, the restoration of all, a notion justified by a cavalier attitude to the biblical text made possible by his advocacy of allegorical exegesis (though what the fathers meant by this and what modern scholars mean by this seem not at all the same thing). The origins of this doctrine of final restoration are held to be philosophical rather than having anything to do with Origen's Christian faith (for which he suffered all but the fate of a martyr): final restoration is required by his philosophical conviction that the end is like the beginning (*semper enim similis est finis initiis*).[1]

---

1. Origen, *De Princ.* 1.6.2

218

This view seems to be carrying less and less weight among scholars. I would point to Fr. John Behr's new edition and translation of Origen's *On First Principles*, a revisionist work of such magnitude that it will be a long time before his approach is assimilated.[2] Behr turns the "philosophy" of which Origen is accused on its head, while at the same time rooting Origen's argument about the beginning and end of the cosmos in his exegesis, taken seriously, not dismissed as arbitrary allegory. Mention should also be made of Ilaria Ramelli's philological, philosophical, and theological arguments in her *The Christian Doctrine of* Apokatastasis: *A Critical Assessment from the New Testament to Eriugena* and her earlier *Terms for Eternity: Aioniôs and Aïdios in Classical and Christian Texts*, which together mount a strong argument against the usual meaning of eternal punishment and in favour of apokatastasis and universalism.[3] The dismissal of universalism as an aberration (however influential) in the Christian dogmatic tradition on Origen's part is less and less defensible.

Nevertheless, so far as the Western Christian tradition is concerned, universalism is, as Tom Greggs puts it, "a minority stream within the Christian tradition. Separationism remains the dominant, majority version of traditional, mainstream Christianity's view of eschatology and of the extent of the atonement." As I began his essay, I found myself uncomfortable, for he uses terms such as "omnipotence of divine love" and "irresistible sovereignty of divine love," terms that disturb me. What Greggs is doing in the opening words is, I take it, to adopt the terminology of those who embrace predestinarianism (he mentions the "Calvinist" position), but I would urge caution about adopting the weaponry of those one seeks to resist (Orthodox theology has a long history of the perils of trying to express Orthodoxy in the terms of Western theology). I shall come back to that later.

To start, I want to emphasize aspects of Greggs's presentation for Christian universalism that I welcomed. First is his insistence on seeing Christian universalism as something quite different from what he calls pluralist universalism, which calls into question the uniqueness

---

2. Origen, *On First Principles*, trans. and ed. John Behr, 2 vols. (Oxford University Press, 2017).

3. Ilaria Ramelli, *The Christian Doctrine of* Apokatastasis: *A Critical Assessment from the New Testament to Eriugena* (Leiden: Brill, 2013); Ramelli and David Konstan, *Terms for Eternity: Aioniôs and Aïdios in Classical and Christian Texts* (Piscataway, NJ: Gorgias, 2007).

of Christ and the absoluteness of Christian claims. What Greggs is advocating is a view that flows from the conviction "that love is the very nature of God (1 John 4:8) and that, since God is love and God is immutable, all of God's actions in relation to God's creation must be consistent with God's nature as love" (p. 202). So the starting point of Christian universalism is to take with absolute seriousness the love of God, manifest on the cross, a theme as fundamentally Johannine as it is fundamentally Pauline.

Second, the passage just quoted from Greggs makes another fundamental point which, it seems to me, is often overlooked by traditional Western attempts to expound the doctrine of the atonement: God created the universe, "all things visible and invisible" as the Creed has it, not just all human beings, however important a role they place in the cosmos, but everything. The created order is not just a backdrop to the ways of God with humans; it is itself loved by God and created to fulfil God's purpose in creating. Too often, Western thought about God and humankind starts from the fall, which took place within the realm of creation, and then proceeds to redemption. Instead, consideration of God and humankind must start with the creation of the cosmos, the whole created order—within which humankind has a unique role as image of God (or more precisely, and importantly for Greek patristic theology, created according to [kata] the image of God) and fulfils that role in relation to the cosmos by being both microcosm and the bond of the cosmos (μικρὸς κόσμος, συνδέσμος τοῦ κόσμου)—and then look to the end for which God created the cosmos: to draw creation into union with himself. This Greggs seems to me to recognize.

Let me return to my discomfort with omnipotent divine love and irresistible divine love. To my ear, this suggests that love is about power (indeed supremely powerful) and is, indeed, a power that is irresistible (not necessarily coercive but with the irresistible attraction of a beautiful woman; Delilah perhaps?). Instead of working with the terminology of Calvinism, Christian Universalism needs to challenge the analogy that lies behind the use of these terms. "God's love is cruciform," as Greggs finely says. God's love is manifest on the cross, not despite the cross, so it is manifest *in* suffering, not despite suffering. There seems to be a tendency, to which the Orthodox are not in the least immune, to pass too quickly from Golgotha to Christ's victory over death in his triumphant descent into hell and his glorious resurrection. But it was on the cross that Christ triumphed over death, and his suffering was part of that. The resurrection does not overthrow the cross but makes its meaning manifest. If this is true, then the language of power, of irresistible power, needs to be used very carefully. There *is* a place for it, God is not weak or incompetent, but his power is never to be seen in terms of the coercion that marks the worldly power with which we are familiar: "My Kingdom is not of this world," as Christ declared to Pilate.

If we stick with unconsidered notions of power, then we do indeed end up either with the irresistible power of God's love, leading to an inevitable universalism, or we see God's irresistible power as directing some to heaven and others to hell: *gemina praedestinatio*, an horrific two-faced God. Where else can we find ourselves? Maximos the Confessor is sometimes claimed for universalism, sometimes that he falls short of explicitly endorsing universalism, but perhaps in some way held universalism to be a view that is to be "honoured in silence (*in Schweigen ehren*)," as Hans Urs von Balthasar put it.[4] But both Maximos and John Damascene, his close follower in many respects, see the end of human life as experiencing the love of God in a manifest way. For some this will be the fulfilment of their deepest longing, which has been tested and refined during their life. For others this will be the deepest torment, to know the love of God and yet to have lived in such a way that this is the last thing one wants—to be loved so deeply. On this view, there is not separation between heaven and hell; rather, there is one final revelation of God's love to which all were created to respond but to which it is possible to warp one's human nature so much that response is no longer possible. The two options are not equal: God created human beings for one purpose, not for two.[5]

Another way of approaching this is found in Maximos. One of his fundamental metaphysical insights is his distinction between being,

---

4. For a careful discussion of this question, see Brian Daley, "Apokatastasis and 'Honourable Silence' in the Eschatology of Maximus the Confessor," in *Maximus Confessor: Actes du Symposium dur Maxime le Confesseur, Fribourg, 2–5 septembre 1980*, ed. Felix Heinzer and Christoph Schönborn (Fribourg: Éditions Universitaires, 1982), 309–39.

5. This is my reading of Maximos, *Quaestiones ad Thalassium* 59 (*CCSG* 22, 55, lines 160–70), which is also found in John Damascene, *Dialogus contra Manichaeos* 75, lines 5–24, in *Die Schriften des Johannes von Damaskos*, vol. 4 (Berlin: de Gruyter, 1981), 391–92; see A. Louth, *St John Damascene: Tradition and Originality in Byzantine Theology* (Oxford: Oxford University Press, 2002), 68–69.

well-being, and eternal being (εἶναι, εὖ εἶναι, and ἀεὶ εἶναι). Of these, the first and the last are gifts of God, and the middle term is up to us. If we achieve well-being, then we shall inherit eternal well-being. If, on the contrary, we make ill-being (φεῦ εἶναι) of the being we have received from the creator, then . . . what? Maximos does not, so far as I can see, draw the "logical" conclusion of ἀεὶ φεῦ εἶναι; he draws no conclusion at all.[6] Ἀεὶ εὖ εἶναι and ἀεὶ φεῦ εἶναι are not parallel options; φεῦ εἶναι seems to frustrate God's plan for human kind. Maximos does not, so far as I can tell, dwell on this: he has reached a surd and refuses to incorporate it into his understanding of God's purposes. Perhaps that is as far as anyone can go or should try to go.

I am not sure this is not Greggs's conclusion, for though he speaks of the "Christian universalist view," his conclusion states, "A universalist account of the scope of salvation may well take the existence of sin with great seriousness, but it also believes that sin is not as sovereign a power as the sovereign love of God," and continues, "Christian universalism is the hope that, because of the sovereign loving of God, the extent of the atonement will be universal not only in its potentiality but in its actuality—not only as a work of God offered to all but as an eschatological reality for all" (p. 217). I am not sure how far this differs from saying that we are entitled to hope for the salvation of all; that we are not to incorporate the possibility of finally resisting God's love into our eschatological vision.

---

6. This is my reading of Maximos, *Ambigua* 10, Patrologia Graeca, ed J.-P. Migne, 162 vols. (Paris, 1857–1886), 91:1116A–D.

RESPONSE TO PROFESSOR GREGGS

MATTHEW LEVERING

Professor Greggs "rejects traditional separationist accounts of the eschaton in which the saved and the damned are divided for all eternity, with the former group destined to go to be with God and the latter destined to everlasting torment, the absence of God, or annihilation" (p. 197). He argues that it is supremely fitting that the God who reveals himself in Jesus Christ as supreme love would, in Christ, save all the rational creatures that from eternity he has loved into existence. As Professor Greggs observes, "Since God is love and God is immutable, all of God's actions in relation to God's creation must be consistent with God's nature as love" (p. 202). Because God is omnipotent, his will to save cannot be frustrated. Professor Greggs notes that "to describe God's love as limited only to those within the church, those who choose to follow Christ, or those who are elect makes God seem either impotent—since God's loving is not sufficiently effective to overcome human sin unaided by faith—or capricious—for deciding that some should have eternal torment and others salvation" (p. 203).

I can affirm much of what Professor Greggs says. God is eternal superabundant love, and why would an infinitely good and loving God not will to save all his rational creatures or be unable to accomplish this will? Yet I cannot see how divine revelation warrants the claim that this is in fact what God has done. In my view, judging by divine revelation, we are left with a mystery that will not be resolved until we see God face to face. The mystery is not why people are damned—surely the answer to that question is readily apparent in our own behavior and in the behavior of unrepentant sinners throughout the grim history of human wickedness—but rather is why God permits such a thing and why God does not somehow arrange things in another way. In Dostoevsky's *The Brothers Karamazov*, Ivan says that no matter what else God might do, the very fact that God has permitted the horrific abuse of even one little child means that Ivan, morally speaking, can have nothing to do with such a God. To this point, Alyosha answers only with a kiss. Faith in Christ, who in sheer love endured the penalty of sin for all people in solidarity with all victims of oppression, must suffice as the answer to Ivan. In Christ we know that the victims of abuse will not be victims forever.

Catholics hold that Satan and the demons are fallen angels, rational beings created by God. Yet the Catholic Church does not pray for Satan and the demons. Citing Saint John of Damascus's *On the Orthodox Faith*, the *Catechism of the Catholic Church* sums up the constant teaching of the Church by stating that "it is the *irrevocable* character of their choice, and not a defect in the infinite divine mercy, that makes the angels' sin unforgivable. 'There is no repentance for the angels after their fall, just as there is no repentance for men after their death.'"[1]

The great Russian Orthodox theologian Sergius Bulgakov gets to the nub of the issue when he argues that God, as infinite wisdom and love, never would have created rational creatures without knowing that he could and would save them all; otherwise God would have been creating rational creatures who from eternity God knew would suffer the horrific pain of damnation forever. It would not be consistent with God's goodness to create a rational creature with eternal foreknowledge that the creature will merely come to the unspeakable grief of everlasting damnation. Therefore, Bulgakov explains at length the way in which Satan himself will repent after countless ages in hell. Satan, in the midst of his hellish "infinite number of circles of eternal self-repetition in emptiness," will at some glorious moment turn and start his long process of being restored to a condition of loving God.[2]

In my view, the problem is that Bulgakov is able to present no evidence from divine revelation for his account of how "a condemnation of satanism by Satan himself" will occur.[3] The conversion of Satan is not part of Scripture or Tradition. Professor Greggs agrees that in addressing God's work of salvation, theologians must adhere to the revelation that has been given and seek to address problems from within

---

1. *Catechism of the Catholic Church*, 2nd ed., Vatican trans. (Vatican City: Libreria Editrice Vaticana, 1997), §393.

2. Sergius Bulgakov, *The Bride of the Lamb*, trans. Boris Jakim (Grand Rapids: Eerdmans, 2002), 510.

3. Bulgakov, *The Bride of the Lamb*, 510.

that revelation—even while allowing that some problems are so difficult that we cannot now do more than mark out the revealed boundaries of possible positions. Thus, at least if it includes the fallen angels (as it must for Catholics), I do not think that universalism is an acceptable option, no matter its logical appeal. This conclusion motivates my efforts to find other ways to address questions that arise about the extent of the atonement—questions that have arisen in every Christian community, as shown by Bulgakov's universalism (which is quite obviously a position regarding the extent of the atonement).[4]

In my full-length essay, I grant that I cannot square the circle of God's sovereign priority and permission of some to choose damnation, on the one hand, and God's radically superabundant love for every rational creature, on the other hand. But it does seem to me that if we assume rational creatures such as Satan have chosen hell through their own rebellious and fully knowledgeable actions, then hell as a place of punishment (being separated from God is intrinsically a punishment for rational creatures) can be a place of justice, which pertains to love. It can also be a place of mercy insofar as we have every reason to believe that God is merciful toward everyone, including the damned.

Having written extensively in defense of universalism, Professor Greggs has assessed the biblical texts that tell against universalism, and he does not find them to be definitive. It would be rather pointless for me to enumerate them all here. I consider Paul's statement that "neither the immoral, nor idolaters, nor adulterers, nor homosexuals, nor thieves, nor the greedy, nor drunkards, nor revilers, nor robbers will inherit the kingdom of God" (1 Cor. 6:9–10)—taken as referring to persons who have freely chosen sinful and harmful acts over the love of God and neighbor—to be an accurate expression of Jesus's consistent and firm teaching as well. I think that the Gospels teach along the same lines that we find in Revelation 22:14–15: "Blessed are those who wash their robes, that they may have the right to the tree of life and that they may enter the city by the gates. Outside are the dogs and the sorcerers and fornicators and murderers and idolaters, and every one who loves and practices falsehood." In my view, this is a clarion call to repentance

---

4. See also Dimitri of Rostov, *Jesus Crucified: The Baroque Spirituality of St Dimitri of Rostov*, trans. and ed. John Mikitish (Yonkers, NY: St. Vladimir's Seminary Press, 2017). Saint Dimitri prays to be among the saved when Jesus comes to judge all humans.

and to the need to spread the good news that God has shown his love and mercy toward all sinners in Jesus Christ. I hold that God unites people to Jesus Christ in various ways—some explicit, others implicit—because the gospel of Jesus Christ is good news for all humans in all times and places.

All this would require a much longer discussion. The main point is that, even if I differ from Professor Greggs's conclusion, I very much appreciate his beautiful insistence upon God's powerful love and goodness in Christ Jesus. If that is not the center of the gospel, then I don't know what is.

MICHAEL HORTON

Distinguishing his position from a pluralistic universalism that avoids the particularity of Christ, Tom Greggs defends the Christian universalism enunciated especially by Karl Barth. Accordingly, Greggs holds that Christ's work "is not only universally offered to all human beings but also universally effective for all human beings" (p. 197). There is no final separation of humanity because "atonement is universal and its benefits are received ultimately by all" (p. 198).

More confidently than Louth, Greggs asserts that "Christian universalism in and of itself is never outrightly condemned; in fact, it would be difficult to do so since the word *apokatastasis* is used in Scripture in Acts, when it speaks of Jesus who must 'remain in heaven until the time of universal restoration [*apokatastasis*] that God announced long ago through his holy prophets' (Acts 3:21)" (p. 201). Greggs questions whether Origen's concept of universal restoration (*apokatastasis*) was explicitly condemned by the Christian East at the Fifth Ecumenical Council (Constantinople II) in 553.

With the popularity of Christian universalism in the modern era, there has been considerable effort among some Orthodox theologians (including Sergius Bulgakov, Kalistos Ware, and David Bentley Hart) to treat the *apokatastasis* as a legitimate position in the tradition (albeit a minority report). Whatever one makes of the Fifth Ecumenical Council, it is indisputable that Origen's most controversial teachings were rejected repeatedly by patriarchs in the East as well as by the bishop of Rome.[1] As Michael J. McClymond documents from such sources as the apostolic fathers, Justin, Irenaeus, and Chrysostom, "Many of the

---

1. See the recent study by Michael J. McClymond, *The Devil's Redemption: A New History and Interpretation of Christian Universalism*, 2 vols. (Grand Rapids: Baker Academic, 2018), 1:39–45; for his thorough treatment of the popularity of the concept in modern Russian Orthodoxy, see 2:685–748.

Greek fathers not only affirmed the reality of hell, but also asserted that this was the destiny of *most* human beings. Irenaeus, Basil, and Cyril of Jerusalem interpreted such passages as Matthew 22:14 ('for many are called, but few are chosen') as meaning that the majority will be consigned to hell. . . . Basil concluded that 'it is not the multitude who are being saved, but the elect of God.'"[2] (It is worth noting that Reformed interpreters have not traditionally extrapolated such a definite and emphatic conclusion from Jesus's statement.)

In terms of his constructive proposal, I wonder about its theological method: "Rather than a question of heterodoxy, the questions around Christian universalism are questions of fittingness: How fitting is an account of universalism to describe the work of salvation in Jesus Christ as attested in Scripture?" (p. 201). If heresy names what is "beyond the bounds," then no branch of the Christian church has expressed openness to it until modern times. In my view, Christian universalism stands or falls by exegesis, not by a fittingness that might be constructed merely in view of one's construal of "the work of salvation in Jesus Christ as attested in Scripture." Sound theology moves from exegesis to conclusions, not the other way around.

The Logical Argument

Greggs's argument appears to me to be a series of logical deductions from questionable premises, without adequate wrestling with difficult passages. He states this argument *in nuce*: "Universalism in its Christian form proceeds in the belief that [1] love is the very nature of God (1 John 4:8) and that, [2] since God is love and God is immutable, all of God's actions in relation to God's creation must be consistent with God's nature as love. Furthermore, [3] since God is omnipotent, God is thus omnipotent in God's loving of God's creatures." Conclusion: "The love of God is, therefore, ultimately irresistible for the creature" (p. 202).

Though I admire Greggs's (and Barth's) insistence on beginning with God, I question [1] as I think he (and Barth) means it. Love is indeed essential to God's being, as are justice and righteousness and holiness. However, there is a difference between God being necessarily loving (indeed, love itself) and God necessarily loving (or even creating)

---

2. McClymond, *The Devil's Redemption*, 1:40–41.

any creature. I have deeper reservations about Barth's doctrine of election, especially the post–*Church Dogmatics* II/2 version, which seems to contradict his earlier defense of God's sovereign freedom and aseity in opposition to liberalism. Divine simplicity and the freedom of God to be God—indeed, to have mercy on whom he will—are threatened by Barth's move. For Barth at least, mercy is basically the same as love for God; to love *is* to show mercy (into which God's wrath is absorbed). To be sure, no one deserves God's grace in Christ, but it sounds as if Barth and Greggs are saying that God is bound by his own necessary being to save everyone.[3] Whatever this is, it is not *merciful* love. By definition, mercy must be free—such that if one were to withhold mercy from someone in a given instance, that action could not be considered unjust (Ex. 33:19 with Rom. 9:15).

With the second premise we enter further in the direction of Marcionite territory: "[2] Since God is love and God is immutable, all of God's actions in relation to God's creation must be consistent with God's nature as love." To be fair, he does mention other attributes, including justice, but only as subordinate to the logic of his argument: namely, the *injustice* of the traditional view. The quotation from Trevor Hart is even more problematic in tying God's being (as singularly love) to a human-centered presupposition: "The central Christian conviction that love is the very nature of God, and that the most fundamental relation of this God to all his creatures must therefore be one of love if he is to be true to himself; the concomitant conviction is that this same God must ultimately have the final good of all his creatures in view" (p. 203). Whatever else is different (especially the particularity of Christ), such statements appear to me at least hardly distinguishable from the positions of Schleiermacher and Ritschl.

What if, according to Scripture, God is revealed as having acted in wrath at certain times and places? Is the righteous judgment that brought destruction and death in such instances actually a form of God's love and

---

3. If Bruce McCormack is correct in his reading of Barth, it even means that God's Trinitarian being is logically dependent on the incarnation and election. See Bruce L. McCormack, "Grace and Being: The Role of God's Gracious Election in Karl Barth's Theological Ontology," in *Orthodox and Modern: Studies in the Theology of Karl Barth* (Grand Rapids: Baker Academic, 2008), 183–200. McCormack's interpretation has not gone without challenge, especially by George Hunsinger, but even if McCormack takes it further, it seems to me that Barth gives him the rope.

mercy even to those who bore his wrath? Or are we to believe that these reports are unreliable, measured against the central dogma that God is only love and can only act in a manner that is loving toward creatures? If "God must ultimately have the final good of *all* his creatures in view," does this indeed include Satan, in spite of the biblical assurance that the devil will be "thrown into the lake of fire and sulfur where the beast and the false prophet were, and they will be tormented day and night forever and ever" (Rev. 20:10)? Indeed, "And if anyone's name was not found written in the book of life, he was thrown into the lake of fire" (v 15). Even if one were to interpret such verses as apocalyptic, hyperbolic, or mythological-allegorical expressions of a higher truth, then *of what truth*? Surely it cannot be that God is singularly loving and merciful and cannot but effect the ultimate happiness of all his creatures. It will not do to counsel subordinating (perhaps ignoring) the passages that contradict the premises.

Unique in the history of the church, Barth's doctrine of election begins with questionable premises based on deductions from what he takes to be the inner and wholly revealed being of God in the history of Christ. But why would Jesus's statements provoke the question, "Then who can be saved?" (Luke 18:26). And why would Paul expect that his teaching on election and final judgment would provoke the question, "Then is God unjust?" (Rom. 9:14–18). Would such questions even arise if the view offered by Barth and Greggs was intended? Based on his logical premises, Greggs concludes that a denial of universal election and salvation "makes God seem either impotent . . . or capricious" (p. 223). With footnotes to Schleiermacher and Moltmann, Greggs asks, "How would God be so thoughtless in God's foreknowledge to create a world that never asked for its creation knowing that the vast majority of people will wrongfully exercise free will and be denied salvation?" (p. 230). Greggs's position is more logically consistent than that of Barth, who, on the grounds of God's freedom, refused to assert with certainty that all will be saved. By halting in this manner, Barth opened the door to a grotesque possibility that there *might be* some who, despite being elected by God and redeemed and justified by Christ, nevertheless are finally lost. Greggs's account leaves no question mark. Yet, in my view, it is exegetically and theologically unsustainable.

To me the Barthian project seems like a theology of glory presented as a theology of the cross. Scripture states the truth of God's particular grace and freedom to show both mercy and judgment but then cautions against any further speculation. We cannot tear off God's "mask" of revelation to discover God-in-his-essence. Thus, we cannot extrapolate that what he has done mercifully for some he must do for all.

Finally, we come to Greggs's third premise: "Furthermore, since God is omnipotent, God is thus omnipotent in God's loving of God's creatures. The love of God is, therefore, ultimately irresistible for the creature." Like [1], this premise also conflates God's necessary attribute (omnipotence) with a necessity to act *irresistibly* in every instance.

We have ample scriptural evidence of God allowing his revealed will and sometimes even actions to be resisted. For example, Jesus laments, "O Jerusalem, Jerusalem, the city that kills the prophets and stones those who are sent to it! How often would I have gathered your children together as a hen gathers her brood under her wings, and you were not willing!" (Matt. 23:37). In fact, we all by nature reject the gospel and even the general influences of the Spirit until the Spirit regenerates us, granting repentance and faith in Christ. And we are held responsible for our rejection because it is truly our choice.

In addition, I find theologically problematic a simple identification of omnipotence with irresistibility, especially without stipulating one's intended meaning. Greggs says that Christian universalism is a combination of Calvinist emphasis on irresistible grace and Arminian emphasis on universal redemption (p. 208). "As Thomas Talbott puts it, '. . . If you simply take the Augustinian idea of God's sovereignty in the matter of salvation . . . and put it together with the Arminian idea that God at least wills or desires the salvation of all, then you get universalism, plain and simple'" (p. 208).

There are different varieties of irresistibility. One is physical force, which neither Greggs or myself intends. Another is an intrinsic lure, like the irresistibility of beauty. This is an essential component of the Reformed understanding of the new birth but is by itself insufficient since even the attractiveness of Beauty itself is ignored until the Holy Spirit unseals the eyes and raises those who are "dead in trespasses and sins" (Eph. 2:1–5). Our Reformed confessions and dogmatics affirm effectual grace while denying that this movement of God's omnipotent love involves coercion. Thus it is better to substitute the more traditional language of effectual calling or regeneration for the relatively recent term "irresistible" (the "I" in TULIP).

Yet none of these definitions coincides with the meaning of "irresistible" intended by Greggs (and Barth)—namely, that all will be saved even against their will. Augustinians do not believe that God's "Yes" overrides the creature's "No" but that the Holy Spirit grants the faith through which one is justified objectively before God. The omnipotence/irresistibility assumed by Barth presupposes a competitive (nominalist) view of divine and human agency, while Augustinian (including Reformed) theology embraces an analogical perspective. God's sovereign freedom is not a counterweight to human agency but its only source. Just as we owe the very existence of our creaturely freedom to God's sovereign freedom, even more so do we owe our conversion to his liberating act.

Like Barth, Greggs insists that evangelism remains essential not to save people from an impending judgment but to save them from the existential judgment of their own hearts and fear of death (p. 207). Yet the prophets, Jesus, and the apostles warn of a coming *day* of wrath—not merely an existential-subjective state of feeling lost and condemned but an objective judgment in which those who do not believe in the Son stand "condemned already" (John 3:18). At this point, Calvinists stand with other Christian traditions in affirming that the reality that some do not believe and are therefore ultimately lost underscores the dignity of humanity and the seriousness with which God takes human agency.

Exegesis

To be fair, Greggs does recommend some proof texts. The first is Acts 3:21: Jesus must "remain in heaven until the time of universal restoration [*apokatastasis*] that God announced long ago through his holy prophets" (p. 201). "There are numerous passages (especially in Paul) that point towards universal salvation, enough indeed for universalism to be a quiet but continued strain throughout the history of Christian theology" (p. 210).

Yet in both cases one may follow the traditional exegesis of all branches of the church and say that here Scripture refers to the final sharing of the whole cosmos—not just individual souls but people, not just Jews but Gentiles, not just human beings but the whole creation from elect angels to mountains and streams—in the glory of God. This would be the framework for understanding the Pauline passages Greggs adduces (Rom. 5:18–19; Col. 1:20; Eph. 1:9–10; 2 Cor. 5:19). Romans 5:18–19 contrasts the fate of humanity in Adam with its destiny in Christ, but in verses 15 and 19, Paul refers more narrowly to "the many," and in verse 17 he adds, "For if, because of one man's trespass, death reigned through that one man, much more will *those who receive* the abundance of grace and the free gift of righteousness [οἱ τὴν περισσείαν τῆς χάριτος καὶ τῆς δωρεᾶς τῆς δικαιοσύνης λαμβάνοντες] reign in life through the one man Jesus Christ." Colossians 1:20 refers to the incarnate Son through whom God has reconciled "to himself all things, *whether on earth or in heaven* [i.e., whether humans or angels], making peace by the blood of his cross."

So, too, God's reconciliation of the world to himself in Christ in 2 Corinthians 5:19 refers to the *kosmos* as a comprehensive realm of creation in the same sense as the other "world" and "all" passages. These all highlight the recapitulation of all things (but not necessarily "each and every") in Christ, who is the head of his church. This seems to be the point of Ephesians 1:9–10 especially, as part of the epistle's larger argument that God's ultimate plan is to unite all things (Jew and gentile) into one "new human," that is, the church with Christ as its head. Once more, I take John 3:16 to provide the formula: The whole world is so *loved* by God that he sent his Son to *save* all who will believe (i.e., an elect remnant from every people).

Greggs does acknowledge that "there is in the New Testament, and particularly in Jesus's eschatological discourses, a clear discussion of the existence of hell" (p. 212). However, he concludes that the imagery of the Valley of Hinnom would have suggested to original hearers an existential state (the subjective experience of distance from God) rather than an objective state of final separation. "The twofold claims of Scripture, the universal and separationist, can be preserved *by prioritizing the universalistic passages* in Scripture and seeing the passages on hell as contextual imagery related to an *existential* distance from God for those facing death in the present without the assurance of salvation through faith in Christ" (p. 213, emphasis added).

Like Barth, Greggs's starting point begs the question. The churches of the East and the West have never interpreted the *kosmos* passages as entailing universal salvation. This is precisely what is in dispute, so the burden of proof falls on Greggs to make the case and not just assume his case and then grant it exegetical supremacy. As with any problem, a good theory is one that makes the greatest sense of the most data.

Finally, Greggs notes that in Jesus's teaching in Matthew 25, the sheep are unaware of their works, and there is no mention of faith or the sacraments. Yet he concludes from this that "those who believe themselves never to have met Christ find themselves categorized as righteous" (p. 214). This interpretation seems strained in two directions. First, we do not have to find Jesus's entire teaching on salvation encapsulated in a discourse preparing his disciples for persecution. The bond of the Head with his members is so strong that caring for "the least of these, my brothers and sisters" (Matt. 25:40) in these trials is caring for Christ himself. Faith shows itself in good works, especially to the household of faith. This is the point that he is making here. Second, Greggs fails to wrestle with the fact that Jesus welcomes the sheep into the kingdom his Father prepared for them "from the foundation of the world" (v. 34) and that the goats "will go away into eternal punishment, but the righteous into eternal life" (v. 46; cf. v. 30). Contrary to what Greggs implies (p. 216), this is not a parable or a statement about the existential sense of being either a sheep or a goat but a straightforward warning about a final separation.

RESPONSE TO TOM GREGGS

FRED SANDERS

Tom Greggs's chapter on Christian universalism is a difficult chapter to respond to, not because it is poorly argued (it is not) or because its conclusions are not worth taking seriously (they are). The difficulty lies instead with the fact that in my own work I have consistently proceeded on the conviction that universalism is so obviously false, and so enervating for Christian doctrine, that I have made numerous theological decisions precisely to avoid conclusions that have seemed to me almost axiomatically wrong. It is therefore with some reserve that I engage this essay on Christian universalism at all; having developed the habit of working around the subject on purpose, addressing it head-on feels like swimming upstream.

Nevertheless, there are three good reasons to interact with Greggs on universalism. First, the essay is well crafted. It draws together some main lines of thought from recent arguments in the field, and it makes its case with some modesty, admitting that universalism is a minority voice in the Christian tradition and making its appeals on the grounds of fittingness. The second reason is that in a discussion of the extent of the atonement, it is elucidating to include a position as far out on the spectrum as this, arguing not only for the atonement's universal extent but also for its universal result. As Greggs points out, some pluralist universalisms are, as we might say, even further out than his position, but since they do not make their appeal to the power of the atonement, they are not relevant to the current discussion. Greggs's chapter functions as a claim for the fullest extent of the atonement, instructive in its own right as a coherent thought project, and useful as a reference point for other positions. Finally, the essay is worth interacting with because it draws attention to what I have described as an urgent need in atonement theology: giving a proper systematic account of the significant fact that the New Testament tends to associate universal language with the atonement in Christ.

The New Testament's pattern of speaking universally when it is speaking of the death of Christ is both a hermeneutical crux and a doctrinal challenge. However, the pattern only registers as a challenge if it is recognized as falling out of line with other biblical patterns— that is, if it is something of a surprising or counterintuitive data point. Universal language clustering around atonement passages is a challenge, for example, to doctrinal systems that have decided, for larger systematic reasons, to understand the atoning death of Christ as limited to the elect. Reformed theologians need to be prepared to account for passages from Paul and John, Mark and Hebrews, Jude and Isaiah, that seem determined to sound the note of universal scope in many forms and in distinct vocabularies. There is simply something about the death of Christ which draws this "all" and "everyone" language out of the apostles. Reformed responses are of course available; my point is only that they are necessary because the overall confession of limited atonement makes the presence of this universal language an issue. It is not the case that all Reformed readers are imposing some extrabiblical system on Scripture. Rather, they come to these universal texts from a large number of other texts that give an even stronger impression of the particularity of redemption.[1] Such interpreters have already been prepared by the more comprehensive sense of Scripture to expect a narrowing or particularizing set of claims about the cross; when they find instead claims about Christ dying for all, they register the surprise and marshal explanations both exegetical and systematic.

The universal language that clusters around the atonement in Scripture also registers as a challenge for doctrinal systems that have already developed, as part of their overall construal of the witness of Scripture, the conviction that not all will finally be saved. Coming to these "all" atonement passages, the majority Christian tradition, which has not affirmed universalism, notices the unexpected universality here in a soteriological context. John Stott puts it with terse eloquence in his commentary on 1 Timothy 4:10, explaining the words "the living God, the savior of all men, and especially of those who believe":

---

1. This particularity of redemption is emphasized by the title and editorial framing, as well as several of the contributions, in *From Heaven He Came and Sought Her: Definite Atonement in Historical, Biblical, Theological, and Pastoral Perspective*, ed. David Gibson and Jonathan Gibson (Wheaton, IL: Crossway, 2013).

> The precise relation between "all men" and "those who believe" has perplexed all commentators. In what sense is God the Saviour of all and specially of believers? This is not universalism, since Paul was not a universalist.[2]

Of course, Stott can only assert (rather bluntly) that "Paul was not a universalist" as a kind of placeholder representing the claim that he has synthesized a total interpretation of Paul's theology. To apply it to this passage as the judgment that "this is not universalism" is to appeal to the principle that hard passages should be read in light of clearer or more plentiful passages. But the phrase "savior of all" is really only a hard passage against the background of a biblical witness that has already been construed as tending strongly away from universalism.[3]

Exegetes and theologians come to terms with these texts and their implications in various ways. The pattern of universal language clustering around the atonement is pervasive enough, though, to register as a fundamental issue for theological interpretation. Many of the chapters in this volume can be observed negotiating the issues raised by this pattern of language, and my own chapter places it as the crucial point of departure for investigating the extent of the atonement. Greggs offers an account of Christian universalism centered on an atonement universal in its intent, scope, effectiveness, application, and result. For this Christian universalist account, the problematic passages I have gathered are not problems at all. Instead they can be construed as the points at which something comes to crystal clear expression which was left implicit or even apparently contradicted elsewhere in Scripture. Greggs comes to these passages with his own construal of the overall message of Scripture and his own systematic commitments to an eschatology with a particular nonseparationist shape. They are no surprise, except perhaps for being surprisingly explicit in their confirmation of what is at best only hinted at by more diffuse lines of thought elsewhere.

The conflict between this view and the mainstream Christian view is manifested here in the different approaches to what I have identified

---

2. John Stott, *The Message of 1 Timothy and Titus: Guard the Truth* (Downers Grove; InterVarsity Press, 1996), 118.

3. There is another sense in which 1 Tim. 4:10 is a hard passage on its own terms: it draws but does not explain a distinction between salvation for all and salvation "especially" for believers. This calls for explanation regardless of any larger systematic concerns.

as disputed texts, but the real conflict rests in the divergent overall construals of the biblical message of God and salvation. These are vast issues, having to do with the main burdens of the content of Scripture: the identity of God and the nature of salvation. Christian universalism, on Greggs's account, is "the belief in the omnipotence of divine love as fulfilled in the atonement" (p. 197). It makes the most of identifying God as the God of salvation, to such an extent that God's identity comes to be wrapped up in that "of" relation; salvation is what God is, without remainder. To construe the overall biblical witness as identifying God and salvation in this way is to fold God into salvation in such a tight connection that the distinction becomes difficult to conceive. It is not that God needs to damn somebody in order to remain God but that a confession of atonement-based universalism risks collapsing our ability to recognize theologically the distinction between God's being and act. The distinction between heaven and hell is certainly not the same as the distinction between God and his free acts, but the inability to draw one of the distinctions often registers in the inability to draw the other. When God is confessed as "God for us" without remainder, with no background of "God in himself" out of which divine decrees and acts emerge, we might expect the blurring of distinctions to show up first in a blurring of distinctions about the extent of salvation. Christian, or Trinitarian, forms of universalism are preferable to the conventional unitarian universalisms that have propagated since the Enlightenment. But even in their best forms, universalisms share the risk of subsuming the God of salvation into the mere apotheosis of salvation. If the Christian doctrinal (and artistic!) tradition has sometimes portrayed this distinction too graphically or absolutely, it has nevertheless been following a valuable instinct. That instinct is the sense that in salvation both something universal and something particular, distinguishing, and differentiating are at work.

The task of interpreting the Bible's complex and even surprising witness to the living God's free action in salvation requires us to develop principles of universality and principles of distinction. The Christian universalism presented by Greggs does not require the latter: all means all in all cases and in all senses. I have argued, in contrast, that it is possible to locate the universal element of the atonement in the work of the Son of God in hypostatically assuming human nature. Here *nature* is a universal word, referring to what all humans have. The particular element of the atonement can be located in the Holy Spirit's application of that work to individual persons, bringing about their personal union with Christ. Here *person* is a particular word, referring to what distinguishes one human being from another. One advantage of these distinctions is that they are not ad hoc, devised to solve the immediate problem of interpreting the atonement correctly, but already available because they originate in the deep structure of classic christological and Trinitarian doctrines. To apply them to atonement and anthropology is to consolidate the Christian confession and to marshal in advance the equipment needed to read both the restrictive passages of Scripture and the universal passages.

At one point in Greggs's chapter, he has occasion to refer to the decrees of the fifth ecumenical council (Constantinople 2 in the year 553), where an Origenist version of *apokatastasis* was anathematized. Is it a coincidence that that same council was a crucial point in the development of the theological distinction between person and nature? The fifth council made possible the confession that "one of the Trinity suffered in the flesh" because it drew out the connection between the three persons in God and the one person in the incarnation, as well as the one nature in God and the two natures in the incarnation. I do not think the fathers of the fifth council made a connection between a more systematic account of the person-nature distinction and the rejection of universalism; they had anti-Origenism on their minds for many reasons. But I contend that the theological resources and distinctions refined at that point in the conciliar tradition are the same conceptual tools that make it unnecessary to draw the conclusion of universalism and that enable a more accurate account of the extent of the atonement.

FIVE VIEWS ON THE EXTENT OF THE ███████
ATONEMENT: A CONCLUDING EXHORTATION

ADAM J. JOHNSON

To explore the extent of the atonement is to jump into the deep end of systematic theology—to ask a question that contains a host of questions covering much of Christian doctrine, and this means that we jump into the deep end of scriptural interpretation as well—for to answer this question well entails a set of reflections which canvas both Old and New Testaments. As with any theological question, our goal is to worship the maker of heaven and earth, the triune God, Father, Son, and Holy Spirit, who in the person of the Son became man for us and for our salvation. But the challenge here is a significant one, for in turning a critical eye to this "for us," we ask a powerful and threatening question: Who constitutes this *us*?

The essays and responses you have read do us a great service in charting the waters in which we must navigate, but they do not, of course, give us a final, cohesive answer. Rather, they give us a range of alternative views on the different theological commitments and exegetical understandings that together form the five different answers to the "extent of the atonement" offered in this book.

In this conclusion, I do not seek to provide the "answer key in the back of the book"—it would be presumptuous to conclude so rich a discussion in such few pages. My goal, rather, is to bring your attention to some of the most important questions any theologian, any lover of the triune God, must eventually come to grips with in order to answer the question of the extent of the atonement. But before I do so, I want to situate the question within the life of the Christian, within a life of faith seeking understanding. Answering a question of this scope requires a great deal of patience. And patience, lest it give way to despair and lethargy, needs to be nourished by deep waters.

Patience

In expositing love, 1 Corinthians 13 begins by affirming that "love is patient" (1 Cor. 13:4). It is this relationship between love and patience that nourishes Christian theology. Because we love our God, our neighbor, and ourselves, we are and must be patient. And because God's love precedes our love of him, his patience with us precedes and envelops our patience, nourishing, shaping, and guiding it. We do not wait aimlessly or strive ceaselessly. We are patient—a restful acting and active waiting (though here, too, the spirit is willing and the flesh is weak) in which our love, built upon the love of God, invites and welcomes that which it seeks.

In the case of doctrine, where we are inviting understanding from the Lord, the pattern is the same. In patience, we seek to invite the truth of God by making our minds and souls hospitable to him. In prayer, study, and worship, we seek to break down biases, overcome faulty presuppositions, minimize our many ignorances, so that we might, with the help of God, through Scripture, and by the assistance of the faithful throughout the history of the church, become a fitting and welcoming temple for the Lord, a mind set apart for understanding God and God's ways.

For it is precisely God and God's ways that are the basis of this invitation. Ultimately, there is no other basis for the theological task of the church than the deep and abiding experience of God's love for us. All questions of doctrine are simply this: an invitation to know and understand the one who loves us. This great evangelical truth nurtures and demands our fitting response in the form of understanding and praise. And because of this freedom and calling to know and love the one who knows and loves us, we are in turn free to be patient.

Questions for Further Exploration

In this section, I offer a series of questions that the essays in this book raise, putting them in a clear and suitable form to stimulate your own wrestling with the question as you delve into this topic patiently. In part these can be answered simply by looking back to the essays and responses in this book, but each will call for further reflection in Scripture and theological writings contemporary and ancient.

1. What is the role of the Trinity in the extent of the atonement? One might think that the Trinity is simply a given, and the question is: What did the Trinity decide regarding the extent of the atonement? But that is too simple. As Matthew Levering, in his interaction with Fred Sanders's essay puts it: "The problem here, however, is that the Son's mission ends up seeming more generous—more loving, because more all-encompassing—than the Spirit's mission" (p. 188). As we think about the extent of the atonement, we must take care to think through the respective roles and implications for each member of the Trinity, Father, Son, and Holy Spirit, faithfully upholding the undivided unity of the Trinity in all of God's works.

2. What is the role of the oneness of God in the extent of the atonement? While this question may not have come to the surface a great deal throughout this book, the oneness or unity of God was nevertheless pervasive. Any theological conclusion that posits disagreement, division, or disunity within the doctrine of God and/or divine attributes is out of bounds, and in different ways, the theologians assembled here are all working to affirm the unity of God. What does it mean for God to be one, for his will to be one, and for his attributes to be one in our reflection on the extent of the atonement?

3. What is the content of God's election? The contributors in this volume are clear: God can and does elect. That is not in question. But what is the content of that election? Is it a general election or a particular one? Is it about people groups or individuals? Is it about heaven and hell or about more earthly purposes? Does God elect different things for different people? Does God will that his election be opposable (either in the sense of different eternal destinies for different people or for a specific election for some and a general election for others)? The question here is not what power we have over and against God, for we are not equals. The question is: What exactly does God elect, and what are the implications of that election for his creatures?

4. What does it mean for God to love? One might think that the answer to such a question is straightforward, but it is not. Does God love all equally? Can God both love and send sinners to hell? Can God both love and not elect someone to salvation? Given that

God is love, does it follow that God loves or must love each of his creatures? Given that love is only one of God's attributes, should it have elevated status within our understanding of God's character? If so, how does this shape our view of election? If not, how do the other divine attributes shape both the divine love and its extension to God's creatures?

5. Is God merciful, and must he be merciful to his creatures? In some ways an extension of the previous question, this is nonetheless an important question in its own right. Does love necessarily entail mercy? If God is mercy, must he always be merciful? Can there be attributes within God, such as mercy, that God is free to either be or not be toward his creatures? What does this imply concerning the oneness or unity of God?

6. Is God free, and does he prize the freedom of his creatures? "Be holy as I am holy" (Lev. 11:45)—are we also to be free as God is free? Without falling into the error of Pelagianism, is there some sense in which God values and preserves our creaturely freedom, and how does this play a role in the extent of the atonement? Clearly, we are not saved by works, but what exactly are works both as the apostle Paul and later theologians understand them? Are they any act done by a creature, or are they something like an act done in order to create an obligation? Can faith be a work?

7. Is the atonement primarily forensic? Louth is concerned that Western theologies of the atonement are overly forensic, partly due to the over-influence of Anselm. Is that the case? Does a well-rounded approach to the atonement and the arc of salvation help give a fuller picture of the extent of the atonement?

8. What is hell? The essays in this book include a running set of reflections on this doctrine. Is it a place? A state? A possibility? A homiletical and rhetorical feature of Paul's discourse? Is it the reality embraced by Christ in his substitutionary death? The urgency behind the question of the extent of the atonement is not the good news of those who are elect to salvation—it is the threat that Christ's work is not efficacious or sufficient for some, namely, the threat of hell. How do we, and ultimately the Bible, understand the reality of hell, as the backdrop and urgency of the extent of the atonement?

9. What is the role of mystery within the extent of the atonement? All theology appeals in some way to the role of mystery within the Christian faith. What is the role of mystery in Paul's thinking about election and within Christian doctrine—and does the logic of Scripture allow us to stay silent on this point?

10. What is the meaning of Romans 9–11 and Ephesians 1? While a host of passages were referred to throughout the book, these, perhaps more than any others, are the most sustained passages in Scripture exploring the logic of election or predestination in relation to the atoning work of Jesus Christ. It is here, with careful attention to the context, rhetoric and nuance of the letters as a whole, that we should anchor our understanding of shorter passages in Scripture.

The Way Forward: An Ecumenical Retrieval

But how are we to go about answering these questions? My own conviction is that the best way to do so is modeled by this book. We did not merely seek four or five different views in order to foster disagreement or discussion; rather, we sought to cultivate ecumenical discussion between some of the main traditions or branches of the church in order to model an approach to the theological task. There are great strengths to staying within one's tradition, drawing on a rich heritage of thought and worship, but taking the time and energy to familiarize oneself with the premises, arguments, and nuances of other traditions greatly enriches one's approach to doctrine.

Examples of this are abundant in the chapters and responses you have just read. The Orthodox view raises substantial questions about the approach to the extent of the atonement taken by Catholic and Reformed traditions, for it finds the whole matter foreign. Here is an offer to Catholic and Reformed theologians to consider other standpoints and emphases for the theological task. But to return the favor, Catholic and Reformed theologians have a powerful and compelling invitation for the Orthodox to consider: a host of passages (not merely verses here and there but extended passages, especially in Paul) that invite the church to consider and understand (not merely appeal to the mystery of) God's plan, God's purposes, and God's election.

This is no mere matter of theological emphasis or biblical sources. The authoritative figures we appeal to in order to guide our thought are of great significance. The challenge to properly interpret figures outside (and within) one's own tradition is particularly important as we follow our contributors' arguments. Origen, Augustine, Anselm, Thomas—these and other theologians featured prominently in the attempt to explore the extent of the atonement. And it was no mere matter of each theologian appealing to the great theologians of their respective tradition: there were brief but thoughtful exchanges in the responses that belied the depth of interaction our authors have had with one another's traditions and theologians (such as one finds in Louth's interaction with the later Augustine), making for important material contributions to the discussion.

With the history of theology as with the interpretation of Scripture, we, as the people of God, do not approach the relevant texts in an unbiased manner, equipped with the tool of reason to come to our decision. Shaped and informed by our fathers and mothers in the faith (contemporary or ancient), guided by those we have read and been influenced by, softened by prayer and drawn by worship, we seek to be nurtured and transformed through the Holy Spirit leading us in our interactions with Scripture. One of the best ways to do this is by listening eagerly and humbly, though not subserviently, to our brothers and sisters in faith with whom we disagree. At their worst, they are starting with alien principles and falsely interpreting Scripture—but even then they offer us the service of pointing to passages we might be inclined to overlook and prompt us to reexplore our own views and premises from another standpoint. And at their best, by their piety and reason they force us to reckon with our many imbalances, ignorances, and errors.

The invitation here is not to consider anew one doctrinal topic (the extent of the atonement) and not merely the thought of our favorite theologian (whether that be Athanasius, Thomas, Wesley, Barth, or someone else) or our favorite passages or books of the Bible. The invitation is far great than that, for as our God is one, so doctrine is one, and to interpret one doctrine well is to bring the resources of all of theology upon it, to interpret one book of the Bible well is to locate it within the canon as a whole, and to understand a theologian is to appreciate his or her place and influence within the history of theology. The invitation is (1) to engage the theological task once more but from this definite standpoint (the extent of the atonement), and in so doing to dwell upon the doctrine of God, his creative purposes, the whole sweep of salvation, including God's plan for Israel, its fulfillment in the death and resurrection of the Messiah of Israel, and culminating in the life of the church as it awaits the second coming of Jesus; (2) to explore the history of doctrine, reading yet more broadly in our favorite theologians and extending to new figures whether that be the later Augustine for the Orthodox, Origen for the Reformed, or Thomas for the Wesleyan, drawing upon contemporary figures to awaken us to new directions and emphases within these classic figures; and, of course, the matter upon which it all depends, (3) to approach Scripture anew, not merely in its verses, passages, and chapters but in the whole span of the canon, as we listen to the saints of the church both present and ancient to help us in attending to the Word of God spoken to us today in the Bible.

GENERAL INDEX